Retelling/Rereading

Retelling/ Rereading

The Fate of Storytelling in Modern Times

KARL KROEBER

RUTGERS UNIVERSITY PRESS

New Brunswick, New Jersey

Library of Congress Cataloging-in-Publication Data

Kroeber, Karl, 1926–
    Retelling/rereading : the fate of storytelling in
modern times / Karl Kroeber.
      p.   cm.
   Includes bibliographical references and index.
   ISBN 0-8135-1765-6
   1. Narration (Rhetoric) 2. Modernism (Art) 3. Stories without
words. 4. Arts, Modern—19th century. 5. Arts, Modern—20th
century. I. Title.
NX650.N37K76 1992
700—dc20   91-20383
                                                      CIP

British Cataloging-in-Publication information available

Chapter two is a revised version of my essay "Narrative and De-narrativized Art," in *The
Romantics and Us: Essays on Literature and Culture,* edited by Gene W. Ruoff. Copyright
© 1990 by Rutgers, The State University.

This book is dedicated to the memory of my father,
Alfred Louis Kroeber,
who first told me stories of
Hannibal, Pulekukwerek, and Little Spilif.

Contents

Illustrations

Acknowledgments

Comprehensive acknowledgment of my indebtedness for what is valuable in this book, as my dedication suggests, would almost constitute an autobiography. I therefore limit expressions of gratitude here to a few who may be surprised, some perhaps not altogether pleasantly, thus to be held publicly accountable. Leslie Mitchner, however, knows how grateful I am for the time and effort she devoted to the grim task of improving the structure of this book; she hasn't plumbed the depth of my indebtedness for her faith that there was something there to be improved. And I am happy that Andrew Lewis is aware of my gratitude for his superb editing. Diane Wakowski one delightful morning gave me invaluable insights into a contemporary poet's understanding of the heritage of modernism. With neither Larry J. Swingle nor Paul Bové do I remember discussing this book, but the clarity of my thinking and the breadth of my knowledge has been vastly enhanced by all that I have learned from my conversations and correspondence with them. Andrew Cooper and I have reached the happy situation in which neither of us is quite sure who is stealing from whom. Tobin Siebers's interest and mine have overlapped for some time—much to my benefit, not only from his command of contemporary criticism but also from the example of his impressive intellectual integrity. What little understanding of Native American stories I possess owes more than he can ever guess to the scholarly judiciousness, as well as to the profound linguistic knowledge, of my son, Paul Kroeber.

My most unrepayable debt is to the students at Columbia, both undergraduate and graduate, whom I have taught over the past twenty years. Anything useful in this book ultimately derives from the combination of intellectual enthusiasm and moral seriousness by which they have enlivened my classrooms. What I have learned from them far exceeds what I have given in return, and I am happy for this opportunity to express my thanks for the generosity of spirit by which they have sustained my enthusiasm for the teaching of literature.

Retelling/Rereading

Storytelling and Modern Criticism

This book is about storytelling and why in the twentieth century it has been persistently misunderstood. The dominant mode of contemporary literary criticism claims to reveal universal, metacultural principles. Thus, it is the current fashion to define narrative according to ideas of "human nature" (such as Freud made popular) that transcend specific social practices. But every storytelling performance is unique, and narrative's preeminent accomplishment is the articulation of meaning for contingent events without gainsaying their contingency. This fundamental fact of how and why stories are constructed is complicated by an equally fundamental—and paradoxical—fact that is addressed by none of the contemporary essays and books about narrative theory I have consulted: stories improve with retelling, are endlessly retold, and are *told in order to be retold*.

Despite recent work by many feminists, some anthropologists, and a few historiographers who have begun to reexamine the social and cognitive functions of narrative, today's "narratology" continues to reflect the universalist presuppositions that originated in modern art's challenges to traditional narrative forms and purposes. Modernism was the first aesthetic system to ask whether excellent art did not *require* the exclusion of traditional narrative, as it was the first to deny that art should have ethical significance. Since stories always evoke judgmental responses, the place of narrative in modernism could only be uncertain, and that uncertainty led to the misvaluation of narrative by modern and postmodern critics. I feel obliged to discuss, therefore, critical misconceptions about narrative as well

as storytelling in itself; my presentation will explore the diverse
vicissitudes of narrative in the art of our century. My topic, after all, is broader even than the daunting breadth of "fiction." It
includes as but one of its segments history itself.

Yet I cannot damn myself for a fool to have tackled this subject. The more I work at it, the more persuaded I am that nothing would be more salutary for contemporary criticism, both
historical and formalistic, than to recognize how disastrously we
have misconstrued what story is and does. We have blinded
ourselves to some of the most fruitful ambivalences within
twentieth-century Western art. Our misconceptions have obscured the true profoundity of modern art's self-proclaimed
distinction from the art of the myriad civilizations of the past—
and of most of the contemporary non-Western world.

The overwhelming bulk of the world's literature before our
century, and even most of it produced by non-Western cultures
during our century, is narrative. And even in Europe until the
end of the nineteenth century it was assumed that painting and
sculpture *should* tell stories. So one of modernism's most revolutionary acts was to categorize storytelling as "primitive," as an
activity peculiar to "undeveloped" people either lost within or
marginal to "advanced" Western culture. It is almost impossible
to find favorable comments on (let alone celebrations of) narrative among the great modern artists—D. H. Lawrence's advice
not to trust the teller being among the kinder and gentler. T. S.
Eliot proclaimed that Joyce, anticipated by Yeats, had found a
means for superseding the "narrative method entirely". Thousands of nonrepresentational modern canvases, of course, *demonstrated* how little the graphic arts needed story subjects. Such
disdain for narrative, already implicit in Walter Pater's dictum
that all arts aspire to the condition of music, has hardened into
critical dogma and is now so embedded in our thinking that
only through drastic self-criticism can we perceive the form of
this prejudice. One way to wake ourselves up is to examine verbal
and visual tales from cultures directly sustained by storytelling,
which now—significantly—implies the cultures of the so-called
Third World. In their stories the vital social purposes of narrative are conspicuous, and their unfamiliarity may alert us to the
parochialism of our supposedly "universal" critical principles,
which often merely express the historical idiosyncrasy of those
fears and needs we would sooner not acknowledge.[1]

There is nothing literary critics overlook more consistently than the fact that stories are always retold and are *meant* to be retold, reheard, reread, that narrative is a repeating form of discourse—in which every repetition is unique. This paradox gives storytelling a strong claim to be the most important of all modes of cultural discourse. No one can dispute that narrative has been the primary means by which most societies have defined themselves. On the other hand, narrative is also the primary means by which sociocultural boundaries could be crossed, not transgressively, but unobtrusively. Stories are like plant species that move readily but unobtrusively over surprising obstacles, including vast spans of time and space, quietly adapting to foreign environments, and then changing those environments. Narrative is the discourse most amenable to translative adaptations that permit simultaneous retention and revision of its peculiarities. The Cinderella story, for a famous instance, is traceable to temporally remote origins in Southeast Asia, yet the version we know appears to us satisfyingly "native," because in small and unobtrusive ways the story has helped to form our minds. And it is principally through narratives, as has long been recognized, that the great religions of the world have articulated, consolidated, and disseminated their influence.

The uniqueness of modernistic contestations of narrative appears most vividly in the graphic arts, since, as I've observed, even Western civilization took it for granted for centuries that paintings and sculptures ought to tell stories. Our surprise today at this fact reveals how deeply we have internalized some modernist prejudices. Only by radical self-questioning can we recapture insight into authentic problematics of graphic narrative. The rewards of such self-examination could be more than intellectual, for we may expose how our critical "universals" may be disguised contempt for those peoples who still tell stories in words and pictures.

If the intellectual heritage of modernism impedes our appreciation of story as perhaps the most important of all modes of cultural discourse, *how* do we go about reexamining basic principles of narrative?[2] The most intractable methodological problem is the exemplification of genuine principles of narrativity. I have, reluctantly, chosen to restrict my use of illustrative examples. I rely on my readers to qualify my illustrations with their share of our joint knowledge of how complicated are the phenomena of artistic history to which I refer so schematically. Even a light sketching of variations that have been worked on the central functions I emphasize would awkwardly enlarge a book intended to concentrate attention on elemental facts of storytelling and its social purposes.

For example: the intrinsic provocation to judgment in storytelling, sharply perceived by Plato, has been obscured for many modern critics by the promulgation of official, propagandistic narratives by twentieth-century totalitarian regimes, in the West notably by Nazi Germany and the Soviet Union. The pseudo-stories fabricated in those societies to meet official commands, however, have proved ephemeral. Genuine storytelling is inherently antiauthoritarian. Even a true believer in an official dogma cannot help articulating a received truth in his own fashion—for stories are told only by individuals, not groups. Inherent to all such individuation is the potentiality for subversion, especially because a story is "received" by individuals, no matter how large and homogeneous the audience of a telling, each of whom simply by interpreting for himself or herself may introduce "unauthorized" understanding—all the more dangerous if unintended.

The ethical provocativeness of genuine stories, of course, is not invariably "good"—exactly why corporate entities regard storytellers with suspicion. Storytellers cannot be depended on, just because they tell stories, to present exactly the "right" issues in exactly the "right" way. That is why there are excellent stories that this or that person or this or that group consider distasteful. I, for instance, find parts of *The Song of Roland* morally unattractive. But no social situation in which the possibility of telling authentic stories exists is as constrictive as one in which genuine storytelling is impossible. Wherever real storytelling takes place, an essential human freedom exists.

Attention to this primal feature of narrative strengthens recent revaluations of story by feminists and reader-response analysts, such as James Phelan in his *Reading People, Reading Plots*.[3] Phelan's discriminations between "authorial audience," "characterized audience," and so forth, become more interesting when we recognize them as offshoots of the basic fact that every story is to a significant degree "created" by its audience, whose *heterogeneity* may have determined the way a given story was told. The Western Apache, for example, speak of "stalking with story," by which they mean telling a story in such a way to have a specific effect on a particular auditor or group of auditors.[4]

This illustration of a practice found in all societies in which oral storytelling flourishes raises another methodological difficulty. The principle that a story "means" in terms of a specific situation within which it is *used,* and at whom it is aimed, is virtually unrecognized by narratolgists. I have to dramatize that principle. But that requires skimping on the historical specifics that determined the very diverse uses of even the few stories I cite. I cannot demonstrate how the meanings of one particular story took shape under the specific circumstances of its tellings and receptions if I am to explain why the meanings of all stories are significantly determined by their "telling situations." Like the critics I criticize, therefore, I must pass over the diversity of responses triggered by differences of class, gender, intellectual interest, and the like, differences that shape the nature of any story. I do so deliberately, and I recognize (as I hope my readers recognize) the unfortunate necessity of curtailing what should be far lengthier commentaries.[5]

Perhaps the best way to justify my somewhat formalistic criticism of formalistic procedures is to specify the particular modernist attitudes I wish to expose for evaluation. It was, significantly, the archromantic storyteller Sir Walter Scott who was the primary target of E. M. Forster's dismissive wit when, in 1927, Forster lamented the novel's dependence upon storytelling. In a much-quoted passage Forster articulates—under the guise of escaping from "romantic" illusions— an essentially modernist view of story.[6]

> Yes—Oh, dear, yes—the novel tells a story, That is the fundamental aspect without which it could not exist. That is the highest factor common to all novels, and I wish that it was not so, that it could be something different—melody, or perception of the truth, not this low, atavistic form. For the more we look at the story . . . the more we disentangle it from the finer growths that it supports, the less shall we find to admire. It runs like a backbone—or may I say a tape-worm, for its beginning and end are arbitrary. It

is immensely old—goes back to neolithic times, perhaps to paleolithic. Neanderthal man listened to stories, if one may judge by the shape of his skull. The primitive audience was an audience of shock-heads, gaping around the camp-fire, fatigued with contending against the mammoth or the wooly rhinoceros, and only kept awake by suspense. What would happen next? The novelist droned on, and as soon as the audience guessed what happened next, they either fell asleep or killed him.

Even Forster's graceful humor cannot conceal his blatant wrongness about what constitutes storytelling. He is contradicted by the vast body of narratives readily at hand. We ought to be ashamed that Forster's error, along with its overtones of colonialist arrogance, passed unchallenged by subsequent narratolgists. It is important for moral as well as intellectual reasons to expose the unsoundness of this dismissal of narrative as an anachronistic survival of barbaric "primitives,"[7] because the dismissal echoes even in so recent a critic as Roland Barthes, whose favored exemplifications in his longest essay on the nature of narrative are trashy "secret agent thrillers."[8] There were historical reasons, if not justifications, for Forster's attitudes. But it is scandalous to affect such disdain today (especially under the guise of superficial concern) for those who tell stories. Even if one puts aside the moral offensiveness of such prejudices against "primitives," we must recognize that they obstruct comprehension of most of the literary and graphic art produced in the world before the twentieth century (including that in the Western tradition). To judge for ourselves what narrative is and what it can do, we must examine self-consciously our inherited critical biases by looking at empirical evidence of different kinds of story in diverse mediums from a variety of societies— including those traditionally deemed "backward" by nineteenth and twentieth-century Western Europeans—the dubiousness of whose views are enhanced by their tendency to describe "universal" aesthetic principles in crude, chauvinistic terms.[9]

It is, of course, impossible to describe briefly the sources of that complex modernist aesthetic of which Forster's disdain for story is representative. But in the last decade of the twentieth century it seems legitimate to depict modernism as a constellation of complex movements in part defined by resistances it has *already* met and reactions it has *already* provoked. In Fredric Jameson's words, in the first half of this century various forces of modernism

> conquered the university, the museum, the art gallery net-work, and the foundations. Those formerly subversive and embattled styles—Abstract expressionism; the great modernist poetry of Pound, Eliot, or Wallace Stevens; the International Style (Le Corbusier, Frank Lloyd Wright, Mies); Stravinsky; Joyce, Proust, Mann—felt to be scan-dalous or shocking by our grandparents are, for the gen-eration which arrives at the gate in the 1960s, felt to be the establishment and the enemy—dead, stifling, canonical; the reified monuments one has to destroy to do anything new.[10]

Even Jameson's brief list of names suggests how difficult it would be to define the core of such a complex aesthetic. But Andreas Huyssen in a thoughtful and well-received book has provided a roster of characteristics among which several central features of modernism are succinctly but persuasively identi-fied in terms of reactions against its dominance. In modernism

> —The work is autonomous and totally separate from the realms of mass culture and everyday life.
> —It is self-referential, self-conscious, frequently ironic, ambiguous, and rigorously experimental.
> —It is the expression of a purely individual consciousness rather than of a Zeitgeist or a collective state of mind.

> —Modernist literature since Flaubert is a persistent explo-ration of and encounter with language. Modernist paint-ing since Manet is an equally persistent elaboration of the medium itself; the flatness of the canvas, the structuring of notation, paint and brushwork, the problem of the frame.

> —Only by fortifying its boundaries, by maintaining its pu-rity and autonomy, and by avoiding any contamination

with mass culture and with the signifying systems of every-day life can the art work maintain its adversary stance.[11]

One could elaborate at length all these items. Clement Greenberg, for example, in his classic essay "Avant-Garde and Kitsch" begins by pointing out that "Picasso, Braque, Mondrian, Miro, Kandinsky, Brancusi, even Klee, Matisse, and Cézanne derive their chief inspiration from the medium they work in."[12] But two characteristics singled out by Jameson and Huyssen are especially relevant to the issue of narrativity in modernism: the rejection of mass or "popular" culture, and the insistence upon the autonomy of the work of art. These features reflect a rejection or radical reformation of narrative, because storytelling is a social transaction in which the audience "participates" as actively as the teller. Narrative in this sense is art that is inherently "impure," everything but self-sufficient. Nor does it shrink from subject matter entangled with the messy confusions of everyday life. Narrative tends to flourish through association with "popular" culture, and so, although it flaunts its artifice, it does not easily become the purely aestheticized object desired by many modernists.

Whether or not there exists a "great divide" between the modern and what follows it, what we now call the postmodern,[13] some persistent incompatibilities between modernist ideals and traditional narrative comprise an awkward inheritance for recent narratologists. Symptomatic of their difficulty is their preference for identifying story as dependent on, if not a "master plot," then a single, totalizing abstraction such as "desire" or "closure." One of my principal arguments is that storytelling consists in the interaction of impulses that shape and define with counterimpulses that expand and disorder. I find it difficult to deny the argument of Susan Winnett that master-plot formulations relying on "male morphology and male experience" (such as appear in references to tumescence and detumescence) need to be qualified by alternatives, and that a good place to begin would be with a model based on female experience. I share Winnett's view that the essential first move is to abandon the concept of *the* master plot, a single pattern definitive for every narrative. But were I forced to choose one gender metaphor for storytelling, I would opt for the female, if only because narrative is so endlessly proliferative, and what M. M. Bakhtin calls "unfinalizing," a mode of discourse.[14] A major point of this book, however, is that stories are phenomena so profoundly cultural that all explanatory analogues to natural processes, including those emphasized in Freudian psychology, are destructively misleading. Until we give up Causaubon-like faith in a single, universal (because organically founded, "natural") plot as *the* key to all storytelling we undervalue not merely the diversity of stories in themselves but also the significance of the diversity of response that stories call forth.

This diversity should remind us of the fascinating fact that *all* human societies have employed narrative, usually making it the preferred form of expression for systems of moral judgment— systems, of course, often violently antithetical to one another. One reason for such preference I have already stressed: all significant narratives are retold and are meant to be retold—even though every retelling is a making anew.[15] Story can thus preserve ideas, beliefs, and convictions without permitting them to harden into abstract dogma. Narrative allows us to test our ethical principles in our imaginations where we can engage them in the uncertainties and confusion of contingent circumstance. It is not surprising, therefore, that narrative should be of special concern to us as we approach the end of the twentieth century, for the accelerated rationalizing and technologizing of our life has unmistakably increased the difficulty of storytelling—and also the difficulty of understanding what could have made story so important to so many other societies.

But these special circumstances, as feminists in particular now insist, also demand that we scrutinize our least questioned assumptions about how social and interpersonal relations are established and perpetuated. Such scrutiny properly conducted should enable us to recognize the existence of and, possibly, the value in perspectives divergent from those encouraged by the centralizing, totalizing, universalizing trends in contemporary life. Thinking about why such trends are uncongenial to narrative and the different ways in which narrative has been deployed may help us recover the ability to appreciate the significance in activities of persons, groups, and entire societies marginalized not just by technological progress but also, and perhaps more dangerously, by ways of thinking that have too faithfully (if unwittingly) reinforced the depersonalizing qualities of our materially "progressive" society. The perspectives of those "others" also offer hope for realizing the ambition fueling the recent proliferation of narratological studies: to identify what we intuit as a—in Ludwig Wittgenstein's perfect phrase—"family resemblance" among the worldwide, wildly various progeny of the irresistable human impulse to tell stories.

Such perspectives cannot fail to remind us, moreover, that the "autonomy" of modern art and its self-proclaimed distinction from mass culture were ideals more often endorsed than achieved. No recent art can escape from what has been called the *commodification of culture* that has accompanied the industrial revolution. This "commodification" refers to the fact that the emergence of a distinct realm of "aesthetics," and art's hard-won independence from control by political or religious institutions, was made possible by a spreading commercialism that, beginning in the 1700s, penetrated with accelerating thoroughness all aspects of Western European society.[16] One reason for my attention in the next chapter to the British Romantic painter John Constable, for example, is that his narrativizing of "pure" landscape was a choice he might well *not* have made. His freedom to choose was unavailable, for example, to artists in France until later. In England at the beginning of the nineteenth century a painter's financial success and artistic repute depended less on the approval of ruling political and religious institutions, or even the patronage of wealthy citizens, than on an artist's ability to appeal to a more numerous, less affluent audience, often through commercial means such as book illustration or the sale of engraved reproductions.[17]

That appeal depended also on the associated yet, so far, less analyzed development of "consumerism." From the middle of the eighteenth century, commodities such as paintings sold to middle-income citizens carried a "symbolic" importance surpassing that of the objects' "intrinsic" worth, thus giving rise to phenomena such as "conspicuous consumption." This emergence of consumerism is closely associated with Romanticism's celebration of the pleasure of private, inner experience, which became the basis for what has been called "modern hedonism," those impulses driving individuals to seek satisfaction of a subjective "self-illusioned quality of experience," a quality of experience deeply influencing and deeply influenced by developments in the arts.[18]

The commercial success of Romantic painters illuminates the distinctive situation of art in our century, namely, that a work can be simultaneously "high art" and popular commodity—regardless of whether, like some moderns, one at least pretends to find the fact bothersome, or, like many postmoderns, one welcomes it. The efflorescence of consumerism (which a novelist like Italo Calvino perceives even in critical celebrations of readers' "producing" the texts they read) is germane to the analysis of recent attitudes toward narrative, because a story is a social transaction that demands an evaluative response from its audience—the most concrete evidence for which today being that audience's willingness to pay for a copy of the story. In play around every story is a particularized economic-ideological context out of which the special character of each telling and each reception takes its unique shape. From the early years of the nineteenth century in Europe a powerful contradiction in which both artists favoring narrative discourse and those resisting it were ineluctably caught was that the "freedom" to tell the story they wished, or the more radical liberty to dispense entirely with narrative, was founded upon their participation in a consumerist society. In our postmodern era, intensified awareness of that contradiction frequently determines how narrative is reintroduced into both the visual and the verbal arts so as to extend, revise, or oppose modernist transformations in traditional storytelling.

It is a fair if very broad generalization that the Romanticism that preceded modernism and the postmodernism that has succeeded it both originate (albeit in very different fashions) in an assumption that artistic "freedom" is attained by welcoming a "popular" (and therefore to some degree a commercial) function for art. A major tenet of modernism is an at least theoretical resistance to consumerism. This is the ground for the modernist insistence on the self-sufficiency of the work of art, its purity, its autonomy from (hence, inescapably, some degree of antagonism to) the economic, social, and ideological processes that inexorably would reduce the aesthetic creation to another kind of commodity.[19] We ought not to forget the noble aspects of that ideal, even as we learn to scrutinize with suspicion some of its claims. That ideal of self-sufficiency (echoed by the call to concentrate on the "text" in itself, and, ultimately, by the dictum that there is nothing beyond the text) led to a rejection of traditional narrative that has affected every aspect of twentieth-century aesthetics.

A sketch of the sequence of my chapters may help to clarify the relevance of these generalizations. The next chapter contrasts the moderns' turn away from narrative in painting with the Romantics' choice to renarrativize landscape. By 1800 landscape had become the primary a-narrative pictorial genre in the West. Unlike portraiture, "pure" landscape (that excluding the narrative elements which originally had justified representations of natural scenes) flowered only in the late Renaissance. The Romantics' "reactionary" reintroduction of narrative into pure landscape art foretells both causes and consequences of modern ambivalent resistance to storytelling, illuminating with special clarity the significance of its impulse to separate aesthetics from ethics.[20]

In the third chapter I analyze elemental principles of narrative discourse, building upon the work of the two modern scholars who have most thoughtfully addressed both the theory and historical practices of narrative, Paul Ricoeur and Mikhail Bakhtin, and on the work of two important philosophers of history, W. B. Gallie and Louis O. Mink. In the fourth I describe fundamental structures by which narrative discourse develops to fullest significance the polysemic character of words by articulating the possibility of different meanings for identical actions. These descriptions permit me in Chapter 5 to show how the disappearance of narrative in the modern era is to some degree an illusion, a product more of critical opinion than artistic practice. A contrast of Thackeray's Victorian novel *Vanity Fair* with Tom Wolfe's recent bestseller, *The Bonfire of the Vanities* (which was conceived as an equivalent to Thackeray's work), suggest reasons for the rise of the modern "paradigmatic" novel epitomized by James Joyce's *Ulysses*, and foreshadowed by Gustave Flaubert, whose "distrust of words" reflected his "distrust of narrative."[21]

In Chapter 6 I contrast selected narrative paintings to highlight some intersections of social and aesthetic forces that produced the nineteenth-century "crisis of narrative." Pictorial examples allow succinct illustration of how all storytelling "explains" contingent events without diminishing their adventitiousness. If one understands this principle (and most current narratologists do not), then he or she can perceive why the Renaissance turn to "invented" stories depending upon detailed descriptive realism led to a radical reorienting of narrative forms finally realized in the turn toward subjectivism and symbolism in the late nineteenth and early twentieth centuries. How a modern novelist transforms (rather than simply dispenses with) narrative I illustrate in the penultimate chapter through discussion of Henry James's *The Ambassadors*. In the final chapter, through special attention to works by Roy Lichtenstein and Italo Calvino, I present reasons why postmodern revivals of narrative have been tentative and only partially successful in the face of the growing sophistication of popular culture and the pervasiveness of stereotypical imagery as the dominant "reality" in increasingly rationalized and uniformly urbanized twentieth-century societies.

A final word of orientation. I do not in this book usually speak of "making stories" or "making up stories," although these familiar locutions are entirely appropriate. I avoid them only because I work from the axiom, discussed in detail in Chapter 6, that there is no significant distinction between the "fictional" and the "nonfictional." The principles of narrative operating in history and in novels are identical—one reason some of the most valuable analyses of narrative have been made by historians rather than literary critics. But the phrase "to make up a story" accurately suggests the contingent, provisional, performative character of narrating, as well as the teller's need for an audience. One normally makes up a story for others (if for oneself, a self divided pretty clearly into teller and audience) as both contribution and response to a social negotiation. This narrative transaction, the mixing of the reality of interpersonal relations with imaginative construction, is surely one of the most fundamental of social exchanges. Storytelling is perhaps humanity's primary tool for *changing* reality. One reason

it is proper, even necessary, to discuss storytelling in terms of narratives in different mediums and from a wide range of times and
cultures is that no activity is more fundamental to those proliferating sociocultural diversifications that distinguish our species from
all other creatures we have yet encountered—though not from
ones we are capable of inventing stories about.

Narrativity and Landscape Art

Celebrants of modern art claim that only in our century has painting at last realized its true nature, that only now has painting become self-sufficient by becoming nonrepresentational. By giving up the pretence of needing subject matter other than paint itself, by escaping the vulgarism of popular storytelling, painting became serious, intellectually significant. Piet Mondrian exulted that "the exponent of non-figurative art associates himself with the most advanced progress and the most cultured minds."[1] But every cultural success comes at a price, even if it takes time for the cost to appear, as disposable plastics seemed conveniently cheap until we realized that saving an environment polluted by our casual discards will prove inconveniently expensive. What, then, is the cost of modern art's nonrepresentational achievements?

The most useful answer, I believe, is found by dropping conventional terminology, such as "abstraction" and "nonfigurative," to examine, instead, how early twentieth-century paintings were emptied of narrative. A century earlier, at the beginning of the Romantic era, the spreading popularity and prestige of landscape painting had encouraged an analogous tendency to subtract story from graphic art. But this tendency was finally rejected by leading Romantic painters, who chose the opposite path—to renarrativize landscape. The Romantic decision *for* story dramatically illuminates the purposes and consequences of the modern decision *against* story.

Narrative is an enormously important mode of verbal discourse: most of the world's literature is narrative. Literature, of course, is a sequential art, like music. So some critics argue that

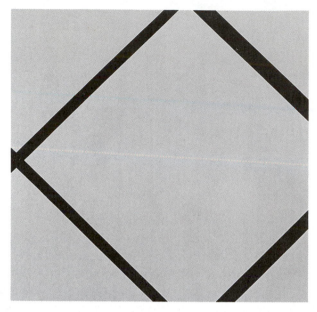

1. Piet Mondrian, *Painting, I* [*Composition with Red, Yellow, and Blue*], 1926. Oil on canvas, 44¾ × 44″. Collection, The Museum of Modern Art, New York, Katherine S. Dreier Bequest.

paintings and sculpture *ought not* to be narrative, since painting and sculpture are spatial arts, static not temporal. Verbal narrative is about action, about change; therefore—this line of thought concludes—narrative painting is a contradiction in terms.

Yet until the twentieth century most people assumed not only that paintings could and usually did "tell stories" but even that they *should* tell stories. Narrative painting was openly referential or illustrative: a picture was expected to refer the viewer to a preexistent verbal narrative. A marvelous instance of this is a medieval mosaic of Jonah and the Whale from a pulpit in Ravello, showing the lower half of a human body protruding from the monster's mouth in the panel to the left, and in the panel to the right the upper half of a human with hands joined in prayer emerging from the same monster's jaws. Could this vivid mosaic be meaningful to someone unfamiliar with the Bible and the Christian tradition, someone who might not even recognize the position of Jonah's hands as indicating prayer?

2. Anonymous, *Jonah and the Whale*, 12th century. Mosaic on pulpit of Ravello Cathedral (Alinari/Art Resource, New York).

One is tempted to say yes. Yet would such an observer know which way to read the action? Might he not read the pictures from right to left and from the monster's point of view—the story of a big one that almost got away?

The Ravello mosaic demonstrates that a picture is worth a thousand words only to those familiar with its peculiar conventions of representation. A picture without a verbal context is quite likely to be incomprehensible, for there are few if any visual cues that are not intrinsically ambiguous. A painfully vivid example of this is the widely published photograph of the family of one of the astronauts watching the *Challenger* shuttle, a picture identified in many newspapers as the family's reaction to the vehicle's explosion, though in fact it portrayed their premature elation at an apparently successful launch. Such mistakes explain why some question whether there are *any* examples of narrative readable purely from images. Wendy Steiner is one of the few critics to have tackled this problem.[2]

She concludes that even paintings that render events with that specificity necessary to narrative—"a story is a specific event carried out by particular characters in a particular place at a particular time" (12–13)—and represent the events "discretely" (so that the temporal unfolding is divided into distinct and ordered and temporally successive parts) are *not* necessarily narrative paintings. What is essential, she believes, to narrative painting is "the continuity of a repeated subject" (14–15). There can be no narrative unless more than one temporal moment is represented by the repetition of one or more figures. Unless a figure, like Jonah or the whale, *re*appears, it is not possible for a viewer to recognize the change or difference that constitutes action necessary for narrative. Only through the recurrence of identical actors can narrative be visually represented (17–19). This argument binds narrative to some kind of realistic representation and the depiction of human or creaturely forms, since the repetition of identical shapes merely produces design. "In visual narrative, the repetition of a subject is the primary means for us to know that we are looking at a narrative at all (21).

A consequence of this view, that we know we are looking at a narrative painting only "because we see a subject repeated, and because reality repeats only in time" (18), is recognition that powerful antinarrative implications lurked within the Renaissance concern for mathematical perspective, representation from a single viewpoint and single moment of time. (25–26, 41–42). What the Renaissance celebrated as "realistic" representation, the illusion of instantaneously perceived, three-dimensional forms, discouraged painters from depicting change. Change cannot appear in the portrayal of one instant from a unique perspective. There is much of value in Steiner's view, but what makes it most fascinating is that—apparently illogically—so many Renaissance painters and their audiences seemed to have *thought* that pictures could and should be narrative.

What skews Steiner's analysis is her conviction of "the all-pervasiveness of the need for a repeated subject in narrative" (19). Taken literally, her definition would allow, for example, the *sequences* of frescoes by Giotto in the Arena Chapel to be narrative, but no one fresco (since no figures are repeated within a single fresco) to be a narrative painting—which neatly if subtly denies narrativity in painting. In the Arena Chapel, furthermore, Giotto represents one important "repeated" figure in a fashion that *conceals* his identity as the same person—an anomaly to be discussed later. Steiner's oversimplification demonstrates the continuing influence of modernist resistance to narrative. Steiner relies on formalist theoreticians who carry forward some central ideas of modernism by treating every aesthetic "text" as autonomous, self-sufficient. Sequential repetition is not *the*, but one of several important features of narrative. To be assessed accurately it must be understood within the total *event* of storytelling, with due attention being given to role of *audience*.

A good storyteller, in whatever medium, appeals to his or her audience's imagination. The most potent effects of story derive not from what is told, what is positively represented, such as a repeated figure, but from what is omitted, not told. Visual omissions may be as potent as verbal omissions. Omissions play a crucial role in narrative because story does not and cannot exist without *both* narrator *and* audience. Narrative is a social interchange that is misunderstood if the actively contributory force of *any* participant is ignored.

The failure of purely formal definitions of graphic narrative lies in their confining attention to what is literally present *in* the artwork, in what may be called formalist graphocentrism.[3] Many visual narratives, like the Jonah and the Whale mosaic, illustrate a preexistent verbal story. Such illustrations bring together, rather than separate, visual and verbal storytelling.[4]

Illustrative reference is crucial in one of our earliest narrative representations, the Mesopotamian Stele of the Vultures, satisfactorily interpreted by an art historian only recently. She suggests we read it not, as had been customary, from the top down, but from the bottom up, and, furthermore, with awareness of the relation of the depictions on the side being read to those hidden on the other side of the stone. Finally, we have to reimagine where the entire stone was physically located. In other words, we cannot "read" the story of the Stele of the Vultures correctly until we recognize that what we are able to see is comprehensible through its relevance to what that perception itself prevents us from seeing (the other side of the stone) *and* in terms of its condition as a social transaction in which its "illus-trative" or "referential" character is the central purpose of its narrative—in this instance, the results of a victory in war.[5]

Since the Stele of the Vultures is a sculpture, I may here di-gress to observe that it is precisely the monument's *place*, its physical site, upon which much of its narratively referential meaning depends: the stele may literally have served as a boundary marker. This evidence of story's linkage to localism dramatizes the contrary *sitelessness* that Rosalind Krauss sees as characteristic of modern monumental sculpture, exemplified by Auguste Rodin's *Balzac* and *Gates of Hell*, of which numerous versions are to be found in museums around the world, al-though no version exists at the place for which each was origi-nally commissioned. As Krauss observes, the "abstractness" of a modernist monument is more than a matter of shape or form, for it is "functionally placeless and largely self-referential."[6] Al-though Krauss's examples are apt, the homelessness, or trans-portability, of, say, many of Henry Moore's monumental figures leaps to mind. There is scarcely a major city in the world *without* a Moore, but virtually all could be interchanged without making the slightest difference. The "localizing" specificity of narrative transaction that determined the form of the Stele of the Vultures is a quality that modern artists and modern audi-ences consider insignificant.

To return to painting: a large number, perhaps a substantial majority, of picture sequences do not present us with simple consecutive orderings. A favorite medieval system is that, for example, of the mosaics of the ceiling of the Baptistry at Flo-rence (whose "Golden Doors" by Lorenzo Ghiberti are sequen-tial in an entirely different fashion). The ceiling's order is that of a ploughed field, left to right, right to left, then left to right again, and so on, an arrangement that assures the juxtaposition of nonsequential units in contiguous registers. But sequencing may be so intricate or obscure that even the most experienced and knowledgeable observer can follow it only with difficulty. In some cases, such as Trajan's Column, described as the most important visual narrative of antique art, one's *inability*—liter-ally—to follow the sequence is part of the intended effect. That is not absurd if one assumes the artists anticipated imaginative responses from their audiences, that they conceived their referential story as a social interchange in which regular order is only one form of narrative activity and in which simple repetition of figures may be a subordinate feature of the narrative sequence.[7]

If we leave audience out of the narrative equation, we may find ourselves denying that Giotto painted individual frescoes properly called narrative. Giotto offers a good test case, because he has been for so long recognized as a genius in visual storytelling. What we learn from his narrative painting should be significant to an understanding of all painted stories.[8] In the Arena Chapel Giotto paints in three horizontal rows stories of Joachim and Anna, the Virgin Mary, and Christ. He seems to have introduced a minimum of specialized or esoteric features, favoring quite conventional representational signals over distractingly "original" details. We can almost say that Giotto depicted the familiar religious scenes the way you and I *think* we would depict them. Despite this accessibility, however, few commentators on the Arena frescoes have felt that the chronological sequentiality of each horizontal row, the register in which we encounter figural repetitions, is essential to their quality as narrative pictures. The chapel is so narrow that it is difficult to see the horizontal progression, and the asymmetrical wall structure to which Giotto adapted his paintings (if he did not in fact help plan the chapel), discourages some merely sequential readings—especially whenever the chapel is suddenly flooded with tourists.

Yet commentators over the centures have praised the narrativity of individual frescoes. To deny the narrative impact of the marvelous *The Kiss of Judas*, for instance, seems perverse. Such individual frescoes *are* illustrative. They refer to celebrated events—indeed, as I noted, Giotto seems attracted to what is familiar and employs unmistakable details for referencing his scenes: Peter cutting off the soldier's ear, for instance. But that *The Kiss of Judas* is illustrative does not preclude its also being pictorially narrative. To the contrary, the obvious referentiality of the fresco permits Giotto to engage us, the viewers, in his representation of the famous episode. Yet Giotto's *The Kiss of Judas*, though instantly recognizable, is not exactly like any other representation of the scene. It thus compels us to imagine the story of that most notorious of betrayals anew. The

3. Giotto, *The Kiss of Judas*, early 14th century. Fresco at the Chapel of Scrovegni all'Arena, Padua (Alinari/Art Resource, New York).

fresco's narrative force derives from its refocusing of our minds on the famous confrontation of Jesus and Judas, seizing the instant following the false kiss—a vividly silent encounter of reactions. Only an extraordinary verbal narrative could equal the moral and psychological concentration of Giotto's pictorial narrative.

This Judas reminds us that no two narratives are exactly alike. Giotto's fresco refers us to a well-known story, but in a unique fashion. Narratives, like conversations, are infinitely diverse. In theorizing about universal principles of narrative we risk forgetting the historical, "localized," facts that determine the final character of every particular storytelling. In the frescoes at Padua we see familiar tales being told through personalized emotional expressions never previously achieved (in good measure because never before *attempted*) in graphic storytelling. Giotto's emotionally provocative narratives are totally different, for instance, from those characteristic of Romanesque sculpture, another graphic form dedicated to storytelling.

In Romanesque churches or cloisters the rows of columns are seldom narratively sequential. If visual narrative depended on sequential repetitions of figures, artists so committed to telling stories in stone (as the Romanesque sculptors manifestly—and brilliantly—were) would have taken advantage of the opportunity offered by columnar rows for "necessary" repetitions— which in fact are almost never used. These nonrepetitive medieval sculptures suggest that by making *use* of referentiality a graphic artist may tell a story in a manner specially appropriate to a visual medium, in a manner not *requiring* sequential repetitions.

Sequential repetition permits one form of pictorial narrative, but a single scene may as fully realize the complex potentialities of authentically *pictorial* narrative. William Hogarth, whose *Progresses* have been cited as the first pictorial narrative sequences not illustrating preexistent stories, uses so many verbal elements (both inside and outside the graphic frame) that he has been charged with being too literary a painter. The seeming paradox disappears as soon as we remember that *all* significant stories are *familiar,* (a successful story is one that quickly becomes familiar). Appreciation of narrative depends very little on curiosity as to "what will happen next."[9] Modernists like E. M. Forster have lured critics into forgetting that all successful stories are, and are intended to be, reheard or reread or reseen, that a story is significant only if it continues to satisfy audiences who already know it.

Many verbal narratives, furthermore, are distinguished by devices that conjoin sequentially disjunctive features.[10] The flashback, elaborately deployed even by Homer three thousand years ago, is the best known of these configurative techniques. Some of these techniques are available to a pictorial storyteller. He, like his language-using fellows, succeeds to the extent that he arouses his audience into imaginative reconfigurings. Illustrative of these elemental (but recently neglected) truths of storytelling is the arrangement in the Arena Chapel, where we encounter more than one story, for the three bands or registers tell the different sotries of Joachim and Anna, of the Virgin, of

Christ. As a result, when one looks at any one painting in a sequence one also perceives above or below it, or both above and below it, pictures that seem to have nothing to do with it or its place in its register. Nobody who spends much time in the chapel, however, will believe that these vertical conjunctions are merely accidental. Giotto has established formal and thematic linkages between the vertically contiguous paintings to enrich and refine the meaning of the horizontal linear sequences.

Christ's baptism appears directly above the crucifixion, the vertical/horizontal play of relationships emphasized by the angels in the top fresco on the left holding Christ's clothes, while below the Roman soldiers to the right prepare to gamble for Christ's robe. The *Marriage of Mary and Joseph* in the top register stands directly above the *Entry Into Jerusalem*, and below that appears Christ's *Ascension*. In the top picture the unsuccessful wooers to the left are excluded, while in the middle Christ enters triumphantly into the city, and, finally in the bottom fresco He ascends from earth toward angels welcoming Him to the heavenly Jerusalem, heralding the possibility of redemption for all. This thematic relation is enriched by a formal pattern. The top picture is compositionally enclosed, the middle one opens its center, both to the sides and in depth, because we see the palm-frond cutters in the background, and this opening of the center is completed in the bottom scene displaying the Ascension—particularly dramatic because this rising and opening movement contravenes the general character of the lowest register as compositionally the densest, as if the real effect of gravity were felt closest to ground level even in the pictures.

Giotto's skill at blending of compositional and thematic features appears in the interplay of vertical and horizontal relations in his placing of the impressive *Lazarus* over the beautiful *Noli me tangere* composition, which appears immediately to the right of the *Lamentation at the Cross*. The figure of Christ vertically "moves" from his upright position at the left of the upper Lazarus scene to the right in the lower *Resurrection*, these vertical orientations contrasting with the horizontal figure in the *Lamentation* directly to the left of the *Resurrection*. We thus see Him die, rise, and move away from the touch of mortality, while the placing of his risen figure directly beneath that of

Lazarus affirms the definitive spiritual triumph over physical death only prefigured in the earlier miracle.

Obvious also is the positioning of the *Adoration of the Magi*, kings kneeling before the holy child, directly above Christ kneeling to wash the disciples' feet. Characteristic of Giotto's special human touch, it seems to me, is his vertical alignment of the camel driver tending his animal, and therefore not looking at the wonderful child, directly above the disciple concentrating on retying his sandal. The wonder of Christ's presence irradiates all the most trivial and ordinary circumstances of common life, even as these details encourage us to imagine the past with its entourage of kings before Christ's birth in contrast to the future faring of humble disciples on foot to preach a greater glory through Christ.

These few examples remind us of what is so obvious that we tend to forget it: visual perception, unlike aural perception, is not essetially sequential. In the Arena Chapel sometimes it is easier for the eye of the spectator to move vertically than horizontally. But it is naïve even with verbal narrative to over-emphasize sequentiality dramatized by repeated characters. Verbal narratives are also configural (a point discussed at length in the next chapter). Through configuration stories conceal as well as reveal, and conceal *by* revealing. Story hides itself by display, and through omissions and internal complication checks its impetus to progression. Narrative makes connections beyond those of any simple logic; it even reveals value in illogical conjunctions by developing the sylleptic or self-contradictory character of much important experience. Narrative tests conventional ways of ordering, calling into question, for instance, what we think of as "normal" cause and effect.[11]

Such challenges are within the reach of a graphic artist. Giotto's vertical ordering achieves an effect analogous to that perhaps no more successfully attained, for example, by Homer when he interrupts the nurse's amazed recognition of the scar on Odysseus's leg with the story of how thirty years before the hero had been injured by a wild boar. Narrative is proliferative discourse. The stories a story gives rise to necessarily complicate, may even obscure, the progression of the original. Both Giotto and Homer, however, depend on the audience's familiarity with what is being told. This appeal to audience participation expresses a teller's commitment to the socially transactive nature of narrative art. That commitment, not any set of structuring devices, is the foundation of all effective storytelling in every medium.

But after Giotto's time, in the Renaissance, there arose ideals of painterly realism and a passion for descriptive accuracy that radically altered pictorial storytelling and encouraged the development of "pure" landscape as an a-narrative genre whose popularity increasingly rivaled "history" painting, that is, narrative painting. These tendencies eventually evolved into modernism's resistance to narrative. But that development was neither smooth nor continuous. An illuminating countermovement in the turbulence was the Romantic renarrativizing of landscape art to redeem the ethical potency of painting. Romantic landscape, therefore, gives insight into the fundamentally evaluative function of storytelling, the function of storytelling that seems least understood by contemporary narratologists.

The narrative features of many of the most famous romantic landscapes are obvious enough—one thinks of canvases of, say, J. M. W. Turner and Eugène Delacroix. But the work of John Constable is even more revealing, because it displays both the artist's original attraction to painting without story and his ultimate reinfusing into "pure" landscape of narrative elements. By himself and by other during his lifetime, and by virtually all commentators since, Constable has been regarded as *the* "natural" painter. His supreme accomplishments are commonly treated as realistic representations of landscape scenes uncluttered by illustration or symbolism. Yet a survey of Constable's career demonstrates that although he never surrendered his commitment to accuracy in the depicting of commonplace scenes, and valued such scenes in and for themselves rather than for what they might signify, his later work complicates with narrative his original representational ideal of a direct, transparent, descriptive naturalism of both theme and style.

Constable's early work, even into the second decade of the nineteenth century, adhered to ideals of naturalistic representation that had flourished in England in the latter half of the eighteenth century. Success in representing with empirical accuracy a natural scene unfalsified by extraneous significations had become an accepted goal by the time Constable began painting. Even toward the end of his life, Constable describes with satisfaction landscape art's attainment of independence from a subordinate role to "history." And in broad outline, at least, Constable's account is correct: the triumph of landscape was through the subtraction of story.

The cultural significance of Constable's starting point is suggested by the international popularity in the eighteenth century of James Thomson's *The Seasons*, a long blank-verse poem almost entirely descriptive in character and which owes much to seventeenth-century landscape painting. Constable, who was all his life an admirer of Thomson, began painting in what may be termed this antinarrative tradition. There are virtually no figures in his early work.[12] But later, in his maturest and finest landscapes narrative features appear.

For brevity I will grossly oversimplify this development, suggested by the familiar observation that the paintedness of Constable's canvases became more overt as he matured. His later works are distinguished by what was called "snow," a flecking of the picutre surface with dashes of light pigment. This characteristic led a contemporary reviewer to remark that "it is evident that Mr. Constable's landscapes are like nature; it is still more evident that they are like paint."[13]

Blatant paintedness accompanies an increasing preference for surreptitious storytelling through the introduction of a few unobtrusive figures, particularly significant in the great six-foot canvases of the 1820s, attaining one climax in *The Leaping Horse*, but observable even in *The Hay Wain*—to which I will principally refer, since it is Constable's best-known work. Critics have insisted on how assiduously Constable labored over the "six-footers" in his studio, "at some remove from nature."[14] Constable, of course, is not the only landscape artist to rework his open-air sketches in a studio. But his unwavering allegiance to the ideal of naturalistic accuracy justifies Ann Bermingham's description of this intense studio painting as productive of a *fictionalized* spontaneity of impression.[15] Constable's later work achieves the *illusion* of transparently realistic representation. As Michael Rosenthal puts it, in the latter part of his life actual appearances lost their importance in his representations of

4. John Constable, *The Hay Wain,* 1821. Oil on canvas. The National Gallery, London (Foto Marburg/Art Resource, New York).

natural phenomena.[16] Yet, paradoxically, in the later works a lower vantage point and visual engagement with the messy details of nature immediately in front of the viewer tend to replace the high perspective and the simpler, less tangled foregrounds of his earlier scenes.[17] Constable forces the viewer to engage with complexities, obscurities, uncertainties, even contradictions in what are portrayals of activities or events, rather than just the reproduction of appearances. It is interesting that scholars insist that *The Hay Wain* had intense personal significance for Constable. Strangely enough, all evidence suggests that nonscholarly viewers are usually unaffected by the canvas's expressivity, seeing it rather as a kind of "objective" representation. This attainment of the *effect* of impersonality, or objectivity, by so intensely personal a work derives from Constable's success in unobtrusively pressing naturalistic description into service to narrative function.

For ordinary viewers *The Hay Wain* is the portrayal of an *event*, tempting their imaginations into constructing what is happening, thereby deflecting attention from the depiction's special relevance to the painter himself. The cart in the stream tells a small, simple, unexciting story, "a tale," in William Wordsworth's phrase, "unenriched with strange events," but for just that reason appealing to the viewer's imagination, urging the viewer, again to adapt Wordsworth's appropriate term, to *make* a story of the incident, to imagine the possible significance of the human interactivity implied.[18] Because the narrative is so undramatic, no more than the wain taking a shortcut through the river to get back to the field where it will be filled again like the wagon in the distance, we are encouraged—especially by the density of details in the foreground through which we "advance" to a more doubtful perception of more distant objects—to imagine all that may surround and be involved in these simple actions within an unspectacular setting. Because its provocation toward story urges us to recreate imaginatively a human meaning of unextraordinary activities, the painting does not strike us as expressive, for it visually *defamiliarizes*, to transfer a term from literary criticism.

The Hay Wain, to put the matter crassly, is addressed to an audience of non-haymakers. Constable's canvas compels our attention to aspects of life that in his day were beginning to be pushed to the background of general social awareness by the onset of industrialized civilization, even as the picture for Constable himself was "retrospective," painted away from the Stour and intended to gain him respect of London connoisseurs, few of whom cared much about details of farm labor. And *The Hay Wain* succeeds admirably in defamiliarizing, for it enables us to regard seriously and specifically—not merely sentimentally or nostalgically—what industrialized society teaches us to ignore. Haying, once generally familiar, has become an uncommon sight in our urbanized existence, both in the direct experiential sense and also in the sense that it has been made culturally invisible by the dominance of ideologies of technological progress indifferent to, if not disdainful of, agricultural procedures. How hay is collected, and what it contributes to our supply of nutriment, few of us now know, or even care to know.

The Hay Wain visually defamiliarizes in order to recall our imagination to a function of our society that we have grown accustomed to overlooking. The painting—in contrast to most of Constable's earliest work—is not transparently descriptive. It goes beyond the georgic tradition celebrating benefits of rural labor, which critics like Rosenthal see as central to Constable's work in the decade preceding the 1820s. The landscape of *The Hay Wain* is made, quite literally, to signify in a new fashion. It means beyond its representational accuracy, and the received descriptive traditions from which it derives, through being narrativized. As story, the painter's visual empiricism takes on a significance not merely subjective, nor, on the other hand, circumscribed by traditional generic implications. Neither expressivity nor symbolic emphasis could so effectively as this quiet storytelling remind us of the importance of a simple yet basic function of our society we have encouraged ourselves to ignore. *The Hay Wain*'s specificity is essential to its effect, as is its provocatively unspectacular narrative. Who could possibly care about a hay wagon—but what *is* this one doing in the middle of the river? By engaging us in imagining the story of so trivial an event, Constable, without subordinating realistic accuracy of observation to either personal or symbolic reference, signifies the value of such overlooked activities. Almost surreptitiously, then, *The Hay Wain* through it story develops a moral position, inciting us to think about what we have thoughtlessly dismissed as not worthy of thought.

A decade later than *The Hay Wain*, *Salisbury Cathedral from the Water Meadows* confirms the progressive narrativizing of Constable's landscapes. Weather and scene as story here become almost obtrusive. But this painting's narrative consists in more than a representation of the English church under threat. The thematic opposition between religious edifice and dangerously lowering cloud over the darkly looming trees above dank burial ground focuses a more oppressively self-reflexive conflict: the conflict generated by man's spiritual aspirations to transform the energy of natural processes, to reduce natural curvatures into mathematized straightnesses. Cultural accomplishment asserts humanness upon natural energies embodied in forces of vegetation, wind, water, oxidation, all the eroding operations of nature that relentlessly wear away the products of our artifices. This painting signifies man's dependence upon the natural systems he utilizes to affirm supranatural culture. The cathedral stands between the graveyard and a rainbow, mythological convenant of hope, but also between the bright wateriness of the meadows and stormy turbulence of the sky, terrestrial and celestial embodiments of uncontrollable evanescence.

The deepest passion informing this canvas is the anguish of the depicting itself. The ultimate complexity of Constable's art, realizable only through narrative functioning thus self-reflexively, consists in making us conscious of implications in his having made out of nature so transnatural an artifact as this painting of Salisbury cathedral. This picture's overt paintedness is profoundly functional; it constitutes the dramatic intersection of activities depicted and the depicting activity itself. This doubling-back of story on its own "telling" required Constable to move beyond the relative transparency and smoothness of his early work,[19] away from that descriptive clarity toward the thickly conflicted style of chiaroscuro distinguishing his late canvases.

This rather complex point has been lucidly addressed by Merle E. Brown, who observes that a painter, say, who treats a painting "as primarily visual, as perception" thereby disconnects his picture from the act of its making, "thus turning it into the sign of an idea, even if the idea is that . . . [it] is *not* the sign of an idea." Brown goes on to note that an image that is "let be" is thereby "turned into a perception, as distinct from anything imaginary" and so can no longer be "so rich and fine as an intuition, but . . . just because it is 'let be,' violated by an idea."[20] Transparently representational landscape painting, Constable discovered, in fact diminished his power to represent the "whole of reality," as Yurij Lotman calls it. By admitting into the representation evidence of the imagining act by which he created it, he could in his painting realize fully the ambiguous meaning for humankind of the ever–self-transforming plenitude of natural phenomena.[21]

The earlier form of his art from which Constable "escaped" roughly parallels what Henry James later objected to as the "mere" life not fully imagined (not fully "composed") in Victorian fiction. As I will suggest in a later chapter, Constable's turn to narrativity to enhance the imaginative efficacy of his work foreshadows James's transformation of fictional story, a transformation founded upon intensified narrative self-reflexivity.[22]

Because he was originally less committed to storytelling than other great Romantic landscape painters, Constable's increasing narrativizing of his scientific naturalism illuminates the significance of the ideology behind what he called his "natural painture," a politics of representation that much modern art later rejected. At issue is not simply Constable's resistance to reformist movements of his day, such as his opposition to the Reform Bill, though of course his "conservatism" founded on nationalistic patriotism is not irrelevant. More important are subtler ideological implications activated by the narrativizing of scene.

These implications derive from the ethical dimension that is opened by storytelling. Because *Salisbury Cathedral* is not just a scene but also a narrative, it signifies with an ethical force it would not otherwise possess. Narrative is intrinsically evaluative.[23] This does not mean that stories should conclude in summarized formulaic judgments. Rather, an effective story appeals in some way to its audience's judgmental powers: the story seems to matter, to be worth hearing or seeing. A good story is one that *deserves* telling. A good story is, to use William Labov's adjectives (to which I will return in Chapter 4), "terrifying, dangerous, weird, wild, crazy, hilarious, amusing, wonderful, strange, uncommon, or unusual" to its audience. In short, it evokes some kind of evaluative response from those who hear or read it. That assessing response (which demonstrates the audience's vigorous participation) constitutes the wholeness and completeness, the total meaningfulness, of a story, its "point," how it transforms the situation that was the originating context for its telling.

Contemporary art critics often overlook this aspect of story because some of the most important twentieth-century painting consciously sought to diminish such evaluative, judgmentally affective responses. Much modernist art, for instance, seeks sensual immediacy of experience and, following Oscar Wilde's assertions, strives to divorce art absolutely from ethical considerations. Constable's work illustrates how Romantic artists tended to bring narrative back into landscape to add evaluative affect to "pure" description. Modernism's programmatic countermovement to exclude ethical issues from aesthetic purity is best understood as an inversion of Plato's reason for banning of art from his ideal republic. For Plato, art was inseparable from narrative, partly because to all the ancient Greeks the supreme artist was Homer, and all stories, even Homer's, inculcated—so Plato claimed—bad morals. Narrative art is dangerous because it contaminates ethical purity. Plato argues that stories are *capable* of corrupting because invariably they evoke evaluative responses, exactly what, in the ideal republic, were to be fully predetermined.[24]

As always, Plato centers our attention on an essential issue, in this instance, that understanding a story is necessarily an ethical activity, an act of assessment. In an "ideal republic," that is, a society in which all ethical problems have already been resolved, there can be no place for narrative art, because there can be no need to raise ethical questions. Plato's logic reveals the special potency of narrative. He objects that stories always deal with change, or at least the possibility of change. For Plato, change is inherently bad, because it is evidence of imperfection. What is perfect, what is absolutely good or true or beautiful, is by his definition unchanging.

Yet even if we agreed with Plato, most of us still live in imperfect societies, in which success, even survival, depends on making judgments in response to shifting circumstances. Imperfection and flux are conditions that demand exactly the sort of understanding that good narrative evokes. A good story does not merely fit particular circumstances to a ready-made formula. Quite the contrary. The judgments evoked by story remain engaged with the specific contingencies giving rise to it and do not abstract themselves into categorizations. This important characteristic of narrative is best illustrated by myth. It is no accident that religions are constituted of myths, because religions must address the consequences that arise from the manifold changes and unpredictabilities in human experience. The Bible, which is predominantly narrative in form, beautifully illustrates the potency of narrative as a mode of discourse that simultaneously articulates and expounds doctrines and principles, while—because of the judgmental responses its stories evoke—rendering those doctrines and principles open to questioning, refinement, subtilization, improvement. The Bible's narrative form has allowed its principles and doctrines to persist vitally, to continue to be effective amid shifts in social

and cultural circumstances. The story of Adam and Eve, to cite
the most obvious instance, explains why the human condition is
not as fine as we can imagine it being, yet does so in a way that
poses problems which enable us, indeed, almost compel us, to
keep reinterpreting the story. Why did God allow the serpent
into the Garden? Was not God malicious to put the tempting
tree in Adam and Eve's way? Is the story misogynous? And so
on. Reinterpretion that is reevaluation does not destroy the
value of story, but rather enhances the story's value. Reinterpretation enables a story to serve as a continuing focus for
the most probing moral questions we can devise, every retelling
and rehearing being—and demanding from its audience—a
reevaluation.[25]

One reason story can be so ethically potent is plain enough.
Ehtical abstractions, the absolutes about which Plato likes to
speculate, have limited value for most of us, because—alas—we
lead such harried and unideal lives, lives entangled with constantly shifting contingencies. Our problem, normally, is not
knowing abstractly what is good or bad, but in figuring how to
apply our beliefs to specific situations, in making quite particularized, if necessarily and admittedly provisional, judgments.

As narratives localize and specify, they necessarily evoke
ethical implications that, as Plato detected, may bring into
question even the moral doctrines that the stories seem most
directly intended to enforce. Stories can thus arouse "unintended" moral effects because the very act of narrating pushes
abstract principles into the dust, heat, and pollution of the
arena of contingent experience. Throughout most of history it
has been engagement, not some fugitive and cloistered "aesthetic" appeal, that justified art—until the end of the nineteenth century.

The contrary choice of many early twentieth-century
painters, their resistance to narrativizing, their exclusion of the
ethical from graphic art to provoke untrammeled intensity of
pure sensory experience for the viewer, is bound into modernism's often-remarked abandonment of depth for increased attention to surface. This, as Meyer Schapiro has observed,
assures that "what makes painting and sculpture so interesting
in our time is their high degree of non-communication."[26] Modern noncommunication is "interesting" because deliberate, not

a failure of skill. And communication logically *can* be disregarded once the transactional quality of narrative has been dismissed. The intensity and immediacy characteristic of modernist painting denies not merely the illusion of visual depth, but also the unfolding in imaginative time that permits a configured wholeness of *response* gradually to emerge.

Modernist excision of the ethical from art is carried out in the name of absolute aestheticism. Aestheticism, as idealistically articulated by artists such as Vasili Kandinsky, Kasimir Malevich, and Piet Mondrian denies the authority of any political or economic or religious or philosophical system to shape art's methods or purposes.[27] Many modern artists invert Plato's hierarchy of philosophy and art but speak in Plato's disapproving tones as, like him, they banish narrative. Story can have no function in an aesthetic program that speaks definitively on the place of morality—even if that place is no place at all. Many societies, of course, have censored or banned narratives as potential challenges to authority (for the good reason that such challenges frequently begin in stories). But only with the rise of modernism do we find storytelling programmatically eliminated to free aesthetic activity from ethical purposes of *any* kind.[28] Such "liberation," of course, may contribute to a *de-*moralized society in which the most inhuman brutalities become not only imaginable but even ignorable.

Leaving that issue aside for now, I want here to point out that the Romantic "return" toward narrative as exemplified in Constable's painting is significant because so contrastively unobtrusive. Romantic renarrativizing of landscape was undogmatic, undoctrinal—because these are inherent qualities of storytelling, qualities enabling it to assume extraordinarily diverse forms, so diverse, in fact, that even its "obliteration" by modernism may be to a degree illusory, a trick of critical misperception.

We should not overlook the coincidence of the rise of "autonomous" landscape art in Western culture with the development of the conception of the artist as an "original" creator in the modern sense, a conception with important implications for storytelling. Previously in the West, as in all preliterate societies, stories were told, not authored. Tellers presented themselves as retellers authorized by a story preexistent to any teller, as we

5. Kasimir Malevich, *Suprematist Composition: Red Square and Black Square*, 1915. Oil on canvas, 28 × 17½″. Collection, The Museum of Modern Art, New York.

have observed in the case of Giotto. Each retelling, therefore, besides establishing relationships among an immediate audience, rearticulated relations of the present to the past. Especially with the advent of printing, the primacy of the teller linking now to then has been usurped by an author presenting a new story, legitimized by its immediate impact rather than its previous existence. The effect of this development in the graphic arts is suggested by the tendency of later critics to characterize landscape representations by painter rather than subject, *a* Ruisdael, *a* Claude, *a* Turner.

As teller functions are subsumed within author functions, narrative is perceived less as transmission and more as creation, and its primal function of making sense of contingencies without denying their contingent nature focuses increasingly on singularities of subjective, psychological experience. In fiction, as I will point out subsequently, a result of this transformation is a shift from syntagmatic to paradigmatic narratives, which intensifies the symbolic, "universalist" implications of story. The paradoxes in this development find substantive respresentation in modernist transformation of Romantic landscape art.

The importance of landscape in the development of modernist painting is visible not only in Paul Cézanne's landscapes but also in Pablo Picasso's work at Horta de Ebro in the summer of 1909, a season that has been described as the "most crucial and productive" of his career, because these landscapes (which include *Mountain of Santa Barbara, Horta de Ebro, Factory at Horta de Ebro, Houses on a Hill,* and *The Reservoir*) "constitute Picasso's first fully defined statements of Analytic Cubism (marked by 'reverse perspective,' bas-relief, modeling, and consistent *passage*)."[29] As Picasso's titles demonstrate, to paint a landscape is to paint a singular locale, some unique physical configuration (which implies a world constituted of individualized places) considered interesting because individual. All the contributory streams to the surging tide of seventeenth and eighteenth-century landscape painting, from topographical depictions of the houses and grounds of the wealthy to the late neoclassic craze for the "picturesque," accentuated artistic emphasis on individuation of scene. Romantic painters like Constable (however much they renarrativized) affirmed in their landscape art the importance of particularized visions of singular, heterogeneously constituted locales within a diversified and always

6. Pablo Picasso, *Houses on the Hill, Horta de Ebro*, 1909. Oil on canvas, 25⅝ × 31⅞". Collection, The Museum of Modern Art, New York, Nelson A. Rockefeller Bequest.

changing natural world. Yet, despite the promise of particularity in the titles of Picasso's landscapes, in the works themselves (as in Cézanne's) the originary point of specific physical situation is transformed into a painterly "abstraction" as "essential" or "eternal" or "universal" forms replace uniqueness of scene as the dominant interest. Simultaneously, the modern artists intensify emphasis on their reconstructive artifices, so that, finally, the "fact" depicted, the natural locale, disappears within the dramatic event of the portraying, the subject represented is subsumed within the act of representing.

This valorizing of the artist's depicting action is analogous to that development in literature by which transmissive tellers were superseded by creative authors. In both processes subjective intensity encouraged essentialized, symbolic effects more "abstract" than the earlier ectypal negotiations between painter and audience through scene, or between teller and audience through tale, which produced works of art that are not self-sufficient in the modern sense.[30] Yet intriguing linkages between contrasting Romantic and modern handling of landscape, illustrated, for example, by Constable's *Salisbury Cathedral* and Picasso's *Reservoir*, imply a hidden continuity that affected the special character of the later art's innovations. Important to that continuity is a narrative impulse overlooked by recent critics who ignore or misunderstand the socio-cultural functions of storytelling.

Social Foundations of Narrative

Although narrative is again coming to be regarded as a significant mode of discourse, there is disagreement about how such discourse is constructed. Some critics, such as Roland Barthes, have suggested story structure is analogous to sentence structure, but only Paul Ricoeur, so far as I know, has thought through the fallacy in this simplistic analogy. He observes that because every sentence comes into being as a speech act, escaping from the mere virtuality of language as system, *langue*, there is "no way of passing from the word as lexical sign to the sentence by mere extension of the same methodology to a more complex entity. The sentence is not just a longer more complicated word. It cannot be defined adequately by its opposition to other sentences, as linguistic units of a lower order, i.e., phonemes, can be.[1] A discourse constituted of sentences, Ricoeur concludes, is therefore not a semiotic structure. This startling point is founded on the following line of thought.

A semiotic structure, Ricoeur observes, has an analytic, "combinatory power based on the previous oppositions of discrete units" (11), and must be apprehended analytically. Discourse structure, to the contrary, is synthetic and to be understood through synthetic processes of apprehension. Discourse, moreover, is temporal: it actualizes a timeless linguistic competence into a time-occupying actuality comprehensible only as a performance, a historical event. Ricoeur perceives discourse to be utterance, to be understandable as what is now commonly called speech act. This is a basic point at which his analysis and Bakhtin's converge in diverging from the structuralist bias of Barthes, A. J. Greimas, and their disciples. The meaning of discourse as historical speech act (or what Bakhtin calls "speech experience") depends on its referentiality, a dimension of its accessibility to its addressee. And any utterance refers not only to nonlinguistic actualities that may be apprehended by those who hear or read the utterance, its addressees, but also refers back to its utterer though specific grammatical procedures, shifters such as pronouns, verb forms, adverbs, and the like. This self-referentiality of utterance, however, is distinct from the semiotics of language system exactly because the latter lacks the accompany external reference. In *langue*, signs refer only to other signs within their encompassing organization. In performance alone, in utterance, in acts of speech does there come into being that complex mode of triple referentiality to speaker, hearer, and world spoken of that constitutes "nonsemiotic," synthetic, response-provoking, "real" historical meaning.

Although Ricoeur distinguishes speaking and writing, he does not contrast them, and his general definitions of discourse apply equally to what is written and what is spoken, for he regards writing to be a *fulfillment* of the dialectic of event and meaning inaugurated by speech. For him, writing fixes not the event of speaking as event but as what he calls the "intentional exteriorization" implicated in a speech act (27). In written discourse it is *manifest* that the writer's intention and the meaning of what he has written *may* not coincide, as normally they will *seem* to coincide in oral discourse.[2] But the possibility of this disjunction (because the writer probably is not physically present to the reader) does not authorize concern solely for an "intentional fallacy," a misreading founded on unverifiable assumptions about what an author may have intended. Against that danger must be weighted always the symmetrical risk of a "fallacy of the absolute text," which is the "fallacy of hypostatizing the text as an authorless entity," that is, a text produced by no human intention (Ricoeur, 30). It is worth noticing, *en passant,* that in present-day society filled with advertising propaganda, and self-serving bureaucracies of every kind, the fallacy of the authorless text is far more likely and dangerous than the "intentional fallacy," a critical by-blow of modernism's insistence on the "autonomy" of art.

The crux of Ricoeur's argument is that a written text, just like an oral performance, is *by* someone, *to* someone, and *about* something. If we lose sight of any one of the three elements in this social transaction, we falsify the text. A predominant mode of falsification afflicting recent criticism arises from concentration solely upon the text, *what* is said to the exclusion of *who* says it to *whom*—and to what purpose. This exclusivity reduces the text from historical artifact to something equivalent to a natural object.[3] Ricoeur, probably because of his commitment to hermeneutic principles, finds that the best way to keep all the essential elements of discourse in uniform critical focus is to center attention on the responsive part of the speech-act process, the audience.

Spoken discourse is normally addressed to another person or persons literally present, but written discourse addresses a more dispersed audience, unknown readers, potentially any future reader. Writing is speech liberated from the physical constraints of oral communication. The price of that liberation is a dependence on some material support, clay, stone, paper, film, computer memory. But inscription makes discourse more self-contained, and, thereby, powerful beyond the here and now. The power in this "iconicity" of writing facilitates metamorphosis of reality by *distanciation,* a distancing of reality from itself to augment its potency (Ricoeur, 43–44). This is the most significant attribute of discourse, for it allows us to *change* our apprehension of reality, thereby differentiating us from animals that are trapped within a given sensory situation. As Ricoeur phrases the point in his famous essay, "The Hermeneutical Function of Distanciation": "Just as language in actualizing itself in discourse goes beyond itself in the speech event, so speech in entering into the process of understanding goes beyond itself in the meaning. This surpassing of the event in the meaning is a characteristic of speech . . . the very first distanciation is the distanciation of the saying in the said."[4] Writing, it must be stressed again, enhances the capacity of oral utterance to go beyond itself in being understood, but that potency is always present in speaking, in which begins the human power to distance reality from itself. For Ricoeur, distanciation is implied in the nature of the primary unit of utterance out of which all discourse either oral or written, is built—the sentence.

For clarity of exposition I will continue to treat Ricoeur's position as fully congruent with Bakhtin's, but at this point one must note that Bakhtin is more radical. Ricoeur focuses his attention on what Bakhtin regards as "secondary" or "complex" discourse genres, with little stress on the primacy of utterance, which is Bakhtin's principal interest. For Bakhtin, the sentence is not a primary unit, so he spends little time analyzing sentences as such, which he considered to be determined by the nature of their utterance. Bakhtin's view in no way invalidates Ricoeur's approach to sentence form. Bakhtin would only insist that we recognize the Ricoeurian dialectic of the sentence as derivative from the more basic dialectic of utterance, which is not at all determined by or definable in terms of subject, predicate, or any syntactic form, but simply by change of speakers. This position, which foregrounds the sociality of human beings, enables Bakhtin to explain with unique clarity the emotional and ethical necessities of narrative discourse through emphasis upon what he calls the "expressive intonation" of performance. But Ricoeur's understanding of the nature of the sentence is valuable for bringing us toward a Bakhtinian sense of story as dialogic utterance. Ricoeur's analysis escapes from the categorizing limitations of structuralism that have dominated recent Western criticism of narrative—while sustaining one of the most valuable goals of structuralist efforts, to find systematic means for describing narrative discourse.

Ricoeur suggests that one may think of sentences as consisting of a dialectic between subject and predicate. A sentence *predicate* designates a type, a kind, a class; it universalizes. A sentence *subject* identifies an item; it singles out. Sentence structure consists in interactions between identifications, the singularity of, say, *James, gravity, pain, French revolution, everything, economics,* and the universality of, say, *vaporizes, runs, believes, tells, grows, colors, contrasts* (Ricoeur, 10–11). This dialectic between subject and predicate may be regarded as a microcosmic version of discourse structure; a story, for example, can be described in terms of the "universal" action of a particular agent.

Ricoeur's description can be utilized to escape the reductionism of structuralist analyses of stories. Folklorists' classifications of "motifs," for example, are usually categorizations of predicates only, as is true of the famous "functions" of Vladimir Propp. Propp was explicit that fairy tale structure was to be defined through its actions, variations in agents being of no importance.[5] But as soon as we think of a dialectical play between "universal" actions and "particular" actors we understand one reason Propp's classificatory scheme is unsatisfactory, especially for a literary critic, who commonly seeks formal differences between works with similar motifs or themes. So far as a work of art is recognized to be a unique entity, the critic who relates it to other works of art must concentrate on, in Wordsworth's phrase, "similitude in dissimilitude and dissimilitude in similitude." But Propp's system, like that of most major folkloristic classifiers, focuses exclusively on similarities.[6] Ricoeur's description of the dialectic of sentence structure provides a model for analyzing narrative discourse, moreover, that enables a critic usefully to juxtapose works radically different in size, form, cultural function, genre, and artistic elaboration, and to do so without unduly compromising the individual integrity of each work. Let me try to illustrate this feature by citing the most extreme instance I have been able to unearth. This is a very brief Ojibwa tale that makes use of a theme that in the Anglo-American tradition is best known through Shakespeare's *Romeo and Juliet.*

> Once the Sioux and Peoria Indians violently hated each other. They lived on opposite sides of a lake. A young Peoria woman, named "Whence-The-Sun-Rises," fell in love with a young Sioux, called "Full-Standing." They made arrangements to go off together. One day, while her parents were away, the young woman was secretly carried away by her lover. When his relatives learned what he had done, he was not allowed to bring the woman into their home because of their hatred of the Peorias. Nor was the woman allowed by her angry parents to cross back to their home over there. And so they stayed in a canoe on the lake until a storm came up and they were drowned. Coming to the surface of the water for the last time, both shrieked. And even today during storms one can hear that shriek on Lake Peoria.[7]

Ricoeur's singular-subject/universal-predicate scheme gives us a way to say something a little more useful than Shakespeare's great romantic tragedy uses the same theme sketched in the Ojibwa tale—which is just about the depth of insight usually offered by folkloristic classifiers. For instance, the enormously greater length and complexity of Shakespeare's play can be seen in the light of Ricoeur's dialectic as specifically functional: the length of the play derives from the extensive use of mediating events and characters, various kinds of "go-betweens" (those getting in the way as well as those trying to help) such as Friar Laurence, Tybalt, Mercutio, the nurse, and so forth, whose "mediations" permit intricate complicating of the basic dialectic. This complicating reflects the playwright's interest in complex social systems of power that are "threatened" by the intensity of the lovers' concern for one another. Their doom appears to arise from "mischances," but in fact reveals how the very intricacy of social arrangements, which clearly display the channelings of violence described by René Girard,[8] assures that the concentrated intensity of such passion as theirs will be "self-destructive."

The stark, almost summarized Ojibwa story, on the other hand, concentrates on how natural passion is self-doomed if it arouses social ostracism. The point of this tale, one might say, is that there can be few or no mediations between group and individual in a tribal community struggling to survive in a dangerous natural world. On the contrary, some of the brilliance of Shakespeare's play derives from his dramatization of how a complicated society that has divorced itself from nature creates the deadly illusion of freedom for individual passions. Artistically, of course, there is no comparison between these "works." But if we recognize that their "predicates" link them while the dialectic interplay of "subject" with "predicate" distinguishes them, we can juxtapose the tale and the play to make a contrast that enriches our understanding of the singularity of each, despite absolute differences in size, form, and artistic intricacy. This perspective enables us to remark, for instance, on the functionality of Shakespeare's extraordinarily rich poetic language, which is necessary to articulate the complexity of a society that destroys the passion of the young lovers, even though it is that richness of language which makes possible the romanticizing of their passion. The Ojibwa tale, on the contrary, must be stark and linguistically plain because it displays

the futility of romanticizing—one might even say of metaphor—in a world in which the natural and the social so directly
intermesh.

If the Ricoeurian dialectic of the sentence provides us the
means to usefully contrast works so incommensurate, its value
is more impressive when we bring together incommensurate
texts more nearly equal in length and artistic quality, as may be
illustrated by two "versions" of the Orpheus story from different millennia and different parts of the globe, that of Ovid in
his *Metamorphoses* and a Nez Percé story, "Coyote and the
Shadow People." (The texts of those will be found in the appendix.)

In a commentary on the Nez Percé story Jarold Ramsey attributes to it an "affective resonance" beyond that of any other
Orphic tale, deriving principally from the protagonist's inability to resist *touching* his beloved wife, the failure expressing the
tragic paradox of Coyote's (Orpheus's) situation: "He has been
seeing his dead wife for some time now, but now that she appears to be fully tangible, seeing is not enough. To return to life
again is to touch and be touched, ultimately in a sexual sense . . .
if he *could* 'take the long view' and restrain himself, the reality
of his feelings for his wife would surely be suspect."[9] Ovid has
little interest in this tragic paradox, and his art does not focus
on the expression of such complexity. So in his telling Orpheus
only wishes vainly to return to Hades, then departs cursing the
gods and turning his love to "tender boys." Ovid's version cannot support the stunning conclusion of the Nez Percé story, in
which Coyote reenacts with ritualized detail his original journey
to the long-house of the Shadow People—to no avail.

That amazing and moving conclusion, although it does dramatize how the "same" story can be told so differently (reminding us that although good stories are retold, they are never
exactly repeated), usefully carries our discussion from Ricoeur
to Bakhtin, for, unlike Ovid's tale, the Nez Percé story is—
among other things—about the possible functions of story.
Coyote's error, unlike Orpheus's which leads only to the introduction of homoeroticism to Thrace, creates death as an inevitable feature of human experience. The stake in Coyote's trial
(though he does not know it until after his failure) is not merely
his personal but the human condition, and whether it will be

defined by an irrevocable obliteration of each individual. Given this context, Coyote's attempted reenactment of his journey seems to dramatize how death defeats a primary use of narrative, the coming to terms with every sort of experience. Its conclusion makes this story about the failure of narrative, as well as about the failure to restore Coyote's loved wife. This self-reflexivity should remind us that every story is simultaneously representation and enactment, conveying meaning but also producing effects, provoking responses. If, as several modern students of narrative assert, telling stories is a way of trying to hold off death—and Scheherazade is the archetypal storyteller—then the deepest tragedy in this Nez Percé account is its portrayal of the ultimate ineffectiveness of storytelling.

The Nez Percé story reveals how Ricoeur's individual subject/ universal predicate pattern shifts critical attention from the grammar of narrative (the structuralists' focus) to what may be called the rhetoric of narrative. This shift enables us to recognize the importance of the congruence of a story's internal form with the form of the telling situation, which congruence constitutes the singular realization of an infinitely retellable narrative. According to the Nez Percé tale, humans are mortal because Coyote touched his wife just once. But the "logic" of this is closed and inescapable, since Coyote touches his wife because he is human. The very feature of phenomenal or biological existence the story resists is thus by it *affirmed*. This self-contradiction is formally accentuated by the failure of Coyote's enactment of the ritual that had restored his wife to him once before, which lands him isolated in an emptiness that seems waiting for Beckett. The resolution or closure that is the aim of the retelling occurs only in the defeat of its purpose. Yet the narrative process itself provides a further reversing contradiction, since the failure of Coyote validates retelling of this story of humankind's continuing—ineffective—resistance to its mortality.

There can be no answer to the question, how often can a good story be retold. Narrative turns back on itself in a productive cycle, not a vicious circle. Humanity exists so long as the possibility of retelling stories is not closed off. As "Coyote and the Shadow People" illustrates, each good story is sustained by its self-contradicting contradictions, in this instance realized through the simultaneous insistence upon the absolute contingency and the absolute inevitability of death. So rendered, this impasse permits the emergence of successively deepening implications. Each retelling of a story permits the articulation of deeper possibilities that exist because they were *not* explicitly expressed in the original telling. This implicit richness of story is precisely the kind of latency one tries to avoid in "scientific" discourse. If we keep that in mind, we understand why explanations of narrative that define it either in terms of its closure or of a "deep" essentialist origin in desire must be inadequate.

The ineffective efficacy of storytelling I describe through the Nez Percé story exists because storytelling is a cultural action, not, like dying, a natural one. Perhaps the worldwide popularity of the Orpheus theme derives from its stark confrontation of natural and cultural, the artificer defeated by the brute force of physical existence. But if so, this reminds us that storytelling is indigenous to every human culture. What that means is fully articulated in Bakhtin's criticism, for his fundamental premise is that all humans live in what he calls an "ideological environment." We do not exist as human beings except in and through the culture of our societies, so human reality is ideological reality or symbolically saturated reality.[10] That premise enables Bakhtin more quickly and rewardingly than other critics to move past the distracting superficialities of particular language structures to deal with what he terms the structures of those structures (1986, 78–79). Bakhtin does not assume language to be prior to forms of discourse, the enabling structurings of acts of speech, such as narrative. He perceives forms of language and forms of discourse as originating in one another.

He insists on this inseparability because he believes that "human consciousness does not come into contact with existence directly, but through the medium of a surrounding ideological environment, which is constantly in a dialectical process of generation . . . [with] contradictions constantly being overcome and reborn." For him, therefore, "every utterance is a social act . . . an historical phenomenon," and, necessarily, ideologically charged.[11] For Bakhtin, the ideological charge of utterance is dynamic rather than fixed. "Literature," he observes, "ordinarily does not take its ethical or epistemological content from *established* systems but from processes of generation of ethics, ideas of knowledge" (1985, 17). It is this active, dynamic rather than predetermined, "socially evaluative quality" of utterance that endows language with its density, its difficulty, and its resonances. The purest form of the socially evaluative quality of utterance appears in what he calls "expressive intonation" (1985, 122). At this point Bakhtin's marvelous illustration of a one-word conversation—two people sitting silently in a room, until one says "Well!" [Russian, *Tak!*]—probably best explains why he insists that intonation is essential to every utterance, and why he perceives intonation as indecipherable except in terms of the nonverbal context, the social situation, which the speech act determines and is determined by—the specific historical, "ideological" circumstances through which the expressive intonation of a speech comes into creative being.

> Two people are sitting in a room. They are both silent. Then one of them says "Well!" [*Tak!*] The other does not respond. For us outsiders this entire "conversation" is utterly incomprehensible. . . . Whatever pains we take with the purely verbal part of the utterance, however subtly we define the phonetic, morphological, and semantic factors of the word "well," we still shall not come a step closer to an understanding of the colloquy.
>
> Let us suppose that the intonation with which this word is pronounced is known to us: indignation and reproach moderated by a certain amount of humor. This intonation fills in the semantic void of the adverb "well," but still does not reveal the meaning of the whole.
>
> We lack the "extraverbal context" that made the word "well" a meaningful locution to the listener. . . .
>
> At the time the colloquy took place, both interlocutors *looked up* at the window and *saw* that it had begun to snow; both knew that it was already May, and that it was high time for spring to come; finally, *both* were *sick and tired* of the protracted winter—*they both were looking forward* to spring. . . . On this "jointly seen" (snowflakes outside the window), "jointly known" (the time of year—May) and the "unanimously evaluated" (winter wearied of, spring looked forward to)—on all this the utterance *directly*

depends, all this is seized in its actual, living import—is its very sustenance. And yet all this remains without *verbal* specification or articulation. The snowflakes remain outside the window; the date, on the page of the calendar, the valuation in the psyche of the speaker; and nevertheless all this is assumed in the word *well*.[12]

I have quoted Bakhtin at length not only because his point is to accentuate the density of extraverbal contexts, but also because his analysis illuminates one of the transformations narrative undergoes in modern aesthetics. As I will propose later, a novel such as Henry James's *The Ambassadors* is organized to tell its story in terms of dialogue-transforming extraverbal contexts that have been constituted by an interplay of expressive intonations. A corollary of Bakhtin's view is that no two utterances, even one-word utterances, can be identical, even though the word or words used are the same, since the expressive intonation of the "historical" moment implicated by each use is individual, unique, unrepeatable. By the same token, as James brilliantly dramatizes, there is no such thing as a "neutral" utterance, one uninflected by intentions and circumstances. Every speaker articulates in his speech an attitude of some kind toward the subject of his speech and a mode of address to whomever he speaks. No utterance, furthermore, can be "indifferent" to other utterances. Every utterance is responsive to and related to other utterances; no utterance is self-sufficient. Every utterance is a link in the historical chain of speech acts forming what we call human communities.

This prepares us for Bakhtin's astonishing observation that—for all the importance of expressive intonation—no utterance can be attributed exclusively to its speaker, because every utterance is produced by interactions between speakers. Utterance is the articulation of a social interaction. This observation compels us to recognize that the listener, the one addressed, the one communicated to, of necessity takes an active role in shaping the utterance, evidenced by the addressee's agreeing or disagreeing wholly or in part, augmenting what is said, applying it, preparing for what it predicts, and so forth. Every good storyteller, therefore, enables a "creative" audience response, because understanding a narrative utterance is an evaluative process that constitutes the utterance.[13]

Michael Holquist has demonstrated that Bakhtin makes of utterance what he does because he operates from a psychology of the self quite different from our common psychological conceptions, yet one that has much to recommend it.[14] Without entering into that topic, I want to reinforce Holquist's point that Bakhtinian "dialogism" most significantly refers to the way that utterance joins my ability to address others (in speech or writing) with their ability to address me. Another speaker or a written page may address me, but in either case the utterance is structured as dialogue because it assumes a respondent. Dialogue implies mutual addressivity; understanding of utterance makes possible responsiveness, which is as active, dynamic, "creative" as utterance, for utterance and responsiveness are an inseparable mutuality of the dialogism intrinsic to human speech acts and responsible *use* of language.

Because addressivity, a turning to someone, is constitutive of utterance, the appropriate critical modes for dealing with the large utterances we call stories will of necessity—besides partaking of methods of historical hermeneutics—tend in the direction focused on by reception and reader-response theories. Bakhtin's approach brings to the foreground, beyond the fact that story response is constitutive of the story, the point that response is inescapably and essentially *evaluative*.[15] This does not mean that the addressees simply agree with the teller's judgments, nor that they even agree among themselves, but that their responses are necessarily judgmental. This feature of Bakhtin's criticism most radically upsets the general bias of formalist-structuralist approaches—which derive, ultimately, from modernism's tendency to split aesthetics and ethics. But Bakhtin's recognition of addressees as evaluators makes his dialogism no mere rebuttal of structuralism, but rather a means for reassessing it in a more comprehensive intellectual context.

Nor is Bakhtin's view discordant with some quite long established ideas about the nature and function of narrative texts. One could argue that he simply emphasizes the social meaning of the implicitness inherent within any explicit statement, indeed within any *action,* an implicitness long ago insisted upon by phenomenologists, leading to observations such as Frank Kermode's that any narrative in revealing one thing thereby conceals something else.[16] This essential implicitness has been somewhat obscured by Freudian psychology's focus upon particular repressions, which are something beyond the more fundamental, intrinsic implicitness that should be the starting point of narrative criticism. The distinction is explained by the German critic, Gunther Buck, who observes that every definite action because it is definite prevents the action from simultaneously grasping all its implications as an action. What is thus implicit is not a defect or a deficiency but a latency that interpretation seeks to bring to light. So what is implicit in all performance can be characterized as "unconscious," unconscious in relation to the consciousness of what the performance specifically intends. But, unlike the unconsciousness of motive traced in psychoanalysis, this is an *essential* implicitness. What is necessarily implicit in a text could not originally have been explicit. It did not *become* implicit. The implicit meaning sought by the literary interpreter belongs to the *normality* of speaking or writing—in contrast to what is *made* implicit by repression. That is why one interprets a text as if the author had communicated everything he had to communicate straight off without circumlocution, why one seeks an accurate text of what the author actually wrote, because only what the author made explicit defines what is essentially implicit *in that text*.[17]

Bakhtin's focus on narrative efficacy as provocation of its addressee's awareness of what is inherently implicit in the telling, on provocation dependent on a story's emphasizing the contingency of the event of telling, and on audience as a complex set of reactional processes, makes his approach convergent with both William Labov's studies of modern oral urban narratives and the most penetrating analyses of story by leading philosophers of history, W. B. Gallie and Louis O. Mink.[18] Gallie observed that to understand what a story is one must understand what it means to *follow* a story, as we all have, and he proposed that following a story is very like following a game, such as baseball or cricket. The analogy lies in the sense of a promised but uncertain outcome, which promise enables the audience to make sense of and find gripping interest in a series of contingencies because it is unable to predict surely their eventual result.[19] Thus, the essential stuff of story is contingency, which philosophers tell us is in itself unintelligible. Hence story is indeed crucial to the historian, who deals constantly with contingencies. The historian's account does not, as Mink puts it, "demonstrate the necessity of events but makes them intelligible by unfolding the story which connects their significance," so that history, as R. G. Collingwood had suggested, is like fiction so far "as it essentially depends on and develops our skill and subtlety at following stories."[20]

Gallie's other fundamental observation, derived from his comparison of following a story to following a game, is that with both we best follow the series of developing contingencies when our sympathies and antipathies are enlisted; what he calls the "basic directing feelings" are brought into play by worthwhile games and stories. That the intelligibility of a story, its meaning, is enhanced by, indeed, is to a considerable degree dependent upon, its engagement of our emotions, is perhaps Gallie's most lasting contribution to our understanding of stories and their functions. The observation frees us from being too rationalistic and too purely intellectual to do justice to the unique capacity of story to render without oversimplifying or reducing to too rigid a structure the complex adventitiousness of human affairs.[21]

Narrative creates patterns that do not diminish the fortuitousness of the contingencies they organize. Herein lies the secret of a god story's infinite retellability. And it is worth noting that Gallie's insight into the essentiality of emotion in story reception helps to justify considering narratives what Mary Louise Pratt calls "display texts," whose function is less to inform than to incite wonder—above all shared wonder at a specific human situation or perplexity.[22]

The concept of display text liberates critical understanding from the limitations of much unsophisticated commentary based in "speech act" theory. Focused as it is on the dialogical interplay of presentation and response, the concept of display text allows one to bypass the reduction of response either to mere personal subjectivity or to mere systems of conventions. It concretizes the element of "creativity" involved by making this quality inseparable from "criticalness," because it emphasizes the differences among those participating in the display and does not diminish the importance of the contribution of any participant. The concept frees us from the crippling misperception of communication as the bland conveyance of "information" from transmitter to receiver, like pouring milk from a pail into a bottle. A display text sets in action a double feedback loop in which the full significance of the original presentation can only be recognized through readers or listeners taking up their responsibility, responding not passively but actively, which is to say, critically and evaluatively. The "creative" response, in what Judith Fetterley calls the resistive reader, may take the form not just of qualification but even of denial. The honorific "creative" is transferable from the originator to audience because the value of a display text depends on its capacity to incite a dialogic response, allowing reversal of the roles of addresser and addressee. The process is made vivid in the criticism of the finest stories, say *The Iliad*. The assessments provoked by the poem produce questions to Homer, as it were, about his text: why, for instance, does Paris vaunt over wounding Diomedes in a verbal formula elsewhere used only by Greeks vaunting over Trojans they have killed? Through his text Homer can "answer" that the debasement of the verbal form reinforces the cowardliness of the action. I cite this instance because it is a piece of artistry that passed unnoticed until *The Iliad* had been actively responded to, subjected to critical assessments, for many centuries. Until brought to light by engaged questioning and responsive readings, it remained implicit.

Louis O. Mink, while crediting Gallie with seizing on the crux of story, its involvement with contingencies in a fashion that engages our emotions, insists on the absolute importance of distinguishing between *following* a story, as Gallie describes it, which depicts a naïve response, that of one who does not know how the story ends (the situation of the spectator at a game), and what it means to *have followed* a story. Mink's insistence on the limits of Gallie's original analogy is far from trivial, for, as he says, in regard to human actions "to know an event by retrospection is categorically, not incidentally, different from knowing it by . . . anticipation."[23]

This is without doubt *the* central question for the analysis of narrative and its functions: "Why do stories bear repeating?"

(Mink, 56). The overriding empirical fact about narrative is that stories *are* retold—many of the best seemingly endlessly. As important, stories are normally *intended* to be retold. As Walter Benjamin pointed out, stories are listened to in order to be retold.[24] Mink's sensible observation, furthermore, is that knowing the full plot of *Oedipus,* or *King Lear,* or *The Iliad* or *The Divine Comedy* or *Crime and Punishment* in no way diminishes our pleasure in or the value of these works. Nor do historians ever complain that their reading of first-rate history—he cites Garrett Mattingly's *The Defeat of the Spanish Armada*—is marred by their knowing how it all came out. "Familiarity," as Mink puts it, "in the case of narrative breeds respect" (48).

Mink argues that story demands we exercise our capacity for *configurational* comprehension, grasping a number of things as elements in a single and concrete complex of elements, with the meaning or value to us of that grasping determined by how we so understand. Aristotle's remark that a play must have a beginning, a middle, and an end, thus, is "a corollary of his principle that a drama is an imitation of a *single* action, that is, that both action and mimesis must be capable of being understood as a single complex whole" (Mink, 50). In one sense, this explanation seems like a truism, as Mink recognizes: one cannot understand a story until one has heard all of it. But it is a truism, as critics like Northrop Frye have recognized, fundamental to criticism, for the ability to grasp complex wholes is the foundation of all successful critical interpretations. What is surprising about Mink's explanation is that it reduces mere temporal succession in story to relative insignificance. As he puts it:

> [I]n the configurational comprehension of a story which one *has followed,* the end is connected with the promise of the beginning as well as the beginning with the promise of the end. . . . To comprehend temporal succession means to think of it in both directions at once, and then time is no longer the river which bears us along but the river in aerial view, upstream and downstream seen in a single survey. (Mink, 56–57).

Mink's position is that narrative comprehends both space and time, allows simultaneously what might be called "vertical" and "horizontal" vision. Storytelling solicits, therefore, a special kind of attentiveness in its audience, a "negative capability" permitting extreme flexibility of response—perhaps most apparent with narrative's "wandering viewpoint." This does not mean that story is simply antithetical to closure. Rather, as Mink observes, it establishes a configurative view that does not cancel the unfolding (or folding-back-into) movements that constitute narrative progress. To see upstream and downstream at once is not to lose sight of the river's eddying flow.

Unless one takes a view like Mink's, it is difficult to explain why good stories become more interesting and more precious when reread or reheard—as indubitably the best stories do. If we regard the essence of story as primarily its sequentiality (what happens next), the high regard for retold stories—a classic is simply a story that is frequently retold—becomes inexplicable. On the contrary, once we have grasped the importance of the configurational understanding of story, that the fluid integrity of narrative is a function of the process by which it is comprehended, its capacity for being retold makes perfectly good sense. Indeed, when one considers a written story, a novel, say, it should be plain that the feedback process by which a reader contributes to the tale will be enormously enhanced by rereading. Before we know the whole, we are more passive recipients in the narrative exchange; rereading, we are positioned to be more "critical." Gallie and Mink thus restore to each member of the audience full partnership in the narrative negotiation. Mink's final example of how in fact we respond to the discovery in Sophocles' *Oedipus* focuses the point admirably: "[S]ince we already know the story, we can only play at following it. In the comprehension of the story as a whole, there are no discoveries and descriptions have no tense" (Mink, 58). Sophocles' play forces it audience to *play:* the "creativity" of the author calls forth "creativity" from his audience.[25]

Sophocles, like Homer, Chaucer, or Dostoyevsky, like all good storytellers, understands the comprehension to which his story must appeal to be successful. Put crudely, the teller probably hopes for fame, for his play to be reenacted, his story to be retold—and resold. But his art will succeed less through arousing curiosity in the naïve about "what will happen next" than through arousing and satisfying our capacity for what Mink calls the power of configural comprehension, a power in the audience that might be termed godlike, for it consists in perceiving succession as simultaneity.

Mink's crucial amending of Gallie strengthens, rather than weakens, Gallie's emphases on the contingency of the substance of story and on the importance of emotion in the reception of story. Mink's "configural comprehension" means understanding the total connectedness of contingencies in a way that does not violate their integrity as "accidental." Configurative understanding means that the significance of the recounted series of event (in fact or fiction) contains the possibility of events having occurred otherwise and of being recounted otherwise. Such implications enhance the satisfaction of grasping in its completeness what we are told "actually" happened. The emotional and evaluative character of our response to a story principally derives from this recognition that the configurative necessity of the narrative conceals other possible but unrealized orderings. Gallie's analogy of the game, although too simple, is helpful in clarifying this process. For instance: on the last play of a football game in which the team for which we are cheering and is one point behind attempts a field goal; when the kick fails we are saddened by the *now* inevitable defeat because there was in the event a possibility for the delight of hard-won victory. The inevitability of the outcome once the game is over does not do away with the adventitiousness of the actions that constituted it. We may through retrospective analysis, therefore, arrive at some conclusion concerning "why" our team lost, but such an explanation does not vitiate our awareness of the game having been made up of accidents. Our sorrow can survive in our analysis—"if only on the next-to-last play the quarterback had not fumbled . . ."

The configurative understanding evoked by narrative includes awareness of the intrinsic implications in the story. Such consciousness that the tale's revelations simultaneously conceal involves the audience in acts of judgment. The social significance of a story, in fact, largely derives from specific assessments by audiences of what they are told, not in terms of some external standard or abstract set of principles, but in terms of the dynamic interplay of the explicit and the implicit in the story itself. Thereafter, of course, the judgment provoked may

itself be judged against various standards and principles ante-
dating or postdating the telling. It goes without saying that we
bring *to* any storytelling a preestablished system of moral and
metaphysical beliefs and a range of commonsense "prejudices"
(as Hans-Georg Gadamer calls them), which form the basis for
how we assess the story. But in the process of receiving the telling, including our retrospective comprehension when it has
been completed, these preestablished systems and prejudices
are aroused—sometimes by being reinforced, sometimes by being challenged.[26] Since our systems of ordering and moral
belief are fortified by entrenched emotional commitments, story-
telling/story receiving solicits powerfully our sympathies and
antipathies to activate those systems so that we may participate
in a transformative realization of what binds us as emotional
individuals to our community.

4

How Stories Are
Constructed

Our response to a good story is incited equally by its configurative totality and the adventitiousness of its constitutent parts. To return to Mink's example (though any good story would serve as well), the power of *Oedipus* arises from our comprehension of the entirety of the protagonist's familiarly strange life, because that understanding enhances our evaluation of the accidents making up his history. However we assess it, the unfolding of that history has compelled us not merely to observe but to bring into play all our human capabilities. Because we know the whole history of Oedipus (as did the audience at the first performance of Sophocles' play), its crucial "discovery" is no discovery, so that the *retelling reanimates* our horrified fascination in its dynamic interplay of fortuitousness and inevitability—an interplay characteristic of all significant experiences.

However often a story is retold, each narrating event is a social construct, involving some identifiable persons, some specific occasion, some special purpose. As Barbara Herrenstein Smith says, "[T]he form and features of any version of a narrative will be a function of the particular motives that elicited it and the particular functions it was designed to serve."[1] In the Robert Georges's schematic presentation, "Every storytelling event is a communicative event. . . . Every storytelling event is a social experience. . . . Every storytelling event has social uses. . . . Every storytelling event is unique."[2] This uniqueness is accentuated by the special *integrity* of the response to narrative of each audience, that reconfigurative understanding that simultaneously perceives the river of temporal sequence from an encompassing "aerial perspective," in Mink's words, and yet, in

Coleridge's phrase, is carried forward less by a "restless desire to arrive at a final solution" than "by the pleasurable activity of the mind excited by the attractions of the journey itself."[3]

These observations recall facts about narrative so obvious that they are easily forgotten—for example, that it takes time to tell stories and that understanding them requires patience and imaginative flexibility, dual points marvelously illustrated by Denis Diderot in *Jacques the Fatalist,* perhaps the shrewdest story about storytelling in the Western European tradition. While a story is being told or read, a patient listener or reader is active, not passive, despite apparent surrender to the flow of the narrator's words, for each member of the audience processes what he or she receives. Our minds continuously imagine future possibilities (what Gadamer calles "fore-conceptions") suggested by what we are being told while reassessing what we have already learned, perhaps enthusiastically, perhaps with distaste or dismay. Narrative receptivity thus continuously unfolds and simultaneously folds back into itself, transmuted by the very process of absorbing the meanings it has initiated. Narrative reception demands what Keats called negative capability, for impatient reaching after absolute certainty destroys the shifting, reconfigurative understanding made possible by story. Enjoying stories means enjoying changing what we think and feel about what a story has already made us think and feel.

In most conversation, certainly in all technical and scientific exposition, a speaker or writer aims, instead, to make all portions of the discourse mean the same thing throughout. And the receiver of such discourse relies on that stability. Narrative, however, presents continuous potentiality for change. A story addressee's pleasure lies in the awareness that each emotional or intellectual response, when succeeded by others, may well participate in a new fashion in later responses, its meaning to be reinforced, modified, even reversed. This perpetual possibility of change, change even in what has already occurred, this constitutes true narrative "suspense," not the simple curiosity over what "will happen next." A story, as every child knows, may improve with repetitions that encourage the active, one may legitimately say "creative," processes of recomprehension and revaluation of contingent details.

Each telling—even of a sacred story—is a unique event.[4] Therefore every story establishes its own history, the history of being preserved by being remade anew with every retelling. Oral tales are usually presented *as* retellings, with tellers, even inventive ones, often falsely disclaiming originality. And all the great originary stories, the primary cultural myths, appear in forms emphasizing that they are to be retold and reheard. The paradox of "unique retellings" is a function of story's resistance to the merely natural. Stories sustain a cultural continuity *through* natural time, in fact, as the basis of history, they are a principal creator of cultural time. All narratives, whether fictional, legendary, historical, or mythical, create a past simply by being narratives. And what that past is for the present moment of the storytelling establishes the basis for a future.[5]

The commonest verb tense in narrative is a form of the past that, through performance or display, serves for its audience as a present. This dialectical situation in which past is present facilitates narrative's capacity simultaneously to preserve and transform, even as story itself persists by being modified in every retelling. In social function as well as intrinsically, narrative sustains and reconstitutes, as Christ's parables, to take a spectacular instance, inaugurate a new dispensation perceived as new because it contains rather than merely rejects or ignores, the old.

We need, therefore, to look carefully into the ways in which storytelling empowers its addressees. One of Wolfgang Iser's key perceptions is that the viewpoint of a reader of (or listener to) a story persistently "moves" or "wanders," because such reading (or listening) engages the reader's or listener's imagination in a process very different from ordinary perception or logical analysis.

> The relation between text and reader is therefore quite different from that between object and observer: instead of a subject-object relationship, there is a moving viewpoint which travels along *inside* that which it has to apprehend. . . . The reader's wandering viewpoint is, at one and the same time, caught up in and transcended by the object it is to apprehend. Apperceptions can only take place in

phases, each of which contains aspects of the object to be constituted, but none of which can claim to be representative of it. Thus the aesthetic object cannot be identified with any of its manifestations during the time-flow of the reading.[6]

Iser's "phases" of a story's total "time-flow" are discrete because narratives include fissures or gaps. "Breaks" in the story, abrupt shifts in action, scene, characters, time, or point of view facilitate the *interaction* of phases or subunits of the narrative, thereby creating a coherent continuity between the immediate, the prospective, and the retrospective. The paradox central to narrative to which Iser draws our attention has not yet been analyzed adequately: the *lacunae,* what is *not* told, constitute the dynamic effectiveness of narrative art. The supreme skill of a storyteller is knowing what to leave out.

This paradoxical character of narrative discourse can be illuminated by an ultimately unenforceable distinction between it and other modes of discourse, as Jean-François Lyotard and René Wellek and Austin Warren have done, though without admitting the final oversimplification created by any such contrast.[7] A discrimination between narrational, scientific, and conversational discourse may be useful when it is focused on the polysemic character of all words, a polysemism, of course, that is not absolute: any word can have a variety of meanings, but no word can mean anything at all.[8] Conversational discourse relies on the context of ordinary social situations to control the meanings of the words being used, thus making communication clear yet flexible and easy. Normal social intercourse restricts but does not eliminate the potential of words to mean more than one thing, which encourages some fluidity and openness of reference without excluding invention and playfulness, such as punning, an elementary dramatization of polysemism. Our grammar in conversational discourse is also conventional but not rigid; space is left for individuality of form and intonation, and metacommentary on language is by no means restricted, though it tends to be exploratory rather than rigorous.

By "scientific" discourse I mean any kind of specialized language used not alone in true scientific work but also in business, commerce, education, or theology, language characteristic of professionalism of every sort. What makes such discourse "scientific" is the deliberate effort to eliminate polysemism. Writers of the purest form of this discourse strive to restrict each word to one meaning. Here, "correct" syntax must be adhered to, even if that means distorting or contorting the language. Ambiguity in either form or meaning is excluded to the extent possible. The obfuscation common to bureaucratic and professional exchanges is a strange case of this: its writers always *claim* their jargon is absolutely necessary for clarity.

Although "scientific" genres have attained overwhelming importance only during the past few hundred years, their rudiments are discernible in every culture. There is good reason for this universality. "Scientific" genres reflect conscious efforts to put language to use for a society (or a segment thereof) that finds itself equipped with only a single linguistic system with which to control a surrounding world of multiple events. Just as one chips a shattered piece of obsidian or flint to make an effective tool, so one tries to sharpen one's language by narrowing, focusing, and refining it.

Scientific discourse is the complement to narrational discourse, which, instead of restricting or excluding polysemy exploits it to extend the multiple meanings of words and develop all sorts of new shades of meaning. In narration, therefore, rules of syntax along with accepted meanings of words are often deliberately twisted, reformed, recreated. Narration seeks out new possibilities of language, and is distinguished by a consistently exploratory verbal self-reflexivity.

It is worth making the rough distinctions between conversational, scientific, and narrative discourse because they lay the groundwork for recognizing why, finally, the only adequate fashion of interpreting a story is through more narrative discourse. "Scientific" analysis, the kind of analysis much twentieth-century literary criticism explicitly or implicitly strives to achieve, destroys story by its very process of examination. This is most apparent in critiques seeking a single, essential explanatory structure, because story is constituted by an intertwining of diverse systems of coherence. "Scientific" critiques ignore gaps, breaks, and omissions that permit the intertwisting of different, even contradictory, linking structures, the macro equivalents and facilitators of the verbal polysemy it is narrative's function to develop. And the purpose of the multiplicity of ordering systems in narrative appears when we identify it as a display text: display makes possible shared participation in the textual dialogue by people whose differences one from the other are sustained by the story.

Even my very rough distinctions between discourses will suggest causes for narrative's dependence on some of its fundamental structuring devices. To illustrate these I will use traditional Native American stories, which have the advantages of being relatively brief and unfamiliar, and so free from preformed interpretive biases. We still lack, moreover, that theory of *text-milieu* that Geoffrey Hartman called for long ago, which would reveal how our analyses of literary principles depend "on a canon, on a limited group of texts, often culture-specific or national." Hartman's observation that "to take the metaphysical poets as one's base or touchstone and to extend their 'poetics' toward modern poetry and then all poetry, will produce a very different result from working from Cervantes toward Pynchon," is even more apt for analysts of narrative who ignore works from cultures in which storytelling is pervasive and vital.[9] Among Native Americans the social functionality of narrative remains prominent even today, and no definition of narrative structure that ignores the social function of story can be adequate. Our stories (since we do not esteem narrative) tend to disguise the interdependence of structure and social purpose, demanding elaborate exegesis that obscures the elemental features of storytelling I wish to highlight. The ethnological significance of my illustrative tales, along with the fact that all were originally told orally, I here simply ignore.

WHY THE BUZZARD IS BALD

There was a man who was killing all the fish. One day he would kill many fish and fill his boat with them quite to the top, and the next morning when he went to the water he filled his boat half full. At length a very large fish came to the surface of the stream and thus reproved the man: "When you wish to eat fish, you ought not to kill more than two or three. As it is, you are killing all of my people." On hearing this the man departed. On reaching his home he thought, "The chief of the fishes said that to me because he thought that I ought to keep away from the water." So he went to another place. On arriving there, he went to a house in which sat a woman crying. He stood looking at her through a crack in the house. At length he said to her, "Open the door," but it was altogether in vain. She paid no attention to him. Then he said, "I am just like an ant." He became that small, and crept through a very tiny crack. When he got within, he said to her, "Why do you sit here crying?"

Then the woman said, "There is some strange being that comes from the country far up above, and when it alights on the ground, it kills the people. It will kill me too, tonight."

The man asked her, "Where does it usually alight?" Then she took him thither. He lay down there, and the woman started home. By and by something bad and cunning alighted. It was very large and tall as well as mysterious. But the man killed it, cut off one ear and the nose, and started home.

Very early the next morning the Ancient of Black-headed Buzzards found the body of the slain monster. He cut off the other ear and piece of the flesh, and he said that he, the Ancient of Black-headed Buzzards, had killed the monster that had been devouring the people. "I was the first [to overcome him]," said he. He carried the ear and the piece of flesh to the chief's house, and said that he had killed the monster. Then they wished to make the Ancient of Black-headed Buzzards a chief. They washed him, making him very white, and seated him on an elevated seat, and they were seated, too.

They sent for the man who had really killed the monster; and he brought to the chief's house the nose and ear of the monster, throwing them down before the chief. And then he said, "Is this sitting one [The Ancient of Black-headed Buzzards] a chief?" No sooner had the words passed his lips than he seized the Ancient of Black-headed Buzzards and thrust his head into the fire. He threw him about at random, making him fall to the ground. And then the Ancient of Black-headed Buzzards was making a sort of blowing noise, just as buzzards now make. And because he was treated thus, his head is bald.

When the chief learned the truth, he gave to the real slayer of the monster the woman whom he had met in the solitary house. And the woman said to her new husband, "Let us go bathing."

But the man refused to go for some time. At length he yielded to her entreaties, although he did not care about going. They went to a small stream. He said to the woman, "Go and bathe," but he sat at some distance from the stream. The woman said to him, "Go and bathe," and on his refusal she took up water in her hand and threw it on him. Immediately the stream became very large, and the man went into it and was never seen again. Then the woman shrieked aloud and went home.[10]

For most readers, I suspect, this tale seems to leave out a great deal. But to imply that it omits what ought to be present would be a mistake. Its brevity I attribute to *minimalizing*, by which I mean the teller uses the least possible detail to carry forward his story. Minimalizing is a feature of all narratives, in Western criticsm it is often called "selectivity." But "selectivity" is a term that draws our attention to what is left in a story, rather than emphasizing sufficiently what is left out, the deliberate "gaps" crucial to the creative reception of narrative by its addressees.

Minimalizing is notable in myths, where it is the source of what many now think of as condensation. But mythic narratives normally are not truncated versions of longer narratives; they are, rather, "pure" narratives that foreground action as action. Thus, in the first sentence of "Why the Buzzard Is Bald" the protagonist appears without a name, merely as "a man." We attend less to him, his motives, his personality, than to what he does and what happens to him. Minimalizing appears in the temporal dimension, too. There is no elaboration of the sequentiality in the Buzzard story: how much time elapses after the warning from the great fish before the man happens on the crying woman is not specified, just as we are not told where her house is located, nor, indeed, who she is. Most startling, we are not told the causes of important events; they "just happen," and no explanations are sought or given in the telling.

These lacunae create a sense of abruptness for a contemporary reader; we fail to recognize that such "absences" appear in all narratives because the "realistic" fiction with which we are familiar conceals them as much as possible. The obvious gaps in "Why the Buzzard Is Bald" are not evidence of its "primitiveness." Narrative tells of some things but not others, and the genius of storytelling is knowing what to leave out—a spectacular example of this is *The Iliad,* which omits most of the Trojan War. Omissions in "Why the Buzzard Is Bald" compel the listener to concentrate on the action as action, event as event, with "meaning" created by what the listener makes of these happenings. Were there nothing left out—if I may propose an impossibility—the audience would be passive because it would have no opportunity for contributory feedback, no opening through which to participate in or imaginatively to create something out of the telling. That the story is not always instantly lucid, that it perplexes, is part of its enforcing on its audience the necessity for a active, constitutive responsiveness.[11]

Compelling the audience to process the storyteller's words accomplishes swiftly and cogently what merely rationalistic exposition could attain only more laboriously at best, and perhaps not achieve at all. The "strange being" the man kills in "Why the Buzzard Is Bald," for example, is truly strange because exactly what the "being" is we are never told, though it would seem to possess some human characteristics. This "absence" of descriptive detail is "supported" by other lacunae in the tale, so that we are made to feel throughout the narrative the difficulty, or even impossibility, of reducing events to any simply formulated explanation. That intractability, rather than a "realism" based in verisimilar detail, permits us to accept the story as "true"; it is true to the nature of "strange" experiences, puzzling or improbable occurrences. Virtually everything that happens is "unexpected," beginning with the talking fish. There is no foretelling that the man would happen upon the woman crying alone, which means that on rehearing or reading, when one knows that he will happen on her, one's response is engaged in wondering why he does, in seeking for possible connections, that is to say, in refining and improving one's interpretive response. But because there is no definitive cause, we can reach no finalized interpretation.

Retrospectively, one can fit the Buzzard, to take another example, into various patterns of pride, excess, and destruction that one comes to recognize as operating in the story, yet even so Buzzard's role remains unpredetermined by earlier events. We overintellectualize if we resist the encouragement of the story to admit the contingency of what occurs, to recognize that the unexpected *can* happen. Stories come into being to help us face the fact that there are contingencies, not to eliminate them.

Even after we have heard "Why the Buzzard Is Bald," or read it, so that we know what is going to happen, a rehearing or rereading increases the significance of its emphasis on the adventitious. A point of the story seems to be that one can never be sure of what is going to happen, even though actions do produce inexorable consequences. The paradox assures that questions and problems posed by the story do not disappear as we grow more familiar with it but, instead, tend to deepen and become more puzzling, demanding reinterpretation, that is, a return to the story, another retelling or rereading of it. This is characteristic of all good narratives; narrative discourse evokes renewal of itself—new tellings, new receptions—by means of its blanks, breaks, absences, what it does not tell.

In "Why the Buzzard Is Bald" each episode turns on circumstances of violence, danger, fear. The power of the tale to trouble, to be affectively meaningful, is helped by its structuring to arouse mingled feelings of terror and horror, to excite an emotional as well as intellectual response to what is monstrously mysterious, above all, to an intersecting of the unexpected and the rigorously logical. There is more than one kind of strangeness in the story, and as the tale progresses one's unease grows at the increase of unpredictably threatening powers, including the "strangeness" of what is most familiar—man himself. An appropriate response, a valid interpretation, then, authenticates the import of *questions* the story poses.

Significant criticism of storytelling, therefore, must take the form of another storytelling if justice is to be done to the interlocking—yet never perfect fitting—of intellectual, emotional, and ethical patternings, each itself subject to slippage. Much contemporary analytic criticism fails because it explains narrative discourse in terms of "scientific" discourse, which endeavors to narrow down to formulaic definition the diverse modalities of complexity inherent in storytelling's "semantic saturation," its enhancing and complicating of verbal polysemism through polytropic macrostructurings.[12]

It is difficult for us not to try to reduce the mystery central to a story such as "Why the Buzzard Is Bald" to an explanatory summary, because our intellectual concerns are with the "clarity" of answers. A "scientific" approach will tend to explain away narrative chasms and perplexities, setting forth more or less definitive answers to questions raised by the relationships—or lack of relationships—among imagined events. But an abiding paradox of narrative discourse is that, though demanding interpretation, it resists finalized interpretation—remaining explicable only in narrative terms. This is why even analytic critics recognize that no "moral" is ever adequate to an efficacious narrative—as with the tale under discussion the etiological title manifestly is not the whole story, despite its dramatization that excessive killing only empowers carrion eaters.

This is not to deny, of course, that stories have both "points" and patterns of structure. If one wonders, for instance, in "Why the Buzzard Is Bald," why the man enters the house by shrinking to the size of an ant, one may notice throughout the tale the dramatic function of size. The fish that speaks is very large, as is the mysterious being, and the water the man finally "enters" becomes large although beginning as small drops. Here is a discernible pattern, even as the image of comparison itself, an ant, is a creature of the soil, whereas the buzzard is a sky creature, and the fish a water being. Both patterns, moreover, are relevant to the recurrent motif of excess.

The tale begins with the killing of many fish, then people suffer, as the fish have, death from above. The boastful carrion eater is humbled, but playfully thrown waterdrops become the large water into which the man vanishes—as retribution for his overkilling of fish? Scavenging buzzard is falsely made great, then thrown to the ground and permanently defaced on the small evidence of ear and nose from the corpse. One could go on, but the lesson is clear: the story is constituted by interactions among diverse systems whose dynamism would be diminished were the tale explainable by one essential underlying structure.

The translation that is our text provides a way of registering the relation of a specific word's connotative complexity to larger interplayings of form, since no narrative—because it is "semantically saturated"—can be adequately translated literally. Any interpretation of even a literal translation carries one rapidly to the point where subtle densities of the original language can no longer be overlooked—something that need not happen at all with scientific or conversational discourse. In "Why The Buzzard Is Bald" the movement from man killing fish to woman splashing him with water drops may be more bound up with the concept of "home" than is suggested by the free translation I am citing. The tale's two final sentences end with *kidedi,* "home," which appears to echo the story's third sentence, literally translated by James Dorsey and John Swanton as "and then fish very large one scolded him went home." This should remind us of how often the narrative treats of intrusions into diverse homes. High-flying Buzzard's punishment is evidence of the evil consequences of laying claim to a place to which one has no right. Honesty and proper respect for balances of nature are one and the same: the natural world may be home for all, however diverse, so long as the different characteristics of "home" for each are respected.[13]

Some such judgmental interpretation is necessary because "Why the Buzzard Is Bald" is concerned with excessive acts disruptive of natural balances, such as overkilling of fish. It is the purpose of narrative, the reason for telling stories, to evoke evaluative responses. This point, as several commentators have recognized, was first emphasized by William Labov in his descriptions of inner-city storytelling. His comment in his original research report is worth repeating at length.

> Beginnings, middles and ends of narratives have been noted in many accounts of folklore or narrative. But there is one important aspect of narrative which has not been discussed—perhaps the most important element. . . . That is what we term the *evaluation* of the narrative: the means used by the narrator to indicate the point of the narrative, its *raison d'etre,* why it was told, and what the narrator is getting at. There are many ways to tell the same story to make very different points, or to make no point at all. Pointless stories are met (in English) with the withering rejoinder, "So what?" Every good narrator is continually warding off this question; when his narrative is over, it must be unthinkable for a by-stander to say, "So what?" . . . There are a great many ways in which the point of a narrative can be conveyed—in which the speaker signals to the listener why he is telling it. To identify the evaluative portion of a narrative, it is necessary to know why this nar-

rative . . . is felt to be tellable. . . . Evaluative devices say to us: this was terrifying, dangerous, weird, wild, crazy; or amusing, hilarious, wonderful; or more generally, that it was strange, uncommon or unusual—that is worth reporting. . . . [w]ithout it [this concept of tellability] we cannot begin to understand the things people do in telling narratives.[14]

What Labov calls the "tellable," D. A. Miller the "narratable," and Ross Chambers the "point," is what Mary Louise Pratt has identified as making up a "display text." Story is story because it allows the addressee to participate in and to share in an evaluative social negotiation.

In complex literary texts, as Chambers and Miller demonstrate, "display" qualities are often created with a degree of subtlety that calls for highly sophisticated analyses to reveal a fundamental narrative "point." But even with so brief a tale as "Why the Buzzard Is Bald" it is apparent that the story's formal configurative integrity, its wholeness, can adequately be described only if we take into account the detailed judgmental responses it provokes. It perplexes (or "interests") because it engages us in judging some very specific events that upset the mechanical application of standard formulas of assessment. A good story—one not arousing a "So what?"—incites the opposite: *That* was worth hearing." The worth is defined by the rewards offered to evaluative interpretation, which, of course, may consist of negative as well as positive judgments.

Individual judgments provoked by a story, indeed, articulate each respondent's peculiar relation not just to the story but also to his or her "interpretive community," thereby often strengthening the community. But as often the evaluations serve to separate individuals from their community, bringing out antagonisms between it and them. This is why the meanings of stories are inseparable from their social functions.

One might argue that the largest "break" in "Why the Buzzard Is Bald" is its conclusion, because that, too, poses questions. Such openness is particularly characteristic of oral storytelling, since the completion of any one telling literally establishes the place for another telling. No one story is *the* definitive story. Just as stories are intended to be retold, every story implies other stories. However conclusive the ending of a given story, it does not and cannot exclude the possibility of a subsequent story. Storytelling is a proliferative activity. "Inconclusive," question-provoking endings merely render visible this fecundity, that the closure inherent to narrative as a whole creates new "openings," possibilities for other stories that, in fact, are a major empowerment of any story's successful social functioning. The central purpose of storytelling is to facilitate tellings. The end of any story makes possible more storytelling, which is, needless to say, encouraged by whatever is enigmatic or debatable in a particular conclusion.

We must carry our understanding of this power beyond the immediate, or first circle, of a story's understanding. The worth of "Why the Buzzard Is Bald" to me certainly differs from its worth to a Biloxi listener. But the one response does not cancel or supersede the other.[15] In this phenomenon of equally valid but diverse receptions originates narrative's unusual capacity to cross social and cultural boundaries—even though story is ultimately untranslatable! Translation helps to prevent me from attaining an authentic "Biloxi-meaning" from "Why the Buzzard Is Bald." But the story, even in translation, may strongly affect me, even though I come from a society that, far from regarding "natural" and "supernatural" as overlapping realms, has banished the faintest possibility of anything occurring outside the order of natural laws. The implications of story's power thus to penetrate such impressive linguistic and cultural barriers have been insufficiently noticed—one reason I use unfamiliar Native American stories. Narrative crosses cultural boundaries by changing and adapting. A story such as "Why the Buzzard Is Bald" has for the Biloxi a point, provokes specific responses, but these are not fixed but generative and proliferative. That is why it readily "adapts" itself to the totally dissimilar responses of, say, a contemporary academic literary critic. Because "Why the Buzzard Is Bald" is constructed to arouse heterogenous evaluations, it possesses the potential for appealing (perhaps in ways surprising to its teller) to a members of a community different from that for which it was originally intended.

The capacity of a story by changing to cross cultural limits is a function of narrative's existing only by being made anew. That is why minimalizing, leaving out, is so determinative of story's satisfactory retellability. When a whole tale has been comprehended, one is free to test, develop, reinforce, modify, or overturn connections between diverse parts of the narrative that as hearer or reader one has constructed. Rehearing or rereading a good story, therefore, can be a more active experience than a first hearing or reading, because the breaks in the narrative allow a vigorous reengagement, a creative reassessing of what has become in part one's own construction.[16]

Walter Benjamin's speculation that the listener to a tale listens so as to be able to retell it touches a profound truth. Even readers today often want to be able to "retell" a good story, that is, to possess it so that they can further renew with others its pleasures. But such positive engagement depends, paradoxically, on a "negative capability" of reception. Only such receptivity gives the listener the mastery to retell a story (perhaps quite differently), and the opportunity to enjoy it again (but perhaps in a quite different way). This is why the most significant psychic activity evoked by narrative is rooted in its silences—why the storyteller's highest skill is in leaving out.

A feature of narrative construction that I call (following Lotman) *segmentation* appears most conspicuously in narrative repetitions. Just as stories are repeated, so many stories are built up of reiterated elements. One must grasp a story as a whole to understand it, yet narrative totalities are made up of subordinate elements perceivable as whole entities. It is worth remembering that "to tell" means "to recount," that telling is linked to tallying. Etymologically, storytelling is associated with enumerating; the tellers we are most likely to encounter nowadays work in banks. Accounting is putting in order, and the telling of one's beads is analogous to the telling of a tale, which is an ordering of discrete events. All well and good, except that "hardly any concept is less clear than that of 'event,'" as Louis O. Mink puts it. As he goes on to say, "[T]here is no particular difficulty about the concept of a complex of events whose parts are themselves events. Uncertainty sets in when we consider the limits of application of the concept. . . . [I]n fact we have no idea whether there are minimal or maximal events, and no knowledge of any standard or preeminent descriptions of any events."[17]

Suggestions that architecture provides a model for story

structure may derive from a desire to sidestep Mink's problem of defining "events" without denying that every narrative is composed of distinct subunits. A Norman castle overawes with its vast unity in part because one perceives it to be constructed of "small" units that are huge stones. The analogy may remind us that powerful stories need not be "seamless" structures. If it is difficult sometimes to define the events that are its constituent parts, narrative nonetheless can exploit its specially disjunctive coherence—although at the risk of being condemned by modernist critics for a "looseness" inferior to the "tight" systematics of plot.

An Arapaho story, "Raw-Gums and White-Owl Woman" (the text will be found in the appendix) enables us to examine how and why stories are composed of discrete units. "Raw-Gums" begins "naturalistically" with a winter camp circle of tents near a river lined with cottonwoods and snags and an ordinary husband and wife pleased with their new baby.[18] Out of this unfolds what appears to be a hostile supernatural force, as we discover the baby to be a cannibalistic destroyer of the tribe's chiefs. But when ejected from the camp the baby is transformed into the beneficence of spring, which eliminates winter, personified in White-Owl Woman. The second portion of the story, though dealing entirely with suprahuman figures, Spring and Winter, employs the same incrementally repetitious form of telling characteristic of the first, "realistic" part of the tale. The two major segments parallel and contrast both formally and thematically, as for instance, through repetitious tellings of eating rituals, Raw-Gum's role reverses from that of devouring threat to savior.

The two halves of the story could be and doubtless were at times told as separate tales. But joined, the meaning of each part is altered and enriched. Each part provides a perspective for judging the other. To juxtapose distinct episodes that do not *have* to be so related intensifies the significance of each.

Because the second part of "Raw-Gums" follows upon the tale of the cannibal infant, the audience is invited to connect seasonal cycles and tribal order, natural processes and social processes. We might not think in this way were the winter-spring second half of "Raw-Gums" left out or told elsewhere as a separate entity. To state the matter inversely, by adding the

White-Owl episode, the teller of "Raw-Gums" encourages us to consider the "naturalness" of cannibalism. After all, if it is natural for the young season (spring) to do away with its elder (winter), is it also true that "good" older people, leaders, chiefs, ought to be "cannibalized" by younger elements in society?

A crux in the first segment of the story is the council after the death of the last chief. At the invitation of the cannibal child's parents the assembled men eat the food provided, but return no solution to the problem the parents have discovered. The council gives the responsible parents of Raw-Gums no aid, though they have been assembled to advise. These older people should "move on" in more than a geographical sense. The drifting apart of the useless council begins to modify our feelings toward the cannibal child. And when, wrapped in fat and literally thrown to the dogs, he leaps up suddenly a vigorous young man chanting "A skeleton! A skeleton!" our earlier reactions of simple horror become more complex, at the least mixed with awe. But our original feelings do not totally disappear, and our response to the renewal of spring here personified, therefore, is oddly ambiguous. We do not, as a rule, attend to the sinister aspects of spring. Yet "A Skeleton! A Skeleton!" dramatizes forcibly the indifference of nature to the sanctities of human memory, just as the dead cottonwood is troubling in being both so appropriate and so inappropriate a repository for the bones of the cannibalized chiefs. Our feelings are pushed in the opposite direction, however, by White-Owl Woman's giving of herself to destruction, accepting the triumph of Raw-gums, which suggests a model (however unusual) for social behavior, the very gruesomeness of the embodiment contrastively defining the unnaturalness of cannibalism.

Ambivalences in our response to the story are thus directed by interrelations between its two main parts, which must to a degree function independently. The light each total segment casts on the other deepens its meaning beyond what comparison or contrast of details within each part could achieve. The functional integrity of whole episodes is the foundation for what Iser calls the "wandering viewpoint" in narrative. The term implies not randomness but psychic shiftings created by transformations in the audience's "angle of vision" upon events within a story. And structuring of episode relations such as we find in "Raw-Gums and White-Owl Woman" encourage reorientations of our ethical and emotional attitudes created by earlier responses.

The segmenting of story structure is so simple and obvious that it is easy to overlook its importance, or to feel that it requires explaining by subtler and less obvious features. But Lotman is correct that among the "profound laws relevant to *every* narrative text . . . segmentation . . . is one of the most important."[19] Discrete narrative segments permit effective repetitions of diverse kinds, because only the distinctness of some "unit" (person, act, place, or even phrase) allows sharp recognition of recurrence. Verbally formulaic set pieces—in oral texts such as I cite or that Albert B. Lord describes in *The Singer of Tales*— give a dramatic structure to discrete units, and the incapacity of recent literary criticism to account for their effectiveness reveals how dim our understanding of story functioning has become. Trained by modernism's preoccupations with naturalistically rendered immediate experience and rigorously limited and particularized sensory impressions, a contemporary reader is ill-equipped to make much of any kind of repetition.[20] If, however, one remembers the function of story is to be retold, it becomes easier to recognize that reiterations operate on a macrolevel somewhat analogously to rhyme and refrain in poetry. They call attention to the formal ordering of the narrative. Such attention provides the audience means for reappraising earlier large-scale interpretive acts on the basis of later structural developments, a process more difficult to achieve in discourse that does not thus draw attention to its own evolving and self-complicating *form*.

Repetition in storytelling, furthermore, allows structural and thematic equivalents of punning, which is a deliberate exhibition of polysemism. Verbal repetition, as psychologists have noted, has a tendency to free words from their merely designatory function. Macrorepetitions analogously encourage new ways of interconnecting a story's themes and structures, permitting the audience simultaneous awareness of what the tale refers to and how it does this referring. This constructional reflexiveness allows story to act as "a primary cognitive instrument . . . for making the flux of experience comprehensible."[21] Even so simple a tale as "Raw-Gums and White-Owl Woman" thematizes its reiterative mode of telling. We come to appreciate that Raw-Gum's repeated cannibalistic nightly forays and the repeated question-and-answer contests with White-Owl Woman are representative of natural differences-within-repetitions with which human societies somehow must come to terms. Every winter and every spring is unique, but their recurrent sequence is unfailing, and viable human societies must accommodate to both uniqueness and recurrence.

Audience awareness of narrative form as part of narrative subject, most plainly visible in repetition and through segmentation, often is the basis of story's social efficacy. Reiterated acts in "Raw-Gums and White-Owl Woman," for example, lead to the realization that Raw-Gums is not merely an *external* force, that he is a "true" offspring of the ill-organized group camped by the river. But his potency derives also from his embodying an overwhelming natural power, the power of renewal that appears so dramatically in every newborn child and throughout the physical world every spring. That is why, when he has proven what he is to White-Owl Woman, she offers herself to his destructive rebirth. As Percy Bysshe Shelley phrased it, "Winter does not quarrel with the Spring." Effective societies will behave analogously. Instead of trying to repress inevitable forces of life's repetitive innovations, they will accept without undue fear the threat that every new human life poses, for, as the story shows, repression produces social monstrousness—cannibalism.

Not all narratives reveal as explicitly as "Raw-Gums" the independence of the interdependent segments constituting them as narratives. Yet all stories are built up of units and subunits possessed of a self-integrity permitting their use for reflexive effects deriving from their wholeness, rather than merely from details within them, or from their merely subserving a single, essentializing structure. Commentators on William Makepeace Thackeray's complicated novel *Vanity Fair* (which I cite because it is the subject of the next chapter) have frequently analyzed the work's structure as built upon contrasts between episodes (more than one critic even drawing diagrams of such episodic patterns) centered on the two antithetical feminine protagonists. Despite the elaborateness and subtlety of the Victorian novel's manipulation of these "segmental" interrelationships, the fundamental principle Thackeray employs is identical with that we observe in the Arapaho tale.

Segmenting, simple and open or intricate and disguised, facilitates the recursiveness of narrative through which the audience's anticipations and retrospections keep open all portions of a story for continual reassessment. Segments may be considered as macrostructural equivalents of the substantive contingencies stories tell about. Segmenting assures that a story may at any time—within a given reading or hearing or at any subsequent rereading or rehearing—produce new meanings and affects by aiding the addressee to reconceive the point of the tale's structure. Here the analogue between literary narrative and music (rather than architecture) may be helpful, not merely because both are sequential arts but also because of the emotionality each excites. Since there are but few tones, the affects of music must be evoked by carefully organized repetitions. In analogous fashion, narrative develops its primary affects through an interplay of subordinate wholes operating to a degree as self-sufficient units within the unity of the total story.

Both the possibility of retelling and the constant play of prospective and retrospective reassessment incited by narrative would not be possible in stories of substantial length unless they were organizaed into integral, subordinate units. For effective participation in a storytelling event an audience needs discrete mediative structures that organize the multiplicity of contingent details of which the story treats. These mediating structures possess enough integrity that under different circumstances they themselves could be "whole stories." Herein lies the secret of the "proliferativeness" of narrative. Every story is constituted of many smaller stories or potential stories, and in this respect the conclusion (however decisive) of any specific telling is never more than provisional.

The segmentation of mediative elements has been the principal focus of structuralist analyses. Both Claude Lévi-Strauss and Vladimir Propp, the most celebrated of such analysts of narrative, built their systems on the premise that stories were built up by articulations of discrete units, these being the ground, for instance, for distinguishable mythic "layers," in Lévi-Strauss's terminology. The weakness of the structuralist approach, indeed, springs from a tendency to ignore all other aspects of narrative construction.[22] Minimalizing, leaving out, for instance, plays little part in such structuralist systems. And the idea of change through reassessment by the audience runs counter to the structuralist focus on the text in itself, as undetermined by the historical specificities of retellings. The text also is usually treated by structuralists as temporally rigid—the "structure" sought being, if not a spatial form, then a timeless formula—epitomized by Lévi-Strauss's mathematized definition of myth.[23] The greater simplicity of Propp's system, however, illustrates structuralism's limitations more vividly. According to Propp, the units of which all fairy tales are constructed *invariably* recur in the *same* order: the fairytale is a formula. This absolutism tends to obscure the importance of the structuralist focus on narrative "bundles" of discrete and "reusable" subunits, as I will try to suggest by a brief comment on a Dakota "Blood-Clot Boy" story (see the appendix). Because this tale has already been analyzed by Elaine Jahner, I concentrate on what structuralists tend to ignore: how audience participation may be empowered by narrative segmentation.[24]

Jahner grounds her discussion in the physical circumstance of the traditional telling situation of this story: the teller sits among a circle of auditors within the circularity of a tipi that is part of a round gathering of tipis. So the story's themes of insider/outsider, belonging/excluded are manifested physically in the story performance. By pursuing the connotations and polysemic functions of some of the crucial Dakota words in the tale, Jahner highlights the significance of its patterns of movement, which are dramatized by the contrastive stillness of the speaker seated within the concentric circles of society, dwelling, and audience. An equivalent combination of contrast and reinforcement appears in the singularly decisive break within the story (equivalent to the division between the "cannibal" and "White-Owl" sections in "Raw-gums") at the conclusion of the killing of the bears. The first eleven episodes could certainly be told as a separate story,[25] for one can hardly miss the conclusiveness of the last sentence in episode eleven and the introductory quality of the first sentence of episode twelve.

> The rabbit now moved into his old home and as he still
> had his magic arrow, he provided meat in abundance so

that the three, including the little bear, lived without want.
12. And then one day Blood-Clot Boy declared his plans.

Because the subsequent adventures of Blood-Clot Boy to the
West are not a necessary sequel to the first segment, the audience is alerted to reversals and parallelisms between the two
parts as coordinate subunits of the whole (as with the two segments of "Raw-Gums and White-Owl Woman") rather than
simply as items in a sequence.

Here appears another cause for story's capacity to gain from
being *re*heard or *re*read. Because a story is made up of relations
not just of detail to detail, and detail to totality, but also of relations of intermediate structural units, it easily extends into the
highest level of discourse the sylleptic orientation characteristic
of its treatment of individual words. "Segment-relations" articulate a story's themes through its systems of structuring,
thereby suggesting how changes in form might affect subject
matter, or vice versa, further opening the story to audience "remaking." The more familiar a story, to state the point over-
simply, the more one is likely to be aware of the arbitrariness of
its construction, so that one's imagination can respond more
alertly to connections (realized and unrealized) of structures to
themes.[26] The "looseness" of story condemned as "primitive" by
modernist critics (such as E. M. Forster) principally refers to
segmentation. Structural "tautness," so often cited as a virtue of
autonomous contemporary texts, discourages "reshapings" by
readers—the activity encouraged by the reiterative divisions in
a story such as "Blood-Clot Boy."

Diverse tellings of a given story may foreground distinct implications of the tale, because the purposes of a specific performance can be accommodated by particular adaptations of the
story's construction. The so-called looseness of narrative makes
possible its openness to this enabling arbitrariness. Segments,
and blocks of segments, marked off by pointed "breaks" in a
narrative perhaps reveal most vividly the intersecting of macro
(structural) and micro (stylistic) levels in narrative.[27] But such
intersecting occurs everywhere in stories, illustrated, to cite my
earlier example, in *The Iliad* when the language of Greek
heroes boasting over a slain opponent is "falsely" employed by

Paris to brag of his cowardly wounding of Diomedes. These conjunctions are the very heart of storytelling, whose purpose is to enhance our control both of our actual experience and our capability for articulating experience in language. Another story, "Grasshopper in Love with Deer," (see the appendix) because it emphasizes the characteristic of *inversion* may help us to understand the centrality to narrative of this intersecting of the "levels" of language and structure.[28]

The major peripeteia in "Grasshopper in Love with Deer" is the linked killing of Wies (Deer) and the feeding of his body to the adulterous Djahdjai (Grasshopper), a revenge reversing the process of sexual betrayal carried out for so long by Djahdjai. The reversal fulfills emotional desires built up in the audience by her treachery. So skillful is the inversion that in our satisfaction at the "justified revenge" we are likely to overlook the mixing of human and animal attributes, until the closing etiological turn compels us to recognize the subtle meaningfulness added to this narrative through the manipulation of emblem names.

We are familiar with fictional names as emblematically significant, Dickens's Dedlock and Joyce's Daedalus, for example. These names function as "proper puns," simultaneously identifying an individual character with a prototype or with an act or object or quality, the relevance of the identification established by what the character is or does. We are less accustomed to the animal naming we find in this Modoc story, which is very characteristic of Native American narratives, in which a name refers simultanously to a species of animal and a human being. Both kinds of emblematic name facilitate intersectings of verbal and characterological levels of narrative, providing loci for those processes of reversal which Aristotle first emphasized as cruxes of dramatic representations. Aristotle's observation comes to mind because in this Modoc story, unlike my previous examples, there is dramatic irony in the audience's awareness of something a main character does not know. The male protagonist's ignorance of Grasshopper's adultery helps to arouse our feelings for him and against Djahdjai. We see in this story a beginning of narrative use of subjectivity, which—enormously intensified—becomes a focus of the modernist transformation of story. Yet there as here, other nonpsychological factors also operate significantly, because storytelling is an inclusive, multi-combinatory mode. Thus the first concrete evidence of Djahd-jai's infidelity, which the husband fails to recognize, is the wearing out of her moccasins. For us today, probably, the sexual connotations are most impressive, but the detail should also fasten attention on the economics of the little group. Moccasins are made by the man for the women from deerhide. Djahdjai, then, not only sexually betrays her husband but also subverts the economics of this family.

One notices that Djihens's (Ant's) spying does not lead to an immediate revelation. Only after a second observation does she speak to her husband, and her warning is at first fruitless, for the husband plainly doesn't wish to believe her. Although the virtuous wife Djihens has been distinguished from the evil one at the very beginning of the story, when we are told of Djahdjai stealing Djihens's roots, the storyteller is alert to the danger that sin and sinners may be more attractive than virtue and the virtuous. The delay in Djihens's revelation makes us feel that her motive is not mere personal jealousy, not even concern solely for the family's economic well-being, but genuine, therefore complex, affection for her husband. She does not want to tell the truth he does not want to hear. The man accuses her of lying out of jealousy, but she "always knew what he thought." All of this helps us to feel that the man loves the unfaithful wife more than the faithful one, but that the latter is not merely a victim—one notices how impressed Djihens is by the power of Djahdjai's love song. The story, in short, is arranged to allow us to experience the evolution of subjectively experienced conflict-ing moral and emotional needs that *require* "turns" in all di-mensions of the narrative.

The evidence of his hunting failures brings the man to be-lieve Djihens, and the second half of the tale reverses the first, as the deceiver is in her turn taken in by a series of deceptions. On his first spying venture the man only cries with jealousy, confirming the power of his fondness for Djahdjai and strengthening our emotional sympathy for his desire to be avenged. This development is clinched when Djahdjai returns home after vainly having sung for Wies. At this moment when we might pity her, her greedy hunger, in a tale built around food-gathering, makes it impossible to regard her merely as victimized by love. As she unwittingly savors Wies's flesh in a new fashion, we feel she has been justly trapped by the insatiability of her selfish appetites.

It is at this point that the resonances of condensation attained through the use of animal names and attributes works most efficaciously. The characters are not, as in the Greek fable of ant and grasshopper (a version of which I am persuaded is being challenged by this story), animals anthropomorphized. The Modoc tale uses animal features to symbolize complexes of physical, intellectual, and emotional characteristics. Thus Djahdjai's "jumping around" registers her promiscuity as both physical and psychological. Stag qualities superbly embody Wies's masculine sensuality, the confidence, for example, of sheer beauty of physical being, against which his rival, though he may kill Wies with a poisoned arrow, can only weep in jealous impotence. For a contemporary reader the details pertaining to sexuality, the long roots, the moccasins, the poisoned arrow, the wife with two holes, are likely to dominate attention. But we mistake the functions of such details if we treat them as purely psychological. For, broadly, narrative always contains "indefinitely many ordering relations, and indefinitely many ways of *combining* these relations."[29] In "Grasshopper in Love with Deer," the animal-human characterization reinforces the potency of the self-inversion of the story as a whole. It reflects on the microlevel of name what Lotman has called the syntagmatics of heterogeneous episodic elements—as opposed to the syntagmatics of homogeneous elements in nonnarrative modes of discourse.[30] Every element of the story works to activate in the audience's imagination a unified complex of experiences implicating sociological, economic, biological, as well as psychological, dimensions of human relationships—what Bakhtin calls metaverbal context. Most simply, of course, but most significantly also, the animal characteristics by which psychic qualities are given physical manifestation serve to link the human cultural conflicts to inescapable natural pressures.

"Inversion," then, means a turning back upon itself of the whole of a narrative, or any of its parts, including the whole of a narrative "segment," but also smaller elements such as diction and character. This multileveled self-reflexive twisting is inescapable because narrative deploys verbal polysemism as a means of exploring the necessarily polytropic structures of social relationships. The revelation provided by the peripeteia in "Grasshopper in Love with Deer," for example, is simultaneously a revelation of the true nature of "Grasshopper," the creaturely aspect illuminating the humanly characterological, while the characterological gives human meaning to the existence of the familiar but alien creature. The Modoc story shows how a word, a name, the linguistic feature making possible "confusion" of person and creature, also can give unique insight into the complex basis of our desires and fears, that arise, in the final analysis, from the simultaneous antipathy between and interdependence of biological and cultural forces.

Narrative discourse could justly be described as a turning of language upon itself, hence the importance of emblematic names, since "proper puns" directly serve to interlace thematic, structural, and verbal systems of organization. Narrative tests what language can do, how it can and might function in the world, untwisting and retwisting this most useful of all human constructs, inversions serving to keep operative in all its aspects language's recursive powers. Storytelling, because it is an event of social sharing, never abandons attention to the narrating process itself, even though a story is composed of references to and comments upon actualities outside its verbal construction. This is probably the core paradox of narrative discourse: an artifact radically distinct from any natural nonhuman reality, narrative's prime value lies in its seeking to accommodate human words to natural conditions, and vice-versa. Narrative articulates human possibilities within conditions it recognizes as significantly determined by nonhuman forces.

These qualities suggest that storytelling may be no minor tool in humankind's evolutionary success, particularly if we follow the argument cogently set forth by Morse Peckham.[31] His line of thought begins in the linking of language to imagination as the source of its capacity to operate independently of the natural world, activating what Ricoeur calls the power of distanciation. This makes it possible for human beings to respond effectively to "random" phenomenon (as animals more bound to instinct cannot), fruitfully to exploit "negative feedback" from an environment. A function of storytelling, then, would be to prepare us not merely to tolerate but even to seek out situations of "disorientation," circumstances in which established "rules" of response are inadequate or inoperable or improvable.

I am attracted to Peckham's approach because the ubiquitousness of storytelling in human cultures implies it possesses evolutionary value. But I want to emphasize that the basic characteristics of narrative I have discussed in this chapter—minimalizing or leaving out, segmental repetition and contrast, and inversion—all derive from story's existence as a social negotiation, as a shared "display." As Ross Chambers has insisted, every narrator must "earn the authority to narrate in the very act of storytelling."[32] In societies in which storytelling is esteemed, it is customary for a narrator to be authorized by the story—hence the common disclaimers of originality by storytellers. But in any society, the meaning of a story is significantly determined by the specific social interaction that a particular telling embodies. Stories, therefore, are one of our best means for appreciating other peoples' ways, and are "our most useful evidence for coming to understand conceptual presuppositions quite different from our own."[33] Even when emerging from social conditions with which we are entirely familiar, stories, through their multileveled developments of the implications of polysemism, enable us to grasp as no other discourse will the uniqueness of a particular configuration of sociohistorical circumstances. Narrative assures that we will not forget that, as Gerald Bruns puts it "[I]t is not wholly accurate to say that words mean; better to say that situations mean and that words mean as they occur in them."[34]

This explains the importance of the evaluative function of story. As the tales I have just cited illustrate, stories present us with individual beings—not abstract forces nor transcendent powers—as *responsible*. The assessments called forth by narrative are not the mere application of generalized rules, the fitting of particular events into preformed categories. Quite to the contrary, stories lure us into imagining ethical problems from the point of view of individuals involved in a unique complex of circumstances. If we judge Grasshopper severely, we do so not abstractly, and not from a distant perspective, but more

responsibly, from within her particular situation and influenced by some sympathy with what feeds her appetites. This
arousal of power to judge and yet simultaneously to understand sympathetically what we judge in all its specificity suggests why every society has found storytelling an indispensable
activity. As Hannah Arendt puts it, "[S]torytelling reveals
meaning without committing the error of defining it, . . . [and]
brings about consent and reconciliation with things as they really are."[35] If we grant this, however, we must recognize that
modernism's contestations of narrative are no trivial stylistic peculiarity but a profoundly serious and unusual event in human
history, both the causes and the implications of which demand
more thoughtful analysis than they have as yet received.

5

Syntagmatic and Paradigmatic Fiction

Unprofitable as it may seem to compare a transient bestseller such as Tom Wolfe's *The Bonfire of the Vanities* with one of the classics of English fiction, William Makepeace Thackeray's *Vanity Fair,* aligning the two works can tell us much about what lies between them—modernist fiction. Wolfe's title reveals his awareness of his Victorian predecessor in satiric analysis of an overly affluent society, and his comments about his book urge a comparison: "I wanted to prove that it was not only possible but desirable to write the kind of novel that had been classified as dead for the past forty years, . . . an honest book about the city, as Thackeray did in *Vanity Fair.*"[1] The form of Wolfe's fiction, however, is closer to that of the modernist synchronic novel, which replaced the diachronic novel favored by Victorian storytellers. Wolfe displays little understanding of how, in fact, a Victorian like Thackeray told a story, or of the extent to which his own work is indebted to technical innovations of modern novelists. This makes *Bonfire,* for a critic with a strong stomach, useful for illuminating *why* modern fiction (so far as one can encompass so diverse a phenomenon under so abstract a rubric) turned away from central features of traditional storytelling, above all, substituting "author function" for "teller function."

Casual reviewers have compared *Bonfire* to Victorian fiction because of the length of Wolfe's novel, the number of its characters, and its satiric slant. Only the first parallel has even minimal validity. *Bonfire*'s attention to financial matters and the mildness of its explicit eroticism perhaps distinguish Wolfe's work less from other bestsellers than from "serious" and "important" contemporary novels, which tend to be as vague about the details of money-grubbing as Victorians were about sex. Wolfe is open about this contemporary literary taboo; one suspects the attraction of *Bonfire* for some readers is its explanation of how today one can go broke while being paid a million dollars a year.

Although money is a focus of both Thackeray's and Wolfe's satire, its social function is exactly reversed in the two books, the chief problem in *Vanity Fair* being "how to live well on nothing a year." What seems to link the two novelists as social satirists utterly divides them. Apparent similarities of length and number of characters are likewise misleading. Thackeray's work is longer both in sheer number of words and, significantly, in the span of time that it encompasses. *Vanity Fair* also includes a far greater number of characters more precisely distinguished both sociologically and functionally. Wolfe is incapable, for instance, of Thackeray's discrimination between a self-made tallow merchant and a self-made wine merchant living on the same square. The difference is due not merely to Wolfe's lack of talent, but also to a shift in twentieth-century fiction away from the use of narrative to articulate sociological discriminations. Novelists in our century prefer imaging psychological distinctions with sensory immediacy. The shift produces quantitative changes. Whereas Wolfe's cast includes half a dozen major figures along with a number of totally subsidiary ones, Thackeray's over a dozen principal personages share his stage with more than twice that number of secondary and tertiary figures whose personalities and roles are somewhat developed, along with more than a hundred stylized, "walk-on" characters.[2]

These differences reflect the absolute contrast between the story structures of the two works, as is illustrated by Thackeray's—and his characters'—interest in how people change: "What a difference," observes Becky Sharp to George Osborne, "eighteen months' experience makes!" (14:139). The centrality of transformation in personality is dramatized by Thackeray's focus (quite different from Wolfe's), on protagonists who appear first in their late teens or early twenties. There can be no gradual development or deterioration in the personalities of Wolfe's figures, because he focuses on a single incident meant to be symbolically representative; his novel deals with the events of a few weeks, in fact, principally with just a few days, in the life of a single protagonist. Thackeray's work recounts, along with a variety of public events, the histories of his several protagonists over the span of more than a decade. Thackeray's novel is typically Victorian in thus being oriented diachronically, while *Bonfire* adheres, without Wolfe's seeming to be aware of what his form requires, to a major strain of modernism's anti-Victorian, synchronically structured fiction.

The prototypical modern synchronic novel, of course, is Joyce's *Ulysses*, a very long book concerned with a single day. Because Wolfe does not so concentrate his action, even if he possessed Joyce's ear for verbal nuance he would be unable to dramatize as Joyce does the intricate resonances of carefully rendered linguistic details. Joyce's reverberative "playing" with words is possible because he has transformed story (as Wolfe wishes not to) to escape the restrictions imposed by the continuous, "historical" narratives forming both warp and woof of *Vanity Fair*. Accounts of changes occurring through processes of time are replaced in *Ulysses* by patterns of paratactic coherence. As Harry Levin says of Joyce's characters, they "move in space, but they do not develop in time." Transformation through time is elided in synchronic fiction, which substitutes the intersection of diverse story fragments that bring together (or dramatically split apart for contrast) a variety of personal experiences presented in their immediacy *as* experiences, not as full stories.[3]

This does not mean, of course, that *Ulysses* is any less an artifice than *Vanity Fair*, nor that Joyce's book more transparently renders nonlinguistic reality. If anything, the opposite is true; the difference is that for Thackeray's conspicuous *teller* Joyce substitutes an invisible but ever-present author—and not one merely paring his nails. Simultaneously, *Ulysses* more persistently than *Vanity Fair* demands from us an imagining of the immediacies of sensory experience, and that requires a radical reshaping of the narrative structuring upon which the Victorian novel is built.

The contrast between *Vanity Fair* and *Ulysses* is especially revealing because Thackeray employs a favored Victorian device of multiple stories. The device was favored because it efficiently deepens the power of a diachronic novel by embodying at the highest structural level continuous mobility of viewpoint, thus enhancing narrative exploitation of polysemism. This flexibility entails consistent emphasis on differences in temporal perspective, the fundamental form of that emphasis, of course, created by the narrator's use of the past tense. Joyce's novel multiplies by fragmenting the limited number of stories constituting the Victorian novel, most obviously by giving dominance to the present tense. This creates the impression that there is no "story" at all in *Ulysses*. And there is, indeed, no "traditional" story, because *Ulysses* substitutes a paradigmatic form for Thackeray's syntagmatic form. One might think of the difference as an emphasis on the "vertical" rather than the "horizontal" axis of Mink's image of the configurative comprehension induced by narrative.

The distinction is clearest in the later parts of *Ulysses* in which the narrator almost totally disappears and indirect discourse is mostly replaced by diversely separate articulations, but throughout the entire novel the focus is on *disjunctions* between holistic archetypal references, centrally, of course, the Odysseus story, and the multiplicity of fragmented, mundane experiences of ordinary Dubliners on a single June day in 1904. That gap constitutes the imaginative space in which a synchronic fiction can explore the "universal," or at least generic, significance of utterly "trivial" quotidian events. That space is created by the telling, not of a few sequentially coherent stories, such as the narrative of Becky Sharp's existence as a governess at Sir Pitt's country estate, but a multitude of intersecting pieces of stories of diverse Dubliners.[4] Equivalently, the "story" of Bloom's, or Stephen's, day is constituted of many disjointed bits that on the level of mundane actuality have virtually no unity beyond the progress of the day—hence the novel's openness to accidents and irrelevancies. The unity of these stories is to be found on a plane of symbolic meaning—a plane virtually absent from *Vanity Fair*.

Wolfe's *Bonfire*, which attempts to use what is in essence the Joycean form for a simplified Thackerayan telling, can take full advantage of neither method. Without an imaginative opening to the symbolic from the mundane that Joyce creates, *Bonfire*'s "commentary" on the society it depicts can be little more than journalistic, since Wolfe has left himself no time for Thackeray's "historical" developments. The disjunction between the ordinary and the archetypal, "parallels that never meet," in *Ulysses*,[5] created by shattering into multiple fragments temporal stories,[6] enables Joyce to compel his reader into imagining meanings for the intersections he portrays that go far beyond those likely to occur to the characters themselves. But these imaginings never diminish the immediacy of the experience of those intersections. Thackeray, committed to developmental story sequences, uses a historical process rather than myth to magnify the significance of his characters' "insignificant" lives, so that the meaning of what happens to them is more or less as comprehensible to them as to a reader of *Vanity Fair,* and in more or less the same fashion. It never enters Leopold Bloom's head that he is a contemporary Odysseus; Thackeray's narrator never allows us to forget Becky Sharp is always aware of being what her society calls an adventuress.

Thackeray's characters evolve syntagmatically, "horizontally" through time. We recognize them through repetitions of certain characteristics and notice how these change or do not change in the course of their history. Joycean figures do not operate in this historical dimension. We identify them through emphasized peculiarities of speech, behavior, or demeanor represented with the sharpness of acute sensory perception, and perhaps through the paradigmatic functions of these "separating" details. Thus we "know" Bloom in part through the various ways in which what he does relates to his symbolic prototype, "vertically" out of natural time, through the presentation of his acts and thoughts in all their casual physicality. Thackeray stays on a single imaginative level; he seldom asks us to make such symbolic or metaphoric connections. His narrator ties events together by likeness and association, *developing* significance in terms of explicit connectives, favoring deliberate similes, and consistently appealing (if sometimes subversively) to recognized, conventional, and supposedly unproblematic modes of linkage between the particular and the general. *Ulysses*'s "arranger" (as David Hayman names the Joycean function replacing the conventional narrator) superimposes upon such syntagmatic evolution paradigmatic, metaphoric systems, so that, "language patterns . . . pre-empt other offices of narrative."[7] This *should* occur in a paradigmatic novel, because in it all meaning is grounded in the sensory actuality of experience as it happens—so the novelist uses words in a fashion analogous to that of a "sensual" poet like Keats or Spenser. An important dimension of the sensory immediacy of *Ulysses* is the attention the text solicits to its manner of representation. The significance of what Joyce's words refer to is strongly determined by their mode of reference—most obviously in the stream-of-consciousness passages. Thackeray, to the contrary, prefers verbal transparency.

Tom Wolfe's spurious archaism also illuminates an associated modernist revision of novelistic characterizing. Without either Joyce's mythic or Thackeray's historical perspective, Wolfe's unselfconscious (and hence illegitimate) "objectivity" can do no more than present people as stereotypes. Dependent on mere verisimilar accuracy, he tends to characterize people by the clothes they wear. If they dressed differently, they would for Wolfe be different persons. The point merits attention because Thackeray, a draughtsman sensitive to appearances (see Figure 12), in illustrating his novel advertised his falsifying of the dress of his characters by making it accord with contemporary fashions (the mid-1840s), not that of the Regency period when the action occurs.[8] Thackeray is not afraid to fictionalize overtly, because he commands a traditional narrative mode. Wolfe, uncertain about *how* he is telling his story, relies on a naïve, reportorial literalness that betrays his effort to fictionalize.

Wolfe's difficulty, however, highlights possible causes for modernism's revision of the traditional techniques for representing the significance of fictive characters. The "realism" of Thackeray's method of characterizing depends, George Lukács argues, on a rendering of major figures as typical because intensely individualized, the prototype for this paradoxical representation being Cervantes's Don Quixote. Lukács means that Quixote captures precisely and completely in his personality the vital play of key social forces operative in early seventeenth-century Spain.[9] There is nobody, in fiction or out of it, like Quixote, because he so profoundly embodies the most urgent social conflicts of Cervantes's day. Analogously, Becky's and Amelia's individualities, in part through Thackeray's consistent contrasting of their lives, are never fully separated from their representativeness. Lukács's point ceases to be paradoxical as soon as we admit that what we call individuality is no transcendent quality but one culturally defined and determined.

It might seem that Leopold Bloom possesses this kind of typicality, but he is in fact "representative" in a different fashion. His outstanding feature, his ordinariness, is conceived and represented in terms of his subjectivity. Bloom's ordinariness appears through the genuine or absolute uniqueness of a life imagined in terms of the singularity of its immediate sensory and mental impressions. This experiential uniqueness escapes the categorizations that constitute the ground for typical personalities as described by Lukács such as Becky Sharp or Don Quixote. In the very process of recognizing that Becky, let us say, is a "selfish adventuress," or Amelia a "sentimentalizing parasite," we begin to feel how inadequate to each character are such valid categorizations—just as the true description of Quixote as an idealistic madman speaks scarcely at all to what makes him so fascinating a figure. Leopold Bloom exists only as a peculiar set of self-contradictory qualities, realized through such subjectively fragmented actions that we do not "comprehend" him in terms of disrupted characterological categorization. Possibly one can classify him, as a Jew, for example, as one might classify Stephen in *Ulysses* as "pretentious young aesthete," but in fact I think few readers do so. One good reason, beyond his presentation through "disjointed" subjective impressions, is that Bloom's "representativeness" is embodied in a sylleptic relation to his prototype, Odysseus. *That* kind of representativeness, of course, is unavailable to Thackeray, who works on the plane of "historical" narrative.

Joyce's deliberate shattering of traditional narrative enables him to conceive of "characters" as individuals possessing representative value in a new fashion. *Pace* Virginia Woolf, there was no sudden change in human nature at the beginning of the twentieth century. Nor did modern novelists reconceive human nature. They altered the art of narrative to address changes in the cultural situations within which human beings were defined as individuals. Joyce's art, which many critics, following T. S. Eliot, refer to in a shorthand manner as "mythic," is neither simply mythic nor simply historical, but both at once because a conscious simulacrum of mythical synchronicity.[10] The simultaneity assures that each Joycean character is a kind of contradiction. Again the most obvious and important instance is Leopold Bloom, who is both a Ulysses figure and in his individualized ordinariness an anti–Ulysses figure. The endless interest of his character arises not from his "Lukácsian" typicality but from his existing for us at one and the same time as a re-realization of Odysseus and a parody of Odysseus. That irreconcilable contrariety (refracted by a multitude of personal idiosyncrasies) permits us to reconceive meanings we have been taught to attribute to the "historical," the "mythic," the "ordinary," and the "archetypal."

The Joycean method allows an immense gain simultaneously in imagined sensory concreteness and in power of self-contesting symbolic reference. Its most direct loss is in its isolation of character from character, for it registers personal identity less as an interplay between persons, as a social phenomenon, than as a psychological integrity founded on a subjective, inner (and therefore hidden) life. Personal identity is presented almost entirely in terms of autonomous processes of consciousness and unconsciousness, impinged on and affected by but not grounded in interactions with other people, and in this sense is dehistoricized.

Lukács's "typicality," which he takes to be universally true, I would argue derives from and applies principally to the literature of the seventeenth through nineteenth centuries in Europe. This literature was founded on a concept of individual identity constituted by social interactions between people, a concept easily adapted to significant presentation in syntagmatic narrative form. Even the prototypicality of *Don Quixote* points to the historical limitation of this conjunction. Every critic recognizes the double failure in the novel of Quixote's first expedition by himself: he accomplishes nothing and his activities are not very interesting. Not until he joins with Sancho does his individual personality begin to emerge effectively—the same being true, of course, for Sancho. Each realizes himself in relating to the other. This rendering of individuality through socialized interdependence dominates European fiction for the next 250 years. In Thackeray's novel, for example, the "reality" of both Becky's and Amelia's personalities depends on the novelist's interplaying of the two through the temporal developments of their stories. Any present moment in *Vanity Fair,* as in *Don Quixote,* appears as an intersecting of past and future through the storytelling itself. This syntagmatic form differs radically from the continuous present of sensory concreteness Joyce employs as the ground of the paradigmatic narrative of *Ulysses,* so radically that it is difficult for us to resist thinking that Joyce has entirely abandoned storytelling, when in fact he has, instead, altered it—albeit drastically.

"Distancing" is a primary effect of the "telling" characteristic of syntagmatic fiction that flourished before the paradigmatic/ synchronic novels of modernism. The latter foreground *immediacy,* evoking the reader's imagination of sensory experiences. This feature of modernist fiction tempts one to draw parallels with modernist painting, which notoriously emphasizes the canvas as a direct, "depthless" sensory phenomenon. But the analogy can be misleading. One normally comprehends language, whether in hearing or reading, by ignoring its perceptual character, of which one becomes conscious only with a misprint or misspeaking. The purpose of modern painting's emphasis on paint as paint, with the rejection of illustrative or referential subject matter (a principal form of "depth"), was to liberate art from such conceptualizing responses fostered by all literary practices. It is more useful, therefore, to observe that the preference for "showing" over telling in modern fiction chiefly seeks to empower readers to *imagine* sensations and perceptions as in the very instant of their occurrence. This ambition for direct effect requires getting rid of the unabashed storytellers earlier novelists had favored.

Bonfire in this respect, too, is rather awkwardly modernistic, being told predominantly from restricted points of view. Most of the action comes to us through the perspective of the protagonist, Sherman McCoy, and whatever is not so represented appears only through the consciousness of some single character or another. Representation for Wolfe is almost unfailingly representation from a single character's point of view, because his focus is the psychophysical stimuli that provoke a particular experience. This makes *Bonfire* radically different from *Vanity Fair,* which comes to us through a storytelling narrator.

Viewpoint in the Victorian novel is perpetually moving within the medium of the telling—a process well suited to the syntagmatic development of stories and appropriate to its usual focus on localized social contexts rather than specific sensory stimuli. At any moment in such a telling the perspective from which an action *and its context* is perceived by readers can slide into a different, even quite opposed, perspective. A simple but instructive example is the account of how young William Dobbin, taking refuge from his schoolmates' ridicule by reading the *Arabian Nights,* comes to fight the school bully, Cuff, who is beating little George Osborne.

> Down came the stump with a great heavy thump on the child's hand. A moan followed. Dobbin looked up. The Princess Peridbanou had fled into the inmost cavern with Prince Ahmed; the Roc had whisked away Sinbad the Sailor out of the Valley of Diamonds out of sight, far into the clouds: and there was every-day life before honest William; and a big boy beating a little one without cause. . . .
>
> "Take that, you little devil! cried Mr. Cuff, and down came the wicket again on the child's hand. —Don't be horrified, ladies, every boy at a public school has done it. Your children will so do and be done by, in all probability. Down came the wicket again; and Dobbin started up.
>
> I can't tell what his motive was. Torture in a public school is as much licensed as the knout in Russia. (5:48)

The passage begins with a verbal evocation of sensory actuality that might be part of a modern fiction (note the stump-thump "rhyme"). But it is difficult to think of a modern novelist who would choose a perceiver so entangled in the fantasy of the *Arabian Nights,* thus dramatizing the relation of escapist of daydreams to actuality—a big boy beating a little one without cause. And that mobility is the basis for the truly un-modern narrator's advice that ladies not be horrified. This is where a contemporary critic, perhaps a little flushed from reading too much Barthes, writes "intrusion" in the margin.

But the narrator's aside to his female readers is better described as a modification of the context within which his audience receives his telling. Such a contextual shift complicates the social meaning of the event told. Thackeray's telling is prin-

cipally of how we judgmentally apprehend a situation of relationships. Even the narrator's uncertainty about Dobbin's motive introduces psychological assessment rather than felt
experience. We are not so much invited to share Dobbin's in-
stinctive outrage at gratuitous torture, as asked to recognize
how his response to that immediate stimulus is shaped by a
long-building yearning for revenge and anger at his own torture by his schoolmates. Focus on sensory immediacy would obscure this gradually developed situation of relational realities
with which *Vanity Fair* is principally concerned. As the final sentences in my quotation illustrate, Thackeray's novel asserts that
it is enduring, if often disguised, social systems that determine
the kinds of personal experiences available to individuals. Thus
the ultimate upshot of Dobbin's defense of Osborne's victimiza-
tion is his cooptation by the conventionalized tyranny embodied in Cuff, who becomes Dobbin's mentor. Since it is this ironic
evolution that is Thackeray's primary concern, he needs a narrative form that frees him from too close an attention to depiction of immediate responses to physical stimuli.

One has the impression that there is scarcely a page of *Vanity
Fair* in which the reader's imagination is not required to move
through a variety of perspectives—all the while taking account
of the diversity of contexts making possible those perspectives.
This mobility is most obvious in the narrator's comments on the
effects of his shiftings. Thus he not infrequently remarks on
how different readers are probably reacting to a particular representation, even describing one, Jones, "rather flushed with
his joint of mutton and half-pint of wine," penciling in his opinion in a copy of the text (1:15). In *Vanity Fair,* subjectivity appears chiefly through interpersonal encounters; the inner life
of the individual is normally of interest only so far as it finds
some distinctly social manifestation. And the most significant
aspect of such manifestations is their *tellability,* that they can be
presented for multiple evaluations by the diverse people of a
complexly stratified society. Thus, to cite the most famous examples, when the narrator leaves open the question of Becky's
infidelity to Rawdon, he is not posing a question of fact, but,
rather, drawing our attention to the different possibilities of
assessment of Becky's behavior that a complex society devoted
to Mammon and "without God" necessarily will develop.

To be accurate, one must observe that Thackeray does not always move our perspectives restlessly; he at times gains powerful effects by temporarily restricting himself to a single viewpoint with the attendant immediacy of physical sensations. An example is his portrayal of the final catastrophe between Becky and Rawdon. Immediately after Rawdon's arrest at the end of chapter 51, Thackeray shifts back in time, telling us in chapter 52 of Lord Steyne's and Becky's maneuverings leading to their assignation. In the following chapter we are back to Rawdon's position, as he stoically decides not to trouble Becky that evening and puts up at the Bailiff's house, only the next morning writing her of his plight, then waiting with increasing agitation for her appearance. Because we are here held within Rawdon's situation, we share his revulsion at the shattering falsity of the note (so unmistakably in Becky's style) she finally sends—instead of coming herself to liberate him. We stay fairly steadily with Rawdon's perspective through his climactic breaking in upon Steyne and Becky, so that, again, we share his terrible vision of his house blazing with lights, and the tableau of Steyne bending over Becky, her arms sparkling with jewelry. Yet even in this climax there are modulations in perspective, so that we are allowed to see (as he could not) the light from his house shining *on* Rawdon's pale face (53:514), and Becky's secret admiration for his ferocity even at the moment of her destruction (53:515). The normal fluidity of viewpoint endows such concentrations of perspective with special dramatic force, while the intermittent return to the usual mobility keeps us subliminally aware of the social forces at play through the individual conflicts, so that they are not reduced to the melodrama of mere personal encounters.

To summarize, the central feature of fictional modernism is its replacement of the traditional narrative *teller* with an *author,* either "invisible," or "hidden" within one or more characters inside the story. This carries fiction away from the most complex effects in *Vanity Fair,* which are attained by techniques enabling readers to perceive socially contextualized events in terms of their temporal evolution. The "presentness" of a represented moment in Thackeray's novel usually consists less in a dramatic showing forth of an immediate experience of subjective sensations than in a syntagmatic interrelating of it to past and future situations. This method relies on a degree of community between author and audience, between novel and readers. Telling is sharing. Were Thackeray's attitude toward his readers like that of Flaubert, to cite one of the begetters of modernist fiction, it would not be possible for him to recount his story as he does. To make this distinction, it must be emphasized, is not to imply that Thackeray's evaluation of the excellence or righteousness of his society is higher than Flaubert's. A case could be made that the Englishman is finally a more profound social critic than the Frenchman.

Thackeray subtitles *Vanity Fair* "A Novel Without a Hero," and structures his work around the stories of two young women who fail as heroines, one, Becky, being "guilty," the other, Amelia, being "weak." The novel permits no middle ground: one heroine must "defeat" the other. The shallowly conventional "sisterliness" Amelia offers poor Becky at the beginning of the book *must* be repaid by Becky's conscious humiliating of Amelia before the Battle of Waterloo. Envy is woman's lot because society allows women no role but that of "rival" in sexual competition. So at the end of the book, although Becky tries to restore Dobbin to Amelia, when he returns she must, literally, disappear. Conscious hypocrisy or the self-deceptive hypocrisy of sentimentalism are the only choices for women in a society dominated by vain, stupid, and selfish men who assume the absolute righteousness of disinheriting mothers in favor of sons.

Intrinsic to Thackeray's social commentary, then, is a critique of literary "romancing" against which Flaubert's condemnations may seem superficial. *Vanity Fair*'s condemnations, however, must be more indirect, even devious, since the mode of their representation is one that appeals through storytelling to readers treated as participating together with the teller in a social community. Thackeray's narrator addresses his readers as people "like" himself, which means that each will differ from him and others, having diverse occupations, prejudices, and life experiences, so that their "community" depends on the acceptance of their acknowledged differences. Even by distinguishing a particular segment of his readership by gender, as in the Cuff passage cited above, the narrator *connects* differentiated groups and individuals. This makes the reading of his story a different imagining process from one of reading most modern novels "addressed" to readers undefined, anonymous, and conceived as responding in purely aesthetic terms. The paradigmatic tendency of modern fiction assumes an audience that from a Thackerayan point of view has been depersonalized and desocialized and even desexed. Modern fiction thus parallels modern graphic arts, which likewise assume an "abstract" audience, one appealed to in terms of aesthetic sensibility alone.

This concept of the abstract audience has become so accepted that few readers today know how to respond when addressed directly. When *Vanity Fair*'s narrator particularizes "Ladies" in his observation about Cuff, other readers, in this instance "Gentlemen," are provided with a means of noticing and evaluating how *another* portion of the audience community to which they belong may be responding. That activity, the arousing of awareness in an audience of differentia of responses within it, is one of the most important features of traditional storytelling—and another feature that has been ignored by contemporary narratologists, since modernist fiction cannot so differentiate.[11] But anyone who has participated in, or observed, oral storytelling situations will recognize that awareness by the audience of the heterogeneity of their community as listeners is usually acute. Often an esteemed characteristic of first-rate storytellers in preliterate societies is their ability to tell a story in such a way that it affects differently diverse members of the audience. The modern novelist tends to appeal to an undifferentiated audience, defined principally by one quality only—aesthetic sensitivity.

The loss in modern society of a sense for story as multiply received certainly encourages the critical view that with modern fiction storytelling became devalued. Novelists such as Wolfe seeking a large, "popular" audience therefore claim to recover "old-fashioned," that is, non-modern, narrative interest. But as *The Bonfire of the Vanities* demonstrates, it is not that easy to restore older ways of telling. The changes in narrative we associate with modernism were provoked by profound dislocations in cultural and intellectual life. And the major modern novelists, writers such as Marcel Proust, Virginia Woolf, Gustave Flaubert, D. H. Lawrence, and Henry James, did not, as some critics suggest, simply eliminate storytelling. Narrative may seem to disappear in their work because it has taken on different forms appropriate to new circumstances of telling.

An evident sign of this transformation is—ironically—the disappearance of overt comment on the fictionality of fiction. Almost every page of *Vanity Fair* reminds us that we are reading a tale. So even direct commentaries by the narrator are mediated by their function in the blatant artifice, and references to realities beyond the printed page tend to function obliquely, as the total narrative of Regency England indirectly illuminates English society of the 1840s. All such connections are to be made by the reader (often at the narrator's explicit urging) as relations between an ostentatiously invented tale and whatever the reader knows or thinks about circumstances in "real" life outside the novel. Not only Tom Wolfe, but also James Joyce, would prefer not to tell us, as Thackeray cheerfully does, "that this work would never have been written" (4:41) if George and Amelia had not interrupted Becky and Jos in the darkened parlor. *Vanity Fair*—adhering to a primary mode of fiction prominent from its very inception—unflaggingly insists that we, its readers, remember that the pleasure and instruction we receive from reading it are the enjoyment and information appropriate to a specific kind of artifact, a story.

Thackeray adapts to the exigencies of modern impersonalized publication an intrinsic feature of storytelling, prominent in preliterate societies where groups gather together to tell and listen to stories. The key feature of all such occasions is that one recognizes oneself to be attending to a story, a deliberate artifice, whose artificiality is often enhanced by ceremonious or ritualized behavior. And a primary virtue of that flagrance of artifice is that it liberates the audience to move imaginatively through a variety of sociopsychological positions and perspectives that in actual life would probably be dangerous if not inaccessible. The pleasure and wisdom of story receiving are almost always spiced by references to such risks and transgressions. Much of narrative's potency for ethical comment (and hence its tendency to provoke censorship) derives from this "openness of its artifice." It is our capacity to *imagine* the situation of others, and our courage therewith to yield ourselves to provisional indulgence in forbidden acts and feelings, that permits us both to sympathize with and to pass judgment on what lies beyond the restrictions of conventional behavior and thinking. One possible effect of such sympathizing and judging, of course, may be a reaffirmation of the wisdom of whatever conventional arrangements are already in place. The recognition if not adoption of the prejudice of others is enhanced by awareness that various other members in the audience community may be reacting in very different ways to a story that crosses the limits of what might not be acceptable outside the telling situation.

What I say here, let me emphasize, has nothing to do with Thackeray's interest in or anxiety about any literal relation to oral telling. Thackeray was his own illustrator, as well as a professional journalist, and his conceptions are profoundly print-oriented. But in a printed form he utilizes this feature of all traditional storytelling—that it is presented to be recognized as storytelling. The ease with which Thackeray's narrator enters into his story is a novelistic development of a basic storytelling characteristic. For a Victorian novelist confronting complex modern culture such openness must have had powerful appeal. How better to comprehend contemporary life, with its accelerating processes of self-transformation along with its mind-jarring diversity of groups and subgroups, classes, professions, new kinds of tradespeople, and even exotic persons from distant parts of the globe? Thackeray's "puppet show" only systematizes a condition that all the best Victorian novelists sought to create. This was a scene of reading that would catch up diverse people into a mobility of ever-shifting perspectives through their awareness of being engaged by an artifice, a story, valuable because illusory.[12]

But, as the success of modernist fiction demonstrates, this adaptation of traditional storytelling proved inadequate to the radical potency of new conditions. What is central to modernist transformations of storytelling is revealed by *Madame Bovary,* long regarded as prototypical of modernist fiction. *Madame Bovary* is a fine illustration because it so definitely is not a synchronic novel. Flaubert's novel is of and in time as thoroughly as Thackeray's, its most powerful effects deriving from the representation of the life *history* of Emma and Charles. Yet the two nearly contemporaneous works could scarcely be more different.

To my mind, the primary difference between the two is intensity. The relaxed telling of Thackeray's novel is replaced in Flaubert's by a continuous demand on the reader to respond to precise evocations of highly specific sensory and emotional detail—perhaps the demand being most powerful when the social situation is most trivial or boring. *Vanity Fair* tells quickly or entertainingly past the routine banalities of life, "leaping" from one more-or-less exciting event to another, whereas *Madame Bovary* dwells on the dull, the repeated, the undramatic—with the same painful precision that it devotes to the violent scenes, such as the failed operation on Hippolyte's foot or Emma's death.

The ultimate source of this intensity is Flaubert's identification with his protagonist, first noticed by Charles Baudelaire, and frequently commented on by later critics, most notably, perhaps, Jean-Paul Sartre, who felt that the irksomeness of Flaubertian characters reflects the author's self-hatreds. Be that as it may, identification by the reader (reflecting that by the writer) is the ground for the stylistic intensity of *Madame Bovary*. We imaginatively feel the sensations of the characters and the emotional resonances they evoke as if we *were* the characters, not an audience being *told* about them.

These intensities of identification account for Flaubert's dependence on free indirect discourse, *erlebte rede,* quasi-direct speech, in which one is unsure whether the source of the utterance is the narrator, the character, or both at once. Is it Emma or the narrator (or both) we hear, when, in response to Rodolphe's clichés "something gave way in her . . . The sweetness of this sensation revived her past desires, and like grains of sand under a gust of wind, they swirled around in the subtle breath of the perfume that diffused over her soul"?[13]

The function of this sylleptic perspective is clarified by its contrast to Thackerayan traditional telling, which normally assures a distinction between narrator and character that precludes Flaubertian identification. When the narrator "enters" the mind of a character, we are usually aware of this as an imaginative act reproducing that by which we participate in his storytelling. Flaubert's identificatory storytelling urges more intense alertness to a linguistic representation by which traditional boundaries between articulator and referent, narrator and character, are transgressed. Free indirect discourse permits direct telling of interiorized, subjective conflicts and confusions, wherein irrational impulses and internalized conventions clash secretly. This is why most of Flaubert's free indirect discourse involves Emma, rather than, say, Charles, Rodolphe, or Homais, for they, in their differently unattractive ways, are freer from such interior contradiction.

It is Emma who is wracked, and finally destroyed, by a competition of discourses within her, which nonetheless reflect the social upheavals of which she is a victim. Immersed in rural, agricultural society to which she no longer belongs, she reads novels, which only arouse an unreal vision of an "aristocratic" life as distinct as is peasant life from her uncertain, in-between situation, that of a "middle" class. Into that desperate indeterminacy all readers of Flaubert's novel are drawn by free indirect discourse, which forces us to read "between" the warped romantic sublimity of Emma's sensibility, and what has generated her silly idealizations of romance, the morally platitudinous and repressively prosy discourse of male-dominated French provincial life. Indirect discourse keeps us "between" these repulsive contradictions, urgent to resolve or escape the poisonous impasse, but unable to do so, condemned to the nihilistic horror finally realized fully in Emma's suicide.

The interiorization of narrative telling that appears so clearly with the emergence of free indirect discourse is usually regarded by critics as an "advance" in narrative technique, but it unmistakably arises from increased awareness of the terrors and limitations as well as the joys of the subjective life. Flaubert's quasi-direct discourse forces readers to experience how two discourses, for simplicity's sake identifiable with the superego and the id, struggle not toward synthesis but against one another in a conflict that can lead only to the destruction of the mind within which they compete. In Flaubert's presentation, destruction is virtually assured because neither discourse, romantic or realistic, can prove superior authenticity. However contradictory, neither is "natural"; both are artificial constructs. The only solid authority in the novel is that of the author; and that authority depends on his awareness that either (or any) discourse will prove a traitor to psychological completeness.

Free indirect discourse is a significant but by no means the only way fiction since Flaubert has striven to assure reader identification with the experience of subjective sensations and the artifices of conflictive internalized systems by which they are experienced. The effort is most simply defined as the supersession of teller by author, and is epitomized in a work such as William Faulkner's *As I Lay Dying,* where there is no visible narrator, but rather apparently unmediated representations of distinct discourses of diverse individuals. Such exploitations of the subjectivization originating in free indirect discourse complicate, may even challenge, fundamental features of traditional narrative, but they remain very much within the province of storytelling. This is apparent as soon as one contrasts pure narrative with drama, which in the literal sense must be without *erlebte rede.* This distinction, if only because critics so seldom attend to it, is worth a moment's attention, since it has become a cliché that modern fiction is uniquely "dramatic." That misapprehension has impeded understanding of how and why modern literature transformed narrative.

Storytelling is distinguished by its capacity to compel its audience to adopt multiple perspectives in the process of comprehending it. To cite the most obvious example, any story allows its viewpoint to "wander" each time the speech of a character other than the narrator is represented. Although this is not the subtlest mode of shifting viewpoint, it contrasts usefully to what happens in drama. The audience at a traditional play remains equidistant, imaginatively as well as spatially, from each speaker, but in a novel, or a told story, the audience, more dependent on its imagining (since there are no physical figures present) tends to adapt to the attitude of each speaker as he or she speaks. To comprehend someone who speaks in a story we imagine ourselves into the utterance position of the speaker. While the quality of that imagining may differ, for example, in a work recounted from the first-person point of view from that evoked by a third-person narrative, the audience's point of view, its position of imaginative response, may change as radically and as often in one form as in the other. For *all* storytelling creates a textured dynamic of perspectives internal to the story being told—probably because it is difficult to conceive of a better way of bringing forward for shared consideration the complexities of human interactions in all their contingent specificity.

For our present purposes, however, the key point is that with pure dialogue in a story the audience tends to "identify" with each speaker; free indirect discourse, and its derivatives, intensifies, complicates, and subtilizes that identifying tendency. The result in a novel such as *Madame Bovary,* which depends heavily on quasi-direct speech, is a demand for continuous complex intensity of response, yet still within a narrative mode, one, to be sure, that is predominantly restricted to print and assumes a basic uniformity of "aesthetic" reactions from its audience. But Flaubert, even though he might be described as the first major novelist to write narratively *against* what he takes to be his established readership, requires of competent readers as much imaginative energy of response as Thackeray. No more than James or Joyce or Proust or Thomas Mann does Flaubert appeal directly, transparently, to an actuality other than that of his linguistic fiction. The intensity produced by his indirect discourse, to stay with this major stylistic feature, arises from readers' conscious engagement in a linguistic performance. One cannot respond to the basic sylleptic bind—do these words represent the character's or the narrator's perception?—without recognizing that one has encountered a *verbal* dilemma.

Critics sometimes undervalue this fact because the modern novelist cannot take delight, as a more traditional storyteller such as Thackeray can, in talking about the *inadequacy* of his language. So far as modern novelists seek identification with immediacy of experience they lose the luxury that Thackeray enjoyed when he declared his linguistic incapacities—for example, to describe war (30:282) or a presentation at court (48:463). Modern novelists have sacrificed to their author function the teller function, which made such self-deprecation possible.

The value of this freedom ostentatiously enjoyed by the traditional storyteller—from the position of a metanarrative overview to display the imaginative nature of his performance—has also been underestimated by twentieth-century criticism. Yet the elimination of a narrator that frees an invisible author to dramatize the special intensities of personal experiencing does not carry the modern novelist away from fundamental purposes of storytelling, which may still be used to assist, rather than hinder, imaginative sharing of other people's prejudices.

Modernists are frequently as concerned as their predecessors to render the mobility of perspective that is a primary reward of narrative imagining. In *Madame Bovary,* again, free indirect discourse with its uncertainty over the source of the linguistic expression demands a supple flexibility of response that is a specialized, intensified form of the mobility of responsiveness all stories seek to evoke. In Flaubert's novel (and in this it is plainly a forerunner of modern practices), the perspective movement characteristic of storytelling is consistently narrowed—attaining what might be called the microlevel of immediate sensory and subjective experience—as it is applied to subtly nuanced feelings and expressions of feeling. But that tightening and confining of narrative focus does not do away with narrative—any more than molecular biology ceases to be biology.

It could be argued, for example, that Flaubert simply constricts the focus of what Wolfgang Iser calls the "wandering viewpoint" intrinsic to all storytelling.[14] In *Vanity Fair,* for instance, temporal "displacements" are common, as when we are told of Mr. Sedley's bankruptcy *after* some of its effect have been recounted (18:168). Flaubert, on the contrary, confines himself almost entirely to shifts in personal perspective within a relatively uninterrupted temporal continuity. And more often than not he prevents perspectives from being diffused or blurred by his characters' verbalizations. He substitutes, as Jonathan Arac has observed, ellipses for speech.[15] Because the language possessed by his characters is so trite and conventional, it cannot adequately represent the real significance of their subjectivity—except through ironic presentation, which is but a dramatizing of their language's inadequacy. Most simply, Charles Bovary's dullness precludes his articulating the contraction of mind and the dimness of perception that define his personality.

Thackeray, too, uses relatively little direct speech, but for different reasons. I am not sure that Thackeray's ear for actual speech was particularly acute. Almost all the impressive conversational passages in *Vanity Fair* derive their principal effect from how they crystallize and concretize metaverbal relationships. Becky's "Oh, Sir—I—I'm *married already*" (14:142), carries little personal accent but is superbly precise in concretizing the sociopsychological situation, ironically climaxed by "the most genuine" tears we will see this little protagonist shed. But, because of his confidence in the authorization of his story as story (rather than any Flaubertian consciousness of the linguistic limitations of his characters), Thackeray is seldom drawn to reproduce actual speech.[16] He may appropriately concentrate on expressive intonations of speech as social rather than as a merely personal phenomena.

But Thackeray and Flaubert, despite their differences, are equally true to a fundamental characteristic of storytelling. Unlike the playwright, who can only implicitly enhance speech acts with such material, the storyteller finds both the peculiar psychological origins and the broader, less immediately particularized socioeconomic ambiance of any remark just as articulable as the verbal utterance itself. For a novelist's audience it is as easy to *imagine* these metaverbal determinants, be they subjective or sociological, as the speech act itself, which is virtually the playwright's only tool.

One can state the contrast in another way. A playwright's skill consists to a degree in "remembering" that characters other than a speaker who are on stage must in some way react to each speech—even if they ignore it, they must do so ostentatiously. The novelist, on the contrary, can omit material virtually at will. What is not told does not exist for his audience, however unlike real life it may be to omit what in fact must have been part of a given situation. In storytelling, as I've noted before, skill consists in knowing what to pass over. The tedious teller is the one who omits nothing, who forgets or never knew that storytelling is, like stonecarving, an art of subtraction, of leaving out, which explains why traditional verbal narratives were uninhibited in letting the teller "intrude" into the story he or she tells, in flaunting that the tale depends on a teller. The presence of a storyteller, besides validating a narrative as belonging to a larger social or cultural context (that a story *can* be told implies *some* shared community between teller and audience), provides the most direct means by which changes in audience perspective may be effected. What many twentieth-century critics call an "interruption" by a teller, therefore, is in truth a means of sustaining a continuity in audience imagining necessary to the wholeness of the story, however much the teller dismisses, leaves out, or skips over. It is this feature of storytelling that Thackeray, like other Victorian novelists, avails himself of, but which Flaubert alters, not merely through the characters he chooses to write of, but through a shifting of the traditional relation between teller and audience. Those shifts, it seems fair to claim, reflected transformations in nineteenth-century society, the range and complexity of which I will not rehearse. But the contemporaneous subjectivizing of narrative painting by W. Holman Hunt (discussed in Chapter 6) suggests how mid-nineteenth century European culture pressured every artist toward "microscopic" descriptive detail to dramatize psychic self-encounters, as fundamental reality came to be regarded as psychological. So Flaubert persistently "intrudes" not into his story but into the mind of Emma Bovary.

That Flaubert was correct in judging what fiction needed is evidenced by the triumph of the direction of novelistic art he championed. But the gains resulting from this turn of storytelling entailed losses worthy of attention because they clarify the nature of the transformation. The Victorian commitment to a storytelling narrator, for instance, allows easy access to a range of texts and tales and story patterns outside the immediate telling. As I observed in a previous chapter, every story is a story because it implies other stories. And to be a storyteller is by definition as well as conventional usage to be a master in the realm of what critics now call intertextuality. A storyteller is someone who knows more than one story and is presumed to know a great deal about a great many. For Thackeray, determined to create "the sentiment of reality," intertextual referentiality enhances his ability to keep the reader's imagination constantly shifting its perspective to explore the diverse implications of relatively commonplace events. To cite a simple instance already mentioned, when John Sedley goes bankrupt and his house and possessions are sold, Thackeray reflects on the social response to such events by suggesting that the reader "remember" his reaction when "Dives" went bankrupt (17:159–160). The reference is not to some actual event but to the story of a wealthy man who found himself after death in the flames of hell begging fruitlessly for a drop of water from the beggar he had formerly scorned, a story that reminds us, even as we sympathize with Sedley (and recognize the ingratitude of those like Osborne who turn on him because they owe him so much), that Sedley, too, has been a worshiper of Mammon. At this point, and a hundred others like it in *Vanity Fair,* the simple fact that the novel comes to us explicitly as a teller's tale allows for this kind of direct reference to other stories familiar to the teller and his audience.[17]

This narrative (rather than verbal) allusiveness, functioning locally and syntagmatically rather than symbolically, has attracted little critical attention. Yet without it nonliterate cultures could not rely on narrative as they do. For such allusiveness permits any one tale to give access to an entire body of stories (both already told and yet to be told) that define the culture. One reason we have lost sight of this function of narrative is made plain by *Bonfire.* Wolfe knows no other narratives to which he can with assurance refer his reader. This is not his literary ignorance; nowadays it is not easy to determine what stories a sophisticated writer and a popular audience might share. Modern novelists begin with the assumption that, though they may share a body of similar *experiences* with their readership, they possess few stories in common, or at any rate few that they wish to make positive use of, since, as *Madame Bovary* so famously establishes, the sophistication of a significant modern novelist may best be demonstrated by contempt for "popular" fictions.

A substitute for traditional stories are mass entertainments—as Thomas Pynchon demonstrates with motion pictures in *Gravity's Rainbow* and television series in *Vineland,* following a lead given by Joyce's exploitation of advertising techniques and presuppositions in *Ulysses.* More simpleminded writers like Wolfe carry forward the crudest aspects of naturalistic fiction, relying on "real facts" to empower fictionality.[18] Wolfe thereby points up a significant risk in any modernist storytelling, which, so far as it depends on evoking imagination of sensory immediacies, is constantly drawn toward a literal verisimilitude that threatens the necessary artifice of fiction. A lovely dramatization of that threat and how it may be overcome is Joyce's "Grossbooted draymen rolled barrels dullthudding out of Prince's stores and bumped them up on the brewery float," which evokes the actual sounds of the barrel movements. But by following this sentence with its inversion, "On the brewery float bumped dullthudding barrels rolled by grossbooted draymen out of Prince's stores," Joyce in self-parody shatters the original mimetic verisimilitude and forces on us consciousness of the artifice of his "realism."[19]

Self-parody is more difficult for Thackeray. His teller may comment on his story and on himself, even as teller, but his very presence makes Joycean verbal self-reflexivity awkward, even as it impedes emphasis on direct sensory experiences. This is why Thackeray's expressed aim, "the sentiment of reality," seems so apt a phrase for what his narrative evokes. It focuses on a central difference between his art and that favored by Henry James, for example, who is one of the subtlest expositors of literary modernism, and probably the novelist who with the most critical assiduity strove to define the transformations he felt the narrative art of his predecessors required for useful adaptation to new conditions. James's most frequently cited polemic privileges not verisimilitude but "picture," using the term "composition"—the same word that Roy Lichtenstein later employed to deny the simple narrativity of his paintings. James accuses Victorian novelists of subordinating aesthetic significance to story's engagement with historical contingencies. It is worth quoting once more James's celebrated attack, especially since one of its targets is Thackeray, some of whose techniques James was not above adapting to his own purposes: "A picture without composition slights its most precious chance for beauty, and moreover is not composed at all unless the painter knows *how* that principle of health and safety, working as absolutely premeditated art, has prevailed . . . what do such large, loose baggy monsters, with their queer elements of the accidental and the arbitrary, artistically *mean?*"[20] This makes one wonder how James might have reacted to *Ulysses* with all its accidents— which should remind us that modern literature is no monolith. But our more immediate concern is the fairly common misunderstanding of what James favors in fiction. George Levine, for example, has observed of this passage that "the Jamesian attempt to create illusion sufficiently powerful to make us forget we are reading a novel would have seemed to Thackeray misguided."[21] Indeed it would, since the foundation of Thackeray's artistry is his appeal to his readers to accept his work as artifice, as a story told by a conspicuous teller. But Henry James, whatever Tom Wolfe may attempt, never advocated, or tried to practice, the absurdity of writing a novel that would make readers *forget* they are reading a novel. Certainly his point in the passage at issue is a condemnation of a *lack* of artifice, not an appeal to deluding readers into believing they were not reading a literary work but literally undergoing nonverbal experiences.

It is easy to misunderstand James's argument because, as I will suggest in my discussion of *The Ambassadors*, he had difficulty defining the fashion in which he felt art "competes" with life—largely, as John Carlos Rowe has demonstrated, because his attitude toward his Victorian predecessors was intricately ambivalent.[22] What is at stake in James's condemnation of Thackeray is how a novelist should best thrust the artificiality of his story upon his readers to evoke the paradoxical truth of recognized fictionality. James feels that reliance on the traditional role of teller unduly limits a novelist's power to shape contemporary experiences—citing, not unreasonably, the fact that a traditional teller accommodates all too readily to the contingencies of human existence. This is, indeed, one of a storyteller's stocks in trade: "A funny thing happened to me on the way to . . ." James seeks an art that will supersede nonliterary realities so that we need accept nothing in the fiction as valid *only* because it refers to actualities outside the literary work. Everything in a proper novel must be validated entirely by its linguistic artistry, to be regarded as primarily "true" or "meaningful" solely as part of a purely verbal *composition*. Only artifice recognized as artifice, in James's view, is capable of making a significant commentary on the actualities of experience, and given the complexity of modern life such artifice demands a reconstituting of traditional methods of storytelling.

The artifice that James favors, and his preference is typical of modern novelists, is more absolute and intense than that of his Victorian predecessors. They seemed to him, through their use of traditional tellers, to contaminate their art with historically verisimilar matter, material not fully processed aesthetically, and therefore not capable of arousing fully a reader's capacities of aesthetic response. James's view, however, is in no way intended to weaken or limit the power of his fiction to comment upon, or judge the social circumstances with which it deals. To the contrary, for him, intensification of the aesthetic qualities of

fiction will make such assessments more cogent. There are, in fact, no subtler or more enlightening commentaries on the strengths and weakness of actual European and American cultural structures than James's novels. But these judgments, though as penetrating into real conditions and as critical as any Victorian evaluations, are, unlike the assessments of Thackeray, Dickens, and Eliot, available *only* through an appreciation of their aesthetic form. Jamesian assessments are the more potent for never appearing as mere commentary.

Thackeray's critique of Victorian society, of course, is also in part embodied in his novel's form, which is, *pace* James, the very opposite of "loose and baggy." But *Vanity Fair* also includes, because it functions in the manner of a traditional telling, a substantial amount of direct "conversation" between the narrator and his readers about facts and attitudes of their common life that is part of the overall "telling situation" but that functions differently from passages of "pure" narrative. This difference in function for James spoils the novel's composition. But all parts of Thackeray's work are presented as appealing to his audience's imaginative capacity, and in that sense *Vanity Fair* is as entirely an aesthetic artifact as any of James's novels. Yet far more frequently than James, Thackeray explicitly compares and contrasts the real world and his fictive world. As Juliet McMaster observes, he repeatedly asks "his reader, during the act of reading, to make comparisons from one world to the other, to bring to bear his knowledge of one on the evaluation of the other."[23]

Such evaluative interplay of real and fictive is possible because *Vanity Fair* is so unmistakably a telling, which renders such comparisons easy and natural, since it assumes the artifice of story as a recognized transaction of sociocultural bonding. The modernist like James is a modernist because he perceives how dubious the possibility of such bonding has become; he wants his audience to concentrate more exclusively on their fictive imagining, responding to his story, in a word, as aesthetes. This desire I believe reflects accurately how the society within which he wrote had changed from that in which Thackeray wrote. What both James's practice and his critical arguments tend to obscure is the degree to which the Victorian "comparisons" between real and fictive worlds include awareness of the definition of "real" as not something natural but cultural, that

the "real" itself is a fictive construct. This point needs to be clarified, not to "justify" Victorian narratives, but to make more understandable why their traditional methods required the kind of transformations in it that were wrought by novelists such as Flaubert, James, Woolf, and Joyce.

Most simply, *Vanity Fair* invites the reader's complicity in both the representation and exposure of social pretentiousness, hypocrisy, and emotional self-deception encouraged by patterns of thought and behavior embodied in popular fictional narratives. McMaster notes, for example, that underlying Thackeray's comparisons of the real and fictive worlds is a method of telling that assures "his novels are certainly about Amelia, Becky . . . and the rest; but they are also *about,* and in no superficial way, our responses to these characters."[24] She draws attention to the Victorian's awareness (as well as our own) that one's responses to works of fictions and elements in them are in substantial measure determined by learned habits of reading fiction. Thackeray, she rightly observes, consistently maneuvers the reader into reading self-reflexively about patterns created and confirmed by previous fiction—which, of course, is an aspect of what I have called the novel's narrative allusiveness.

Storytellers do not create out of nothing. They begin from familiar forms, genres, plot patterns, what we may call, after E. H. Gombrich, narrative schemata. These schemata storytellers make anew. This process is fundamental to all narrative art. As Yurij Lotman has remarked, at the heart of every story "lies an event, some happening which contradicts some basic classificatory regularities of the text or of our consciousness in general."[25] *Vanity Fair* is a densely complex tissue of such revisings of familiar narrative schemata. As several commentators have pointed out, almost everything that happens in the vast novel can be identified as a variant on a pattern conventional to the fashionable and popular fiction of the time. Awareness of the deviancy provides the reader with a means of joining the narrator in reevaluating the virtues and inadequacies of *both* inherited fictional structures and the actualities to which those structures have given a specific ideological, emotional, and ethical order.

For readers today perhaps the most obvious of these narra-

tive patterns that Thackeray reworks is that of the sentimental, "chivalric" romance, because the Amelia-George and Rawdon-Becky stories so plainly distort it. But as John Loofburrow, a sensitive commentator on this aspect of Thackeray's artistry, rightly insists, Thackeray's deft disorderings are intricate re-synthesizings, not mere pastiches: "*Vanity Fair* does not wholly discredit idealisms; . . . reality is not the reverse of romance, any more than it is its fulfillment. Chivalry is vindicated, but in deviant ways. . . . *Vanity Fair* reinterprets in contemporary terms the traditions of chivalric romance . . . basic relationships persist, realistic contexts alter their terms. But the patterns are still present."[26]

I do not want to become deeply engaged in the particularities of Thackeray's transformations of his source schemata, well analyzed by critics like John Loofburrow and Jack Rawlins. The important fact to recognize is that such manipulations tend to operate unobtrusively. Leo Bersani is correct in insisting that the "modernity" of *Madame Bovary* lies not merely in its often-analyzed "critique of the expectations imposed on life by literary romances" (*Vanity Fair,* after all, makes much the same criticisms), but also in its "ostentatiously radical critique" of the *literary* modes characteristic of such romances.[27] This Flaubertian "violence" is intensified by Joyce, who relies heavily on outright parody, both of specific popular styles, as with a character such as Gerty McDowell, and in his Odyssean metanarrative. Flaubert can be called a "realist" to the extent that he refused to manipulate conventional literary patterns quietly in the way Thackeray does, but assaulted them openly by making those patterns the determinants of Emma Bovary's subjectivity. This, of course, forces the author to enter her mind. Flaubert's innovativeness, signaled by his emphasis on free indirect discourse, consists largely in his focusing on the clash between Emma's internalizings of "romantic" patterns and the *sensory actualities* she experiences. Against the violent personal immediacy of this intimate struggle, Thackeray's calmer appeal to common imaginings and the evocation of a shared "sentiment of reality" must appear a feeble accommodation to prevailing taste.

That Thackeray and his audience share much in the imaginative realm, however, does not bar the novelist from subverting parts of their common heritage, such as the sentimental popular fiction whose narrative styles it evokes. But this undermining is a far cry from Flaubert's transference of the schemata of Romantic fiction into the structuring of Emma Bovary's psyche.[28] *Vanity Fair* deploys, in order to modify, sometimes drastically, the whole panoply of literary and visual patterns by which the author assumes his readers have been prepared to think and feel—chiefly by earlier fictions. But Thackeray does not make these the structural system by which a particular character undergoes all her subjective experiences. Thackeray's narrator invites his readers to become aware of the possible inadequacies of what they have taught themselves to accept as admirable ways of ordering experience. Amelia Sedley, therefore, can only be a rather conventional heroine, very much like the heroines of the sentimental romances of inferior fiction that were popular in humdrum bourgeois homes. But she is presented in a fashion that makes any intelligent reader increasingly queasy about the systems of thinking and feeling so endorsed.

We know that Thackeray's approach was to give way before Flaubert's, and, with the advantage of hindsight, we recognize that Thackeray's art has some internal difficulties. The most striking evidence is his own inability to write another novel comparable to *Vanity Fair,* even though, as Gordon Ray demonstrated, only in the process of writing of *Vanity Fair* did Thackeray discover a successful mode for effectively engaging his readers.[29] Even Thackeray's basic device of the novel as puppet show may be perceived as a way of *fabricating* a common ground with his readership. In the preface to the book publication following serialization, the implied author describes how the show to be performed already "has been most favorably noticed" in "the principal towns of England." Our attention is directed to "the famous little Becky Puppet" and "the richly dressed figure of the Wicked Nobleman," as if Thackeray's characters had already entered into the realm of popular familiarity ("Before the Curtain," 6). Indeed, the expansion of what had been a mere episode of puppetry in *Don Quixote* into a structuring frame of *Vanity Fair* is evidence of how by the middle of the nineteenth century Cervantes's turning of narrative inward could no longer serve as a comically liberative device.[30]

Granted all this, one must characterize modern literature's turn against traditional narrativism as a necessary, even idealistic, reaction to conditions that made storytelling as traditionally practiced undesirable if not impossible. But that turn, which we may describe as intensified aestheticizing, had necessary ethical consequences, since storytelling is an evaluative transaction. Serious critics recently have charged modern art with being morally nihilistic. Pierre Bourdieu cites Flaubert as the exemplary

> modern artist . . . as indifferent to the exigencies of politics as to the injunctions of morality . . . recognizing no jurisdiction other than the specific norm of art . . . invented too-pure aesthetics, a point of view with universal applicability, with no other justification than that which it finds in itself. . . . [T]he "pure gaze" Flaubert cultivated at the price of breaking the ties between art and morality . . . pushed to its limits tended toward a kind of neutralism, even ethical nihilism.[31]

Bordieu's charge is impressive because it appears in the context of a conscientious effort to describe the circumstances in which Flaubert was forced to practice his art. These are, of course, beyond the scope of this essay. I want only to emphasize that if, following Bordieu's judgment, one finds an ethical power in *Vanity Fair* lacking in *Madame Bovary*, the difference has little to do with the religious convictions of the two authors. Bordieu's point is that whatever Flaubert's beliefs, his *art* inculcates and manifests "ethical nihilism." So far as Flaubert and his successors rejected storytelling they might well have moved in this direction. While I hope that my previous remarks on Henry James suggest that Bordieu oversimplifies, I think he (and likeminded postmodern critics) make it possible to understand why the modernist struggle with storytelling is so significant. And these critics do good service in reminding us that there are inescapable moral consequences in any serious efforts to redefine the functions of art, consequences which it is irresponsible to ignore.

Tzvetan Todorov, for example, has placed the same issues in a more specifically political context in analyzing the causes and significance of Paul de Man's, Martin Heidegger's, and M.

Blanchot's acceptance of Hitlerian ideologies. Pointing out that more intellectuals in the twentieth century committed themselves to absolutist political marxism of various kinds, Stalinism, Trotskyism, Maoism, and that Michel Foucault even briefly supported the Ayatollah Khomeni, Todorov observes that in the twentieth-century West intellectuals, "theoretically the most enlightened segment of the population," have tended to support violent and tyrannical political systems. The structural cause for this phenomenon lies in the social task of the intellectual to criticize existing norms. As majorities have turned to democracy, intellectuals have felt compelled to question democratic values and processes. The foundation for their critiques, Todorov suggests, has been the model of modernist aesthetics, attractive for its emphasis upon autonomy, exactly what the social critic needs. The work of art is "beautiful" or "significant" in and "of itself, not because it contains a particular truth or moral." This "aestheticization of politics" is conspicuous because programmatically enforced in totalitarian regimes, but it is also, through the activity of intellectuals, a force within democracies as well.[32] One need not extend this kind of analysis into insistence that an aesthetic more congenial with narrative would necessarily be more democratically oriented. After all, stories often have incited men to fight for fanatic causes. Yet narrative, rightly understood, is intrinsically antiauthoritarian, always potentially critical of all dogmatic and absolutist doctrines. This is one reason some modern artists could not, and did not, jettison storytelling easily or comfortably. I suggest this ambivalence is foreshadowed by various Romantic renarrativizings and some Victorian difficulties with the narrative mode.

The divorce of ethics and aesthetics that Oscar Wilde championed certainly would have made the writing of *Vanity Fair* impossible, which seems what Henry James desired. Yet most readers of James's novels would hesitate to accuse him of wishing thoroughly to "*de*-moralize" fiction. The logic of Wilde's vision of modernism, however, is no mere glittery paradox, because, as Plato has recognized, to tell stories is to engage one's audience in ethical questioning. The real paradox we must confront is that Wilde himself, for all his aestheticizing, went on telling stories. Not even all twentieth-century *graphic* artists turned against narrative: Diego Rivera, for example, adapted innovative modernist painting styles to the production of narrative murals.

Storytelling was not absolutely nor universally rejected by modernism, but it was often radically modified, most significantly through driving the teller out of the tale. It is not the "author" who disappears from modern fiction but the teller. Schematically: from the time of Cervantes to late nineteenth century the novel, though dependent on invented rather than traditional stories, freely made use of the traditional storyteller's functions. Modern fiction, to the contrary, tends to rely on an all-powerful "author," or what Foucault better describes as the "author function,"[33] which, however invisible, supersedes the traditional narrator, who at most survives as a character, or characters, within the tale. The tendency of modern fiction is, alongside a preference for synchronic structures, toward monologic narrative, sometimes in the form of a literal monologue, perhaps more frequently in the form of a collection of diversified "monologic articulations," as in Woolf's *The Waves* and Faulkner's *As I Lay Dying*.

The Aesthetics of Contingency

Why did not modern painters, instead of struggling ambivalently with narrative, seize on storytelling to celebrate the innovative freedoms of subject and style they championed? In rejecting the Renaissance concept of realism as the representation of a single instant from a single perspective, these artists might logically have embraced storytelling as a liberating mode. Some modern painters, in fact, did just that—notably the Mexican muralists Diego Rivera and José Clemente Orozco. In their great murals they superimposed a variety of modernist Parisian stylistic innovations upon the popular political caricatures of Posada to tell the complexly brutal story of Mexico's recovery of the cultural heritage that had been suppressed by the Europeans.

One's analysis of the fate of narrative in modern art, then, depends very much on which artists one chooses as exemplary. This is, of course, a fundamental methodological impasse in any study that traces specific effects of long-term aesthetic changes. The three painters I discuss in the following pages point to a significant historical evolution that can deepen our understanding of the narrative transformations of modern fiction analyzed in the preceding chapter. But the choice of a different exemplar—Brueghel, say, rather than Vermeer, or Van Eyck rather than Giotto—would modify the trajectory I trace. My main purpose, therefore, is to illuminate a *principle* of graphic narrativity by demonstrating how essential to any story are its representations of accidental particularities.

But aesthetic principles, because they belong to cultural systems, can never be disentangled from history; they are to be understood only through a historically oriented vision. Renais-

sance artists did not (as formalist narratologists like Wendy
Steiner feel they should have) stop telling stories in pictures.
But a Renaissance artist telling a story to a Renaissance audience is engaged in an interpersonal negotiation different from
that which occurred when a medieval artist told a story to a
medieval audience. The difference is epitomized by the difference between those two supreme storytellers, the author of *The
Canterbury Tales* bustling about The Tabard in his "General Pro-
logue," and the author of the *Orlando Furioso* ceremoniously
greeting his noble friends as his very metaphoric ship reaches
port in the 45th Canto. Simple as this distinction may seem, it
has momentous implications—suggesting as it does that a modernist may be expected to tell a story in a *quite* different fashion
from his predecessors, so different, indeed, that we may not
even recognize it as a story.

I begin with Giotto, since he has long been recognized as a
superb narrative painter. In his paintings in the Arena Chapel
in Padua telling the stories of Joachim and Anna, the Virgin,
and Christ, there are two pictures representing Judas Iscariot,
The Kiss of Judas (Fig. 3), and *Judas Receiving the Bribe* (Fig. 7).
Many comments could be—and have been—made on the two
pictures, but nobody has called attention to what intrigues me
most: they do not appear to depict the same man as Judas. This
difference is of peculiar interest, because critics like Steiner argue that there can be no narrative in graphic art unless one or
more figures are *repeated*. If one compares the faces of Giotto's
two Judases, however, one might not recognize that the same
man was being portrayed, for Judas receiving the money, with
the black devil literally grasping his back, is tall, almost handsome, bearded and mustached, weak-looking rather than de-
based. The Judas who seizes Christ just after the kiss is a
shorter man, far bulkier in body, without moustache, unshaven
rather than bearded, with a brutalized, sloping brow.

Is it not remarkable that such differences have passed unre-
marked in critical commentaries, since intriguing explanations
seem readily at hand?[1] Judas receiving the bribe might be regarded as the medieval stereotype of the evil Jew, hooked-nose,
red-hair, and all. Judas seizing Christ might be seen as a representation of moral deterioration, showing the devil having truly
entered the man. But the telling fact is Giotto's disregard for

7. Giotto, *Judas Receiving the Bride,* early 14th century. Fresco at the Chapel of Scrovegni all'Arena, Padua (Alinari/Art Resource, New York).

what we think of as individualizing characteristics to make his figures recognizable. We, as well as his contemporaries, identify Giotto's personae less by their idiosyncratic details of face, figure, or dress than by their idiosyncratic function in a familiar action. We recognize the betrayer because Judas is as Judas does.

This observation raises hard questions about the value of particularization in storytelling. Giotto's work proves that superior narrative can succeed with little particularization—which permits the hypothesis that the nature of any story may be usefully described in terms of the specificities it is able to ignore *without* loss of effectiveness. In the instance of the Paduan frescoes, not only individuality of figure or dress, but also concrete specificities of the natural world and of architecture and furnishings are omitted without diminishing either narrative effect or affect. Giotto's omissions are possible principally, I would argue, because he tells a *familiar* story, referring to what his audience has *already* imagined.

His aim is illustrative referentiality. Depending on his audience's knowledge of the whole story he retells, Giotto can concentrate on what for *his* telling is most essential in each episode. The arm with which Peter in *The Kiss of Judas*, for example, cuts off the soldier's ear, is represented "unrealistically." Its lack of anatomical verisimilitude is irrelevant, because what is emphasized is Peter's act in its contribution to the central confrontation, while ten other disciples try to flee, one being seized by the sinister hooded figure whose back only is visible. This "negative" position and action help to focus the climax of this physical, social, psychological, and spiritual crisis. Yet, this hooded figure is Giotto's purely adventitious invention. This simplified figure is the "negative" focus for an "original" *re*-imaging of a familiar story, one that viewers have previously imagined. The hooded figure permits an innovative modification of earlier imaginative experience that does not violate the boundaries of illustrative reference.

If we return to the other Judas fresco, a quieter, more subtly evocative scene, Giotto's skill at inciting new imagining through simplified particularization is perhaps best illustrated by the jerked-thumb gesture of one priest at the man being bribed. It would be difficult to think of another so commonplace and "naturalistic" an action that could more efficiently express their contempt for the traitor. That it is all too easy and "natural" to behave treasonably reminds us that Judas's act reveals how all betrayals are devilish self-betrayals. Yet it is worth noting that the jerked-thumb gesture is, iconographically speaking, original—at least I have found no source for it.[2] Giotto's narrative brilliance is manifest in his introduction of so casual, so unnecessary, so seemingly accidental, so natural, yet fortuitously expressed, a gesture, which epitomizes judgment and evokes our judgment at once.

The priest's thumb beautifully illustrates one kind of storyteller's inventive deployment of contingent detail—something that need not have happened, something not intrinsically important. Particularizations in stories are most meaningful—and are most meaningfully represented—when adventitious. This is a fundamental paradox of narrative: the meaning of a whole story, which we perceive as the coherent configuration of details, does *not* compromise the fortuitousness of those details. This distinguishes the "order" created by story from other forms of discursive patterning—which render detail *subservient* to larger form. Story is the only mode of discourse that tolerates, even cherishes, the accidental and irrelevant. Narrative's creation of a unity that does not do away with the contingent quality of its particulars explains its fantastic vitality: good stories are endlessly retellable—and are endlessly retold without loss of potency—because they encourage, as no other form of discourse does, dramatization of the significance of contingency *as* contingency.

Because the key specificities constituting narrative's enduring potency are fortuitous, they are also useful for defining diverse modes of storytelling. For instance, Giotto's contingencies are not *themselves* particularized. The thumb-jerk gesture is effective because not in itself elaborated; it is not presented as specially characteristic of the individual who makes it; it in no way rewards examination of *its* intrinsic character. The contingent, one might say, is here stylized. It accords with Giotto's refusal to characterize through individual idiosyncrasy of form, demeanor, or dress, and with the austerity of his representations of architectural and natural detail.

Time and place are schematized by Giotto because they, too, are conceived of and represented as functions of the story's central action. Particularities are not permitted to distract us from the meaning of the organizing encounter of each fresco, each of which is, therefore, self-contained in its referential illustrativeness. No figure, for example, looks out of the picture plane toward the inside of the chapel, toward us, the viewers. We are spectators of an imaging, very much aware of the flat plane of the paintings, which never pose as windows opening into a world other than that painted. What is represented, in short, is the *already imagined* world of the stories of the Holy Family, imaginatively remade through a minimum of original specificities themselves unparticularized.

It is no diminution of the "solidity" or "realism" of Giotto's art thus to insist that as a narrative artist he succeeds by staying in the realm of—and appealing to—imaginations already experienced in the material he retells. So long as there exist common imaginative grounds for artist and audience the transaction of artistic telling may *lose* substantiality through emphasis on merely literal verisimilitude. Attention to the uniqueness of the priest's thumb, for example, would *detract* from the narrative value of the familiar gesture because it would distract us from its function in the retelling.

My second illustration of how contingent detail may be made to function narratively, Vermeer's *Soldier and Young Girl Smiling*, might well be dismissed as possessing what Steiner calls "low narrativity," or indeed, as not being narrative at all.[3] That one may reasonably refer to the painting as either a narrative or a genre scene derives from Vermeer having portrayed an unfamiliar situation: *we*, the viewers, must decide whether or not he is telling a story—a matter about which there can be no debate with Giotto's frescoes. And observe the contradiction that here penetrates into the work "familiar" and its negative. Vermeer's scene is "unfamiliar" in the sense that we do not "know" this soldier and this young woman as we know Judas and Christ. But the circumstance of a soldier talking to a pretty girl is "familiar" to the point of banality. This antinomy of familiarity radiates through every aspect of the picture's enigmatic fascination—indeed, whatever "story" the painting tells is generated by it.

Vermeer uses not only a familiar situation but a familiar subject of painting—which makes possible the characterization of this painting as a "genre" scene. *In* the painting, moreover,

8. Jan Vermeer, *Officer and Laughing Girl* [*Soldier and Young Girl Smiling*], painted perhaps 1655–1660. Oil on canvas, 19⅞ × 18⅛″. Copyright The Frick Collection, New York.

he makes use of common figures, positions, and properties. A seventeenth-century Dutch viewer would immediately recognize the dress and furnishings in the painting as accurate and commonplace. And if that viewer had seen many paintings, as a Dutch person of that period probably had, he or she would recognize a host of themes, motifs, and conventions of representation quite characteristic of paintings of the time, although usually given original twists.[4] And the more familiar that viewer, or any other, becomes with *Soldier and Young Girl Smiling*, the more intriguing, because the more irresolvably antinomian, become these little twists. Vermeer, instead of working entirely within a realm of common imagining, as Giotto does, provokes us to imagine "new" possibilities within a common occurrence. With *Soldier and Young Girl Smiling*, we, the viewers, become as much the creators of whatever story is "in" the picture as the artist himself.

This helps to explain why the Renaissance development of mathematical perspective and instantaneous "realism" did not seriously diminish the production of narrative pictures. The new realism shifted the burden of narrative from the community of shared imagining between artist and audience toward increased constructive activity on the part of the audience— from whom more "creativity" was now demanded. In Vermeer's painting, then, we see the graphic analogue to what Erich Kahler has called the "inward turn" of narrative in literature, the decisive text being *Don Quixote*.[5]

By "inward turn" Kahler refers to the fact that Cervantes's figures are invented, made up out of his own head, not versions of traditional literary or mythological characters. Analogously, Vermeer's soldier and girl are "new," unique individuals, whom we have never imagined before. But the painting forces us to realize that this "inward turn" demands that the reader or viewer respond inventively, that we "make up" a new story out of the familiar phenomena of actual experience we share with the painter. More directly than Cervantes's novel, perhaps, Vermeer's painting enables us to recognize that the imaginative appeal of *this* kind of storytelling requires *description:* the inward turn requires outward display. This kind of storytelling must take place *through* concrete particularizings of its specificities, whereas Giotto's narrativity depends on representing all such particularizings as "mere" functions of his story. Renaissance "naturalism" produced no diminution of narrative art; it produced a different *kind* of storytelling, narration dependent on detailed description. This suggests the possibility that modernism, albeit in a different fashion, did not so much abandon narrative as attempt new kinds of storytelling.

The answer to the question of what we should call *Soldier and Young Girl Smiling*, genre scene or narrative, is that we interpret it by making the scene into a story, by seeing it *as* narrative. There is really no other way to "comment" on the painting, as is proved by the many fine interpretations the work has evoked, all of which, more or less systematically, treat it as a story. This imaginative interpreting is elicited principally by the picture's descriptive particulars, even though Vermeer's canvas includes relatively few details, most not unusual. Their ordinariness constitutes a common experiential ground that makes possible the transactional sharing of a narrative performance. Of course what is represented is not identical with things and people we have actually encountered. We know we are looking at a picture, a representation—which means that the particularization of contingencies must be the primary source of imaginative arousal. *This* chair with lion-head finials we have never seen before. *This* young woman is very much a unique individual, and it is around her that all else in the painting revolves. If Giotto's Judas is to be identified by his *function* in the action in which he participates, it is the sheer contingent *presence* of Vermeer's unique girl that evokes our imagining of what may be "happening" in *Soldier and Young Girl Smiling,* that inspires our creation of a story about her.

It is worth digressing about that last pronoun, even though I cannot pursue its implications fully. It is difficult to think of a painter before Vermeer who made an ordinary girl, no madonna, saint, or queen, the generative center of a visual narrative. This focus on the feminine in its most ordinary form is emphasized by the "defensive" posture of the soldier she faces. More subtly but also perhaps more profoundly than Cervantes, Vermeer brings into question not merely the traditional concepts of the heroic but also the dismissive stereotype of the domestic. The fashion in which new kinds of storytelling in the seventeenth century are associated closely with new attitudes toward womankind, just as Shakespearean heroines are linked to new kinds of comedic forms, ought to be explored by critics alert to the distorted patriarchal bias of much recent narratology.

Let me return to the descriptiveness of Vermeer's painting and its relation to the Renaissance inward turn of narrative, which, as this canvas reveals, involves not merely the artist's inventing but also the audience's. We respond to the details in

Soldier and Young Girl Smiling not merely as accurate representations of experiential facts but also as revelations of the nature
of the encounter with which we are presented. These particularities incite us to "make up" out of our own heads what may
be occurring before our eyes—which of course means putting
into play internalized systems from our culture that determine
our conceptions of how and why things happen to and between
people. Paradoxically, therefore, the representation of details
of setting, dress, demeanor, in this sort of narrative art must be
precise to arouse our constructive imaginings, or, less preten-
tiously, our fantasizing. To contrast this descriptiveness with
Giotto's stylization, recall the priest's thumb-jerk gesture in *Judas Receiving the Bribe* and compare it to the girl's partly open
hand on the table. Hers, too, is a perfectly "natural" gesture,
but one charged with specificity of meaning determinable (not
through its place in a familiar narrative configuration) through
a judgment of its particular relationship to a unique situation
made up of a whole set of "new" contingencies. These include
the "open" glass in her hand, or the soldier's slightly backed-off
position with *his* hand on his thigh turned away from her,
though, like hers, partly open. One might say that we are invited to evaluate the overdetermination of the position of her
hand—as well as of all the other details—in terms of how these
diverse accidents may meaningfully interrelate. The specificity
of the rendering of particularities, therefore, encourages us
to invent what in fact is a narrative "explanation" of what we
perceive.

The effect of Vermeer's "realistic" representation, as critics
such as Lawrence Gowing, Svetlana Alpers, and Edward A.
Snow have emphasized, derives not merely from a verisimilar
rendering of things and actions as we know them from lived
experience but also from adherence to *conventions* of such representation, because these conventions are part of what viewers
(through their internalizations) experientially share with the artist. The more an artist evokes such conventions, even as he
displaces or twists them to original purposes, the more he also
encourages his viewers' imaginative enterprise, even as, in a different but analogous fashion, Giotto incites his audience's engagement in a narrative negotiation by recalling through referential
illustration the totality of a well-known story. Vermeer's very

different narrational technique may be illustrated by the positioning of the soldier's hand on his thigh, a well-established representational convention, registering thoughtfulness and reserve: it is most famously a characterizing gesture of Michelangelo's contemplative figure of the Medici Tomb. The unique situation with the girl's less conventionally open hand so prominent, however, lures us into reassessing the significance of the body-language convention as we perceive this fighting man's hesitancy toward such an inviting girl.

The process of such evaluative judgments appears in modern, even rather formal analyses, such as that of Edward. A. Snow, who perceives the painting as "creating two distinct impressions, the second of which tends to contradict and revise the first."[6] The first, enforced by the picture's composition, is nearly the soldier's view, though as Snow says, his position, "flattened against the inside surface of the canvas," makes us crowd up behind him, finding him as much an obstruction as vantage point. There is, Snow finds, "a cramped, defensive, ill-at-ease quality" in him that contributes to the picture's strong "perspective divergence," his conflicted view contrasting with her openness and radiantly focused attention. The girl, "remote and diminished" when seen through the soldier's gaze, seems to move nearer and gradually to become the dominant interpretive center. Confined within a domestic interior, she nevertheless becomes the fullest concentration of being, while the soldier retreats to a more "peripheral, transitory presence." In sum,

> an initial experience of having an uncomfortably close emotional involvement in what passes between the couple forced on us from the perspective of the male participant gradually gives way to a sense of a more distant, multifaceted viewpoint encompassing the whole (just as the hexagonal shape of the pictorial space counteracts the strong perspective divergence). And the remarkable thing about the painting is that all its facets cohere at this level, in an integrated, sympathetic act of vision.[7]

Snow's interpretive reading exemplifies the *style* of all the best interpretations of Vermeer's canvas, a "creative" style unnecessary for a reading of a Giotto fresco. Snow's commentary consists in a back-and-forth movement, a defining of the relations of physical particularities one to another on the basis of a conception of the whole configuration, but a defining that simultaneously keeps open the possibility of a revisionary interpretation of the relations as examination of them may change one's assessment of the total situation. So here, too, the contingent nature of the contingencies composing a story is preserved—even in the temporal dimension. One notices that Snow interprets as if seeing acts in time, even though time is not literally represented. This "implicit temporality" allows him to form explanatory judgments that do not confine the meaning of the picture within any one "abstract" system of definition—further evidence of the importance in the painting of a narrative force.

The effect of that force is clearest in the protagonist, who seems nobody special, just an ordinary, good-looking Dutch girl. Yet she is *not* just anybody, since she appears completely individualized. We have never seen anyone exactly like her. She is unique and her uniqueness makes her interesting—and mysterious. For it is the unique individual who can never be fully explained, who must remain, like a contingent happening, "unintelligible," as the philosophers say. A story involving a fully individualized figure tends toward the indeterminate, in that the character—however overdetermined by the representation—cannot be defined entirely by the action in which she is involved. There is only one Judas Iscariot, but that individuality of being in Giotto's telling is subsumed into his function within the story retold. So Judas need not look the same when he reappears. But Vermeer's anonymous young girl's individuality determines—indeterminately—the story we imagine from her representation.

The upshot of this paradox is that Vermeer's picture is only meaningful intrinsically. What is happening and how we should judge that happening depend entirely on our reading of the relation of this soldier and this girl. Unlike Giotto's story, Vermeer's story is inherently enigmatic; it can be interpreted, indeed, it *must* be interpreted, but never definitively. Although both Giotto and Vermeer represent in a manner that compels us to combine perception and evaluation, with Vermeer our appraisals develop from what we make of the descriptive details. With Giotto the illustrative referentiality of what we see invites reassessment of a shared familiar story.

A final contrast between the fresco and the easel painting:

the former is painted with total consistency, each part painted in the same way, whereas different parts of Vermeer's picture are painted in different fashions. The contrast is most conspicuous in the representation of the girl, who is painted in what one critic calls a "scumbled, rough" style.[8] Such variation would be senseless in Giotto's story. Vermeer's invented subject arouses an equivalently inventive (what we call interpretive) imagining from his viewers—which may be enhanced by paint calling attention to itself as paint. Giotto's consistency, his transparency of style, his lack of such self-reflexive appeal, is appropriate because of the bond between artist and audience from which he begins. *Only when an inventive artist challenges his audience to invent does awareness of the process of artistic realization become an appropriate evocative technique.*

By now the reader's thought must have raced ahead of my plodding exposition, recognizing characteristics of Vermeer's painting as prototypical of twentieth-century graphic emphases. Modernism's bias away from traditional narrative is an intensification of something already present in Vermeer's art—namely, a descriptiveness that—paradoxically—increases the demand on a viewer's imagination to operate inventively. One "difficulty" of modern painting is that it demands so much from *our* imagination. The modern painter gives us very few guidelines for imagining, "innovating" by refusing to be illustratively referential and even by rejecting conventional modes of representing common experiences. To talk of a painting drawing attention to how it was created recalls many modern artists, such as Jackson Pollock, whose most characteristic works do very little else. But of course the extremity to which Vermeer's techniques have been carried transforms them, even inverts their purposes. Vermeer, the evidence of his surviving oeuvre suggests, would have seen little point in a painting that excluded representation of the human figure, or at least excluded the *female* human figure. It will be worthwhile, therefore, to consider by way of contrast a "reactionary" Pre-Raphaelite effort in the mid-nineteenth century to recover some qualities of medieval art.[9]

William Holman Hunt's *The Awakening Conscience* offers an obvious thematic contrast to *Soldier with a Young Girl Smiling,* while providing a Protestant equivalent to Giotto's religious concerns. But whereas Vermeer's picture may be regarded as a

9. William Holman Hunt, *The Awakening Conscience*, 1853. Oil on canvas. Tate Gallery, London (Tate Gallery, London/Art Resource, New York).

"genre scene," even though incipient narrativity informs all its details, *The Awakening Conscience* forces its story upon us, even as its details are more elaborately rendered, to the point of what has been called hyperrealism.[10] It may seem surprising, therefore, that Hunt's painting only feebly provokes the inventiveness stimulated by Vermeer's canvas. Its insistent narrativity seems to preclude the *sharing* necessary to effective storytelling. A story imposed upon its audience vitiates the social negotiation constituting narrative because it disempowers its addressees. The importance of audience liberty and power is illustrated by Coleridge's Wedding Guest, the most famous story victim in English poetry, who nevertheless initiates the Ancient Mariner's account with a question. And the wisdom and sorrow experienced by the Wedding Guest derive from his freedom to perceive more in the narrative than the simplistic piety offered by the teller.

To use Robert Weimann's terms, Hunt's blatant narrativity reduces the representing process to a representational product.[11] Such a pseudo-story reduces the addressee to a consumer, not an active partner. Nor can Hunt even by the most meticulous stylistic detail recover the imaginative community of a medieval painter with his audience. His picture is not illustratively referential; it depicts an original event, like Vermeer's "unfamiliar" scene, one we could never before have imagined—and which some seem sorry to have been asked to imagine once. Why Hunt's descriptiveness dismays some viewers as theatrical, rather than imaginatively evocative, may be clarified by the example of an analogous Pre-Raphaelite historical painting. John Everett Millais's *Christ in the House of His Parents* is a private imagining of the artist. The picture is linked to Christian mythology through a highly self-conscious allegorizing that enforces on the viewer—beginning with the explicit title—a single programmatic meaning to be read out of each of its carefully fabricated details. We are asked to spell out these allegorical signals, the cross of lumber, the injured hand, John bringing a basin of water, the distraught mother, the sheep, and so forth. Absolute isomorphism between every detail and the meaning of the total composition leaves no place for, let us say, Giotto's enigmatic hooded figure. Nothing in Millais's picture is truly contingent, although it pretends that everything in it is accidental.

For many critics, there are likewise no real contingencies in *The Awakening Conscience*, although it pretends to represent a fortuitous revelation. Around the painting's frame when originally exhibited was inscribed in large letters a quotation from *Proverbs:* "As he that taketh away a garment in cold weather, so is he that singeth songs to a heavy heart." The quotation was reinforced in the catalogue of the Royal Academy exhibition when the painting was first presented to the public by two other Biblical quotations: "As of the green leaves on a thick tree some fall and some grow, so is the generation of flesh and blood" (Ecclesiastes 14:18), and "Strengthen ye the feeble hands, and confirm ye the tottering knees: say ye to the faint-hearted be ye strong: fear ye not, behold your God" (Isaiah, 35:3–4). And all the visual details, if we follow John Ruskin's famous interpretation, serve a single function—to dramatize the sudden realization of sinfulness revealed by the face of the girl whose "numbed heart," in Ruskin's words, has been struck by a phrase in the song "Oft in the Stilly Night," causing her to spring up "in agony," while her seducer, "not seeing her face, goes on singing."[12] Although he does not dwell on the unraveled women's work in the lower right corner, the soiled glove on the floor alongside Edward Lear's musical setting of Tennyson's "Tears, Idle Tears," as well as the clock with its figure of Chastity binding Cupid, Ruskin has been persuasive that every detail is rendered so that we cannot mistake the message they enforce with painful clarity:

> That furniture so carefully painted, even to the last vein of the rosewood—is there nothing to be learnt from that terrible lustre of it, from its fatal newness; nothing there that has the old thoughts of home upon it, or that is ever to become a part of home? Those embossed books, vain and useless—they also new—marked with no happy wearing of beloved leaves; the torn and dying bird on the floor; the gilded tapestry, with the fowls of the air feeding on the ripened corn . . . nay, the very hem of the poor girl's dress, which the painter has laboured so closely thread by thread, has story in it, if we think how soon its pure whiteness may be soiled with dust and rain, her outcast feet failing in the street; and the fair garden flowers seen in the reflected sunshine of the mirror—these also have their language:
>
> > *'Hope not to find delight in us, they say,*
> > *For we are spotless, Jessy—we are pure.'*[13]

Contemplating sinful women tended to make Ruskin fervid, and one may feel even Hunt's melodrama is being exaggerated by "terrible lustre" and "fatal newness," not to mention the startling projection of "outcast feet failing in the street." Yet *The Awakening Conscience* opens itself to this allegorical moralizing as Vermeer's painting does not. No such definitive reading has ever been made of *Soldier and Young Girl Smiling*, indeed, no such univocal interpretation of it is conceivable. Vermeer's painting is as carefully planned as Hunt's, and every detail in it contributes to the total meaning of the picture, *but in contingent ways*. Vermeer's mode of representation endows details with significance without jeopardizing their adventitiousness. In *The Awakening Conscience* all contingency seems to vanish within a system of meaning masquerading as honest narrative.

One understands the negative reaction of modernists to such self-falsification as *The Awakening Conscience* seems to thrust upon us. Such works, interpreted in the Ruskinian manner, encourage an idea that *all* narrative belongs to the domain of crudely popular sensationalism of vulgar moralizing and is antithetical to the purposes of serious aesthetic endeavor. Even more damaging is the fashion in which such a painting encourages the conception of narrative as a vehicle of didactic purposes—story used to make art subservient to conventional dogmas. This damaging conception is provoked by a work such as *The Awakening Conscience*, because, as Plato had censoriously observed, and as I have cheerfully remarked, storytelling inescapably raises ethical issues, because it evokes from its audience judgmental responses. To modernists determined to liberate aesthetic practice from every kind of ethical constraint, Hunt's moralized storytelling seems to be nothing but the debasing of art into propaganda.

Yet a more careful consideration of what Hunt actually attempts in *The Awakening Conscience* may suggest that the relation of Hunt's painting to modernistic antipathy to narratively illustrative art is complexly intriguing, particularly if one recognizes the misleading character of Ruskin's commentary. The painful laboriousness with which *The Awakening Conscience* (like most of Hunt's pictures) is painted expresses the artist's genuine religiosity, but his scrupulous technique also springs from the daring originality of the subject, which anticipates a central focus of modernism. In this painting Hunt attempts to portray an instant of psychological transformation. Such an action had been regarded as an impossible subject for the visual arts, and the Victorian theorists, who (unlike their Romantic predecessors) tended to subscribe to Lessing's dicta on the antithesis between graphic and literary art, had specifically condemned such subjects in painting. *The Awakening Conscience* in this respect, as in others, may be perceived as a challenge to Victorian aesthetic theory.[14]

Striving to depict a purely inner, subjective event, Hunt almost necessarily falls into what Martin Meisel calls a "hallucinatory realism in the rendering of the room and its detail." Such hallucinatory realism might be termed private or psychic symbolism, the imposition of a subjective vector of meaning on a variety of phenomena endowing them with a particular significance as the context of an intense psychological experience. That Hunt thus carries "the inward turn of narrative" to a limiting condition may be suggested by a contrast to *Soldier and Young Girl Smiling*. Vermeer makes use of commonplace circumstances and objects represented in all their familiarity to tell a story comprehensible only from the painting itself— which is, therefore, intrinsically dubious: there is nothing outside the painting by which to test the validity of our interpretation of it. This indeterminacy is articulated through the limits to the descriptive verisimilitude by which contingent features are presented. Details are particularized with more precision than in Giotto's frescoes, but never hyperrealistically. What might be called narrative stylization assures that we cannot be absolutely certain how much significance, or what kind of significance, ought to be attributed to any detail—for example, the girl's partially open hand. Details *can* be thus, if I may be forgiven the paradox, indeterminately overdetermined, because the illusionary precision with which they are represented is recognized to be restricted; the paint provides a "defective" image of what it represents. But exactly such "defects" make the picture's story "open," endlessly retellable, reinterpretable.

Failure to grasp the principle operative here vitiates much contemporary theorizing about narrative art, verbal as well as visual. Skillful narrative artists *exploit* the so-called inadequacy of their medium: neither paint nor words can exactly reproduce the

phenomena to which they refer. It is the use of the "gap" between signified and signifier that allows narrative, in contrast to
other forms of discourse, to develop ever-evolving meanings
from the "accidents" of life—so long as their audiences take
pleasure in awareness that what they see or hear is a story, an
account facilitating social sharing, not a substitute for nonnarrative actualities.

Vermeer allows none of his specificities to become absolutely
(or univocally) determined. That is why no knowledge of the
life outside the painting, from which everything in it—literally—is drawn, will fully explain the relationship it depicts. The
accuracy of the portrayal of familiar objects and circumstances
is of service only in arousing our imaginings about what *may* be
going on *within* the picture. Equivalent specifics in *The Awakening Conscience* are rendered with more intensely illusionary precision because their significance depends on their symbolic
function of contextually dramatizing the protagonist's subjective experience. Because every detail is loaded with the same
meaningfulness, that which (to put it crudely) testifies to her
debasement, insight into which has just come to the protagonist, it may be possible for a viewer to *identify* with her, share in
the psychic crisis she undergoes. Hunt's "hyperrealistic" cir-
cumstantiality is required by his endeavor to enable us to empathize with his protagonist's moment of spiritual revelation. The
photographic accuracy with which physical details of the scene,
all of them, are represented is necessary because those details
are the contrastive ground against which the "inadequacy" of
the painting to depict the kinetic instant of subjective spiritual
revelation is realized—that inadequacy being Hunt's version of
narrative exploitation of the gap between signifier and signified.

What is demanded by Hunt's concentration on an invisible
inner crisis may be concretized by a contrast of his protagonist's
hands with those of Vermeer's girl or Giotto's priest. The con-
science-stricken girl's self-clasped hands seem to impress most
viewers as a less "natural" gesture than that of Vermeer's smiling girl or Giotto's priest, but more important than the gesture's possible conventionality is its revelation of purely inner
distress. Hence its seeming theatricality. It reveals a tension se-
creted within her. The hand gestures in the other paintings are

significantly "other directed," in David Reisman's now quaint phrase, elements in encounters *between* people, whereas the clasping hands in Hunt's picture embody a self-contained psychic conflict. This is why the gesture strikes us as so meaningful within particular and definite limits. There can be nothing "casual" or tinged with the "simply natural" in Hunt's painting, because all details must signal in some way what cannot be seen but which explains, gives special meaning to, everything that does appear. Hunt's story seems aggressively thrust upon us because in his picture the syntagmatic openness of narrative reference is being transformed into paradigmatic symbolism.

What strikes many viewers as offensive about *The Awakening Conscience* results, I believe, less from Hunt's "Victorianism" than from an awkward "proto-modernism."[15] Hunt intensifies to the point of subverting that descriptive particularization on which Vermeer's narrative depends. Spectacularly illustrative of this transforming is Hunt's predatory cat, because the animal under the man's chair so obviously allegorizes (*within* the picture) the relation of the man to the woman. Such allegorizing contrasts with the effect of the map in Vermeer's painting—which might also be juxtaposed to the sheet music in Hunt's picture, for the viewer must spell out the title of the song and know its words to appreciate its exact role in Hunt's story. Once that appreciation is attained, the significance of the detail as a detail is exhausted, its contingentness superseded by its value as a clue to the girl's psychic experience. Vermeer's map's function is endlessly debatable—as the diversity of interpretations of it proves—because it is irreducible to explanation from anything but the dubiousness of the depicted situation. The map's meaning is totally intrinsic, so its adventitiousness is unrestricted, as is highlighted by its reversal of usual coloring conventions: land here is blue, water brown. One may speculate ceaselessly on what this coloring means, because such speculation inescapably becomes reinterpretation of the possibilities of the relation between the man and the woman. The painting's "truth" is undeterminable, because its authority is undiminishable, since purely inherent, however accurately it seems to represent circumstances of seventeenth-century Dutch life.

Because Hunt, unlike a medieval painter, does not appeal to a well-known story, he must, like Vermeer, work from factual knowledge shared with his audience, knowledge of actualities extrinsic to his painting. But Vermeer's *story* consists in what a viewer is provoked imaginatively to construct from his representation. Hunt, who after a time took to calling his picture *The Awakened Conscience,* begins from a complete, in a sense a completed, story whose meaning the viewer is asked to *re*-construct by determining the significance of clues provided by hyper-realistically portrayed particulars—whose apparent fortuitousness we are meant to see *through,* as Ruskin so fervently does. This is one reason why each detail must be rendered with fanatic scrupulosity of illusionary verisimilitude: each detail is meaningful as a clue or symptom—and clues and symptoms are most useful when most precisely described.

Or, if we consider what specificities a narrative may felicitously omit, *The Awakening Conscience* again appears to represent a limiting condition. One has the impression that Hunt has omitted nothing. The impression of course is false, but that it can occur reveals much about the "realistic" mode in which Hunt participates. We feel no detail has been left out because absolutely everything represented seems to possess a definable significance. We recognize intuitively that every feature of the scene—rightly understood—is a clue to the picture's meaning. This is the way Marxists and Freudians approach human phenomena, and why, like the painting, these "masters of suspicion," are a bit oppressive. Story's evocation of possibilities of meaning by representation of contingencies simultaneously adventitious and part of a narrative coherence seems here superseded by some totalizing explanation. Such totalizing interpretations, Marxist, Freudian, Realist, deconstructive, whatever, tend to be—rather than proliferatively fecund—mutually exclusive because dependent on a univocal diagnosis of symptoms. The peculiarity of the responsiveness elicited by narrative is its sustaining with satisfaction the potential of various responses—no one of which precluding any other.

But if Hunt's painting thus encourages reactions negating negative capability, its efficacy emerges from its simultaneous rejecting of a dominant Victorian view of the inevitable destiny of fallen women. Against the girl's sudden insight, all the painting's so meaningful clues also become "meaningless." The material embodiments of the system of judgment fabricated by Hunt's and his viewers' society are displayed as trivial, ephemeral, without genuine "substantiality" in the flash of unseen radiance illuminating her mind. Marxists, Freudians, deconstructionists, any modern systematizers, *ought* to be disturbed by *The Awakening Conscience,* for it calls into question the value of the very method of totalizing interpretation its scrupulously "comprehensive" rendering of physical details evokes.

Hunt, despite his medievalism, in exact opposition to Giotto, stylizes none of his details. We are meant, for example, to notice when looking at the girl's clasped hand the *absence* of a wedding ring. If that device reminds a reader of Sherlock Holmes's observation on the dog that did *not* bark, the association is not so casual as it might at first appear. The "detective story," which emerges in the middle of the nineteenth century, is a type of pseudo-narrative, since as such it does not sustain rereadings once we know *the* solution, what the various clues uncontestably mean. At the conclusion of a detective story we recognize that what had appeared random or inexplicable (like Vermeer's map) in fact belongs to a pattern that could always have been interpreted in *the* right way (identifying the criminal), the one way predetermined by the author. The dissatisfaction of those who like genuine storytelling with most detective fiction seems analogous to that felt by many commentators on *The Awakening Conscience.*

But Hunt is attempting something more than the spurious mystery of detective-story entertainment, and his painting has been much misunderstood, especially by Ruskin, whose public analysis, we should remember, was provoked by confusion in the minds of viewers at the painting's original exhibition. That Hunt's original audience apparently had difficulty deciphering what the painting meant should alert us to the originality of his effort. Ruskin does better than the reviewer who explained the scene as a tiff between brother and sister, but for that very reason he may more profoundly obscure Hunt's central point, that salvation is possible for this "fallen" woman. Ruskin's imagining her wandering, a despairing outcast of urban streets, is in accord with the conventional Victorian attitude toward sinful females—who even Dickens and George Eliot seem to think do best quickly to die, or get transported to Australia. As Hunt defied accepted formal restrictions by trying to represent an

instant of psychological change, so his handling of theme challenges conventionalized Victorian morality. Hunt's painting is
didactic; but it teaches the message of Christ as it appears in the
New Testament (not in Victorian reformulations), notably the
story of the woman taken in adultery: redemption is offered to
all.

The Awakening Conscience reveals how narrative undergoes al-
teration when personal psychology, subjective impression,
comes to be regarded as what is most important, most "real."
Then the physical, the material, can only inadequately represent psychic events. So Hunt, wishing us to identify with the
girl's self-accusatory memory of innocence lost, symbolizes
what she recalls by the greenery appearing in the strange background mirror that blocks the window behind the two figures.
The "green world" of innocence is reflected, rather than being
directly visible to the viewer, whose position is usurped by a
reflection, thereby facilitating the identification necessary to the
dramatization of a psychic, not a physical, event. In this graph-
ically interiorized self-scrutiny the physical details of the unre-
flected room are only a material context that "negatively"
illuminates the true interior, psychic self-confrontation.

Where does that strange mirror, which is the key to the subjectivism of *The Awakening Conscience,* come from? Whatever its
source, its significance is, I believe, best understood through
the analogue of late-medieval Flemish painters, especially Jan
Van Eyck, because of his famous *Arnolfini Marriage.* The name
"Pre-Raphaelite," assisted by Ruskin's prejudices, which ran
strongly in favor of Italianate art and as strongly against the
realism of the Low Countries, has blinded critics to the parallels
between Hunt's techniques and those of early *Northern* painters.
We know he had visited in Holland and Belgium before painting *The Awakening Conscience,* and his letters and autobiography
testify to his interest in Flemish techniques and subjects. Hunt's
religious convictions should have attracted him to early Northern artists, whose scrupulous accuracy in representing physical
details is in fact closer to Pre-Raphaelite techniques than the
work of Italian painters of the Campo Santo frescoes, whom we
know inspired Pre-Raphaelitism. For those of us who have read
Erwin Panofsky on the *Arnolfini Marriage,* it now seems scarcely
conceivable that Van Eyck's masterpiece with its profoundly
significant mirror is not a source for *The Awakening Conscience.*[16]

I do not, however, argue that Hunt had a specific source, but rather that there is an impressive analogy between his picture and early Netherlandish paintings, which operated on the "principle of disguising symbols under the cloak of real things" (Panofsky, 141). This practice helps to explain the curiously self-contradictory character of Hunt's narrative art as reflective of his historical situation. Panofsky has shown that Jan Van Eyck used a technique of intensely realistic contextualism to create "doubly disguised" symbolic significance, explaining the *Arnolfini Marriage* by suggesting the ostensible subject conceals a more significant thematic purpose.

> With the subject thus identified, not as an ordinary portrait but as the representation of a sacrament. . . . we begin to see what looks like nothing but a well-appointed upper–middle-class interior is in reality a nuptial chamber . . . and that all the objects therein bear a symbolic significance . . . the crystal beads and the "spotless mirror" . . . are well known symbols of Marian purity . . . the dog . . . was an accepted emblem of marital faith . . . and the discarded pattens in the lower left hand corner are here intended . . . to remind the beholder of what the Lord had said to Moses on Mount Sinai. (Panofsky, 201)

The difference, of course, is that whereas the *Arnolfini Marriage* evokes symbolic meanings shared by a community, *The Awakening Conscience* appeals to its viewers' ability to understand through the more-or-less generally recognizable (that is, socially commonplace characteristics of dress, demeanor, and setting) purely private, entirely subjective experience, experience that in fact runs against the grain of community opinion and accepted attitudes. This is why Hunt must create a work with which the viewer can *subjectively identify*. Without entering into the emotionalized sensations of the protagonist, one cannot make sense of the picture. Such identifying, like the recognizing of symbolic significance implicit in the details of the *Arnolfini* canvas, supplants other narrative appeals. But the complete subjectifying of Hunt's representation necessarily implies, more concretely than the Van Eyck painting, the importance of particular, contingent actions—the essential stuff of narrative.

Yet difficulties intrinsic to the subjectivizing of narrative are just as disturbingly dramatized by Hunt's picture, which does not merely invert a typical Victorian attitude toward fallen women. It also expresses his personal involvement with the model, Annie Miller, whom Hunt intended to marry, once she had been educated into respectability—which explains the educational books on the table in the picture. The "subjectivism" of the scene with which we are to identify is thus complexly problematic: we today may find more distasteful Hunt's ideal of "redemption" than the Ruskinian attitude his painting subverts. It is difficult for me, anyway, not to feel some satisfaction in knowing that, in the event, Annie Miller did not accept as docilely as Lizzie Hexam in *Our Mutual Friend* the imposition of patriarchal respectability through literacy. Instead, she exploited Hunt's passion and successfully played him false.

What Hunt's obscure painting reveals with peculiar clarity, then, is how focus on subjective experience may complicate rather than eliminate traditional narrative. It suggests that at least one major segment of modernism is less directed to simply doing away with narrative than with adapting it (to a degree that makes its traditional form almost unrecognizable) to exigencies of a totally secularized society in which the most fundamental reality is psychological. When significant action is mental action, what is outward and visible cannot be directly evocative for the audience. It forms, rather, the context within which events in another mode take shape. This alters the nature of the social negotiation storytelling had usually facilitated—illustrated by Giotto's unfailing representations of human *encounters*. As I have observed, narratives are what speech-act theorists call "display texts," discourses that lay out events or situations for joint assessment by speaker and addressee, writer and reader. Stories are meeting places. Narrative is the discourse of encounter. Intensely private experience such as Hunt portrays precludes simple and direct sharing, for the conflict he represents is self-encounter, not only of his protagonist but also of the artist.

Artistic representation of the self-encountering of psychological change confronts each viewer or reader with the need, but also the special difficulty, of trying to *identify* with a subjective experience. What Hunt's painting must do is enable us to think and feel as his protagonist thinks and feels at the very instant of revelation. So to paint, however un-modern the subject of spiritual awakening, opens the way toward the modernist definition of the work of art as valuable when detemporalized to immediacy, made self-sufficient, autonomous, that is, possessed of a significance which the individual viewer can rewardingly experience only through subjective empathy.

In carrying Renaissance perspectival realism to a self-inverting limit, turning narrative entirely inward, then, Hunt gives us insight into modernism's treatment of its audience less as story recipients than as aesthetes. The modern aesthete, as most famously defined by Oscar Wilde, is someone liberated from any ethical engagements with art, a freedom implying transcendence of those social relations between teller, tale, and audience that distinguished the traditional narrative transaction, but left open the possibility of powerful psychological engagement. The validity of Wilde's definition of modernism is confirmed by the practice of many famous modern painters, among whom abstractionists such as Mondrian and Malevich may be cited as representative. The deliberateness with which their paintings dispense with story dramatizes their appeal to viewers as aesthetes, neither conceived by the artists nor conceiving themselves as defined by specific social or moral positions, not as citizens of a particular state or class or ethnic group—or even sex. The audience sought by such modern art would consist of those who appreciate art that transcends the contingencies of social circumstance, capable of profound, but socially untrammeled subjective experience. Desire for such addressees accords with the modernist rejection of Renaissance formal techniques of perspectival realism, techniques appropriate for a narrative sharing with audiences conceived as historically particularized individuals for whom the older communal imaginings of medieval civilization had disintegrated. Modernism's notorious celebrating of "natural" essences, forms and colors purified of "content," uncontaminated by referentiality, on canvases without "depth," embodies the desire of these artists for *de*-historicized, *de*-individualized, *de*-socialized audiences.

What José Ortega y Gasset called the dehumanization of modern art applies most significantly to the character of the addressees it seeks, and seeks to create. Modern art's profoundest abstracting is not of forms but of audience, leaving little place at the center of this style for the traditional transactive encounter of storytelling by which accidents of a public experience might be mutually evaluated. The ethical implications of such a development had to be profound, as is shown in the recent influential analysis of this aspect of moral history, Alastair MacIntyre's *After Virtue,* whose insistence on an inseparable linkage between morality and narrative merits special comment, particularly because he identifies the end of the nineteenth century as a critical breaking point.[17]

MacIntyre argues that the "grave disorder" in the practice and comprehension of morality during our century results from the failure of the Renaissance and the Enlightenment to institutionalize rationalized definitions of moral virtue. The final collapse of "enlightened" rational morality in the late nineteenth century produced as the most influential moral theory what MacIntyre calls *emotivism,* "the doctrine that all evaluative judgments, and more specifically all moral judgements, are *nothing but* expressions of preference . . . or feeling" (11–12). The self presented by emotivism can find "no limits set to that on which it may pass judgment," for such limits could only derive from rational criteria for evaluation, and "the emotivist self lacks any such criteria." The capacity of the self so conceived "to evade any necessary identification with any particular contingent state of affairs" means that this self possesses "no necessary social content and no necessary social identity" (31–32). MacIntyre offers as illustrative of the spectrum of emotivist descriptions of personal identity Sartre's early definition of the self as distinct from any specific role and Erving Goffman's total liquidation of self into role playing. *All* forms of modern self-definition deny identity as conceived by premodern, traditional societies. In these "it is through his or her membership in a variety of social groups that the individual identifies himself or herself and is identified by others. I am a brother, cousin, grandson, member of this household, that village, this tribe. These are not characteristics that belong to human beings accidentally, to be stripped away in order to discover the real me" (33).

MacIntyre concludes that any valid idea of personal identity must begin in recognition that man is "essentially a storytelling animal." Contrary to the modern view, personal identity meaningful enough to permit a viable system of social morality is a creation of storytelling: "Deprive children of stories and you leave them unscripted, anxious stutterers in their actions as in their words. Hence there is no way to give us an understanding of any society, including our own, except through the stock of stories which constitute its initial dramatic resources. Mythology, in its original sense, is at the heart of things" (216). The essential narrative for anyone, MacIntyre claims, is the story of his or her life from birth to death. To be the subject of such a narrative is "to be accountable for the actions and experiences" composing it (217). Personal identity is "just that identity presupposed by the unity of the character which the unity of narrative requires" (218). The correlative is that "I am not only accountable, I am one who can always ask others for an account . . . I am part of their story, as they are part of mine. The narrative of any one life is part of an interlocking set of narratives" (218). Moral behavior can be meaningfully represented and assessed, therefore, only narrationally.

Much as I endorse MacIntyre's claim that human beings are storytelling animals (so that he is quite accurate in describing the damage done to children by depriving them of stories), I find him missing the point that, for all the collapse of rational justifications of morality at the end of the nineteenth century, twentieth-century society has become more, not less, rationalized. This is why story has been so little esteemed. A narrative account reckons contingencies as contingent—an approach unsatisfactory to any systematizing rationalizer, be he bureaucrat or philosophic critic. Stories are usually ectypal accounts and therefore obstruct ideological and philosophical explanations and orderings. MacIntyre is characteristic of our time: he can explain story only in a "scientifically" rational fashion, not in a narratively rational one.

And his difficulties illuminate why twentieth-century literary criticism (with most exceptions occurring among feminist commentators) has done badly with narrative, even today continuing to ignore the importance of processes of retelling and rereading. Narratives open to reassessment, attractive *because* revisable, have small appeal to philosophizing critics, who prefer to the proliferating form of story—a plot. I have as much as possible avoided the term "plot," because I have learned that while academics prefer to talk and write about "plots," ordinary folk and peoples whose societies still honor storytelling commonly speak of "stories." Once again, E. M. Forster in *Aspects of the Novel* epitomizes the modern view. "The King died and then the Queen died," Forster tells us in an endlessly quoted distinction, is a *story*, whereas "The King died, and then the Queen died of grief" is a *plot*."[18] Plot makes sense because it depends on and confirms a conventional view of causality. Plot is admirable because it explains things in a way worthy of the attention of sophisticated intellectuals. Story is inferior, preferred by "primitives" and the "vulgar."

Sophisticated critics, however, might do well to consider the questions about causality raised by David Hume, Werner Heisenberg, and Max Planck. That they do not reveals, besides their ignorance of science, a dependence, as Gerald Bruns has observed, on Cartesian rational systematizing because it preserves for them a sense of being in control. The motive of power is confirmed when one thinks of plot as the hidden, "deep," universal, metacultural structure by which one explains, brings under one's control, the incohoate surface of contingent happenings. The reward of critical distrust of "mere" surfaces is the discovery of what Peter Brooks aptly calls the Master Plot—the single structure from which all other narratives derive and on which they depend. Knowing the master plot, the critic becomes like Sauron, Tolkien's dark lord of the rings.

Another source of critical difficulty with narrative is a contemporary predeliction for ignoring the frank artificiality of storytelling. This undermines MacIntyre's valid argument that how we live is to a degree determined by what stories we, and those around us, regard expressing how society *ought* to function. But stories constitute social being because, properly speaking, they are only told. To refer to "living" narratives is to slide into confusing metaphorical usage. MacIntyre is explicit, however, that he regards "human actions in general as enacted narratives," insisting

> narrative is not the work of poets, dramatists and novelists reflecting upon events which had no narrative order before one was imposed by the singer . . . it is because we all live out narratives in our lives and because we understand

our own lives in terms of the narratives that we live out that the form of narrative is appropriate for understanding the actions of others. Stories are lived before they are told—except in the case of fiction. (211–212)

MacIntyre's problem is that he ignores the distinction enunciated by the Russian Formalists between *fabula* and *siujet,* and popularized for American narratologists later by Gérard Genette's derivative distinction between *histoire* and *récit.* Some inconsistencies in accommodating the foreign terms has encouraged unnecessary complications, and it is simplest to stick to the English terminology used by Nelson Goodman in his elegant "The Telling and the Told."[19] Goodman distinguishes between order of occurrence of events and order of tellings by two sentences telling the same story: (1) Lincoln's assassination preceded Kennedy's, (2) Kennedy's assassination followed Lincoln's. Whereas the first story's order of *telling* is congruent with the order of events as they actually occurred, the second reverses the order of enactments.

The "distortion" or "twisting" of story number two does not make it inferior to or less true than story number one. There is always more than one way to *tell* a story. Narrative facilitates *re*presenting events from different perspectives (of place, person, order of events, or of moral attitude), thereby calling forth different meanings from the same actions. This is the full realization of narrative's emphasis on the power of words to mean more than one thing. But these characteristics exist only because story is telling, not simply living out. One's life and the story of one's life, as every study of autobiography affirms with varying degrees of grumpiness, are never the same. The death of Orestes and the story of his death are quite different, as Clytemnestra discovered.

The last illustration shows that the distinction between the telling and the told applies equally to "factual history" and "fiction." This non-distinction has made story indispensable to most cultures. Storytelling is a tool for investigating, celebrating, and even changing the realities of human existence. Goodman is firm: "[T]he distinction between the order of the telling and the order of the told does not imply truth, or that events told of occurred in a given order, or even that there are any such events" (800). Telling and response in no way depend on some belief in any absolute order of events independent of all tellings. Goodman, aligning himself more with Frodo rather than Sauron, insists, "When I speak of several versions of the same or virtually the same story, I am by no means conceding that there is some underlying story, some deep structure, that is not itself a version" (801).

If my understanding of classical and medieval rhetoricians is sound, they held the equivalent of this "versional" view. Confusion, eventually requiring the Formalists' rephrasing of the telling told distinction, arose with a change in the concept of "invention." *Inventio* meant the new disposition of familiar materials: Giotto's "inventiveness" resides in his "original" way of telling the stories everybody knows. "Invention" in the sense of an individual making up out of whole cloth, as Cervantes does in *Don Quixote,* increasingly replaced the earlier meaning from the Renaissance on, producing intensified concern with the nature of "fiction" and for the value of "description," as I have already observed. One might complicate Sartre's remark that we live in one direction but tell in the opposite direction, by asserting that narrative is a polytropic remaking of singular experience, imagined or sensory. Storytelling is valuable because every tale can be no more than a version. We live once, irreversibly, but our story may be retold endlessly.

Such considerations should make us cautious about judging the role of narrative in so complex a phenomenon as modernism. And the reevaluation of *The Awakening Conscience* I have proposed implies that nearly as important as suppression of narrative in the later nineteenth century was the possibility of storytelling taking on a radically different form. I want to suggest how the that possibility functioned in verbal art, the natural medium of storytelling, by glancing briefly at *The Ambasadors.* I treat that novel as representative of Henry James's innovations, which, in turn, illustrate how and why one major current of literary modernism remodeled, rather than rejected, narrative principles as a foundation for new artistic purposes.

Modern Dialogic Narrative

Henry James's importance to early modernism is often defined in terms of his severe criticisms of his Victorian predecessors. But, especially in his prefaces, James regularly speaks of himself as a storyteller, and in his letters, his criticism, and his fiction usually seems at ease with the tradition of the novel, which he so explicitly, and influentially, worked to change. It is entirely characteristic of him to name the protagonist of *The Ambassadors* after a novel by Honoré de Balzac, and then have another character identify that novel as "an awfully bad one."[1] James reminds us how the anxiety of artists toward their predecessors may comprehend more than simple oedipal jealousy, a reminder useful in orienting ourselves toward appreciation of how modernism might not need to do away with narrativity absolutely even while urgently contesting it.

James's central innovation in storytelling, phrased schematically, is to extend the technique of free indirect discourse, what the Germans call *erlebte rede,* and Bahktin quasi-direct discourse, into the telling process. James thus transforms the teller's function from telling *about* into telling *through* a "central intelligence," such as Lambert Strether. This complicates the narrational activity, making the story of *The Ambassadors* simultaneously the story of Lambert Strether's evolving perceptiveness and consciousness of the events in which he engages. This turn simplifies the tendency toward narrative elaboration of the Victorian novel, diminishing, for example, the preference for multiple narratives—which provoked some to charge that James's novels were no more than inflated short stories.

If in *Madame Bovary* a reader must often be unsure of whose perception or awareness is being represented, the narrator's or a character's or both, the reader of *The Ambassadors* must accept this sylleptic quality penetrated into the unfolding of the story itself, signaled by the narrative being persistently generated by conversational encounters, telling emerging from dialogic interchange. Flaubertian indirect discourse permits the reader to be aware that what a character such as Emma thinks or feels may be mistaken, misguided, or based on misperceptions and that this is truly what she feels or thinks.

By extending this twofold method into the narrative process itself, James offers a telling not merely of what happened but also of what may, or may not, have happened, or what one comes to believe really took place that had been misunderstood or misrepresented. James's observation in the preface to *The Princess Cassamassima* that there could be no story to tell if we were not bewildered is fully realized in *The Ambassadors,* whose narrative articulates the intersecting of different characters' shifting perceptions or misperceptions of what is, or appears to be, going on. This produces an intensification of, not an escape from, the complex interplay of anticipations and retrospections provoked by narrative. James thus carries forward a primary function of narrative, to explore and improve our command of the intricacy of language by which to effect changes in ourselves and our environment, to transform the realities of our existence.

James thus seizes the opportunity of employing the "limitations" of subjectivity to enhance narrative self-reflexivity, to exploit the capacity of words not only to mean different things in different situations but even to mean different things to two people in the same situation. Narrative's capacity to articulate disjunctions between the use of words and the contexts in which they are used is fundamental to its effectiveness in constituting the contexts within which and through which human beings undergo social experiences. Although we have observed narrative self-reflexivity in even so simple a tale as "Grasshopper in Love with Deer," in James's fiction it attains full efficacy, the significance of which Bakhtin dramatized in his analysis of the metaverbal circumstances of his one-word dialogue, *"Tak!"* *The Ambassadors* is a continuous exploration of the interplay between what people say and the contexts that influence both why they say it and how and whether what they have said is under-stood.

James, for all his criticism of his Victorian predecessors, transforms storytelling more by intensifying techniques by no means unfamiliar to novelists such as Thackeray and Trollope than by counternarrative moves. He pays more attention to the pressures of immediate subjective experience and to how com-monplace words shift meanings within microcontexts of dia-logic situations, but the ground of his story, like theirs, is an interplay between extraverbal realities shaping and being shaped by specific ways in which words are deployed in those contexts. By "telling through" Strether he enables his readers to experience the delicate processes by which a specific conver-sational situation determines what he and others mean even as the situation comes into being through what they say. We per-ceive how characters subtly adjust the nature of their shifting interrelations to changes in the medium of those interactions, the artifice of their conversations, which include, of course, meaningful pauses and silences. Only by carefully following, or having followed, the development of such doubly self-reflexive narrativized dialogs can we understand, for example, the sig-nificance of Maria's declaration at one point that "everything" *means* "Strether," or how adultery may be by another character fairly termed a "virtuous attachment," or what is signified by Strether's celebrated admonition to Little Bilham "to *live*,"—all of which examples, like countless others that could be cited, appear banal if not absurd when thus abstracted from the nar-rative evolution of self-transforming dialogic contexts they bring into existence.

This interplay explains James's concentration on quite com-monplace words or exceedingly vague terms, such as "wonder-fully." He is as little interested in the Flaubertian *mot juste* as the Joycean crossword-style pun. He shares with those novelists a modernist fascination with language as language, but his attention (which accounts for a "conservative" streak in his compositions) centers more on the dynamically shifting micro-contexts of familiar terms. This is why his novels so marvelously exemplify what Bakhtin calls dialogic fiction, which is fiction that supports Wittgenstein's argument that the meaning of a word is determined by its usage.

The Ambassadors can be understood as developing the narrative principle of reversal and involution that I illustrated with "Grasshopper in Love with Deer," though of course intensifying a hundredfold the subjectivity of the characters—thereby enhancing the significance of the story's folding back upon itself. This full realization of subjectivities increases the capability of narrative to accommodate the tiniest (but not therefore unimportant) contingencies of social intercourse. The sylleptically doubled story of what happens to Strether being what happens to Strether's conscious perception of what is happening to him must depend on a myriad of incalculable linguistic intersections of personalities and perceptions of personalities. It is no coincidence that the key event of the novel is a purely accidental meeting, because The Ambassadors is the story of Strether's encounters with the shifting unpredictabilities—not of the natural world—but of a humanly constituted world of social interrelations. So far as James's concern is the very essence of such a world, his focus on ultrarefined characters is not merely appropriate but necessary. Just as the deepest interest of "Grasshopper in Love with Deer" resides less in the sheer actions of infidelity and killing than in its self-involuting representation of relationships changed by changes in perception of relationships, so The Ambassadors, despite its refinements of tone and manner and its absence of physically violent incident, is genuinely exciting to anyone ready to follow the novel's depiction of Strether's changing awareness of the dynamic interplay of alertly and subtly conflicting consciousnesses among which he must negotiate.

Epitomizing how James's story of change transforms narrative is the observation on a verbal reaction of Waymarsh's to a remark of the protagonist: "Strether had n't yet got quite used to being so unprepared for the consequences of the impression he produced" (129). This intense concentration on the subjective deployment of and responses to language defines a temporalized social environment that gives the subjective experience its particular meaning—yet the environment is itself affected by utterances deriving from a character's awarenss of its influence. Thus Strether's interlocutor here, Waymarsh, is finally strongly affected by Strether's developing perceptions, and, of course, Strether reacts significantly to his friend's change. What is at issue in their exchange is illuminated by the balder light of Freudian psychology, coming into being even as James wrote, and founded on the relation of analyst to analysand oddly analogous to James's relation of narrator to protagonist. Freudian psychology programmatically seeks to describe how language means for individuals through the contexts by which it comes into being for them. Most simply, the analyst strives to uncover the somatic and emotional processes that determine whatever the analysand is capable of articulating, metaverbal conditions of which his particular usages of language are symptomatic. Exemplary are the words of Freud's patient who couldn't remember the face of a woman in his dream, but insisted, "I know it wasn't my mother." Ideally, at any rate, psychoanalysis would restore to the patient a power of controlling the meaning of his words, freeing his conscious will from subjection to contexts that determine what he can articulate, especially about himself—briefly, to be able to say to himself or others, "That may have been my idea of mother." As Jacques Lacan has shown, psychoanalysis is "the talking cure" in far more than a superficial sense, for its cure is a reempowerment of the individual to give language specific meaning.

James, endlessly curious, is less intrigued by cures than adventures, so his fiction originally and daringly explores what are nowadays termed boundary conditions, where one kind of existence or one kind of action crosses into or is interpenetrated by another—as is so melodramatically the situation of the protagonist of *The Awakening Conscience,* and so intricately the experience of the protagonist of *The Ambassadors.* A story of serious explorations into mental or cultural boundary conditions will necessarily tend toward the subjective, although its value increases so far as the boundaries it tests are more than mere personal limits (as of an analysand)—which accounts for James's preoccupation with the encounters of Europeans and Americans. Narrative, even transformed, "modernized," continues to present itself as an opportunity to share, constitutes an offer to think and feel differently together, addressing the odd fact of our life that, as Carol Gilligan puts it, "we know ourselves as separate only insofar as we live in connection with others, and we experience relationship only as we differentiate others from self."[2]

Narrative tended to remain viable for modern writers only through a radical intensification of its self-reflexive properties—to a degree that it may have become scarcely recognizable as narrative, and, indeed, finally threatened to self-destruct. For the primary condition of modern, urbanized, technological, cosmopolitan civilization is that it has made obsolete the local if not intimate community of narrator and audience in which storytelling had always been rooted. The contemporary storyteller must manufacture some substitute for that community. Unlike the traditional teller, the teller of a modern tale faces the task—to adapt a decisive phrase from *The Ambassadors*—of changing encounters into relationships, because the relational basis upon which storytelling traditionally had relied was yielding to ever more depersonalized connections.

James had good reason to retain a narrator, namely, to ensure that identificatory processes would always be mediated and qualified, so that we are persistently thrown back on our awareness of reading critically about Strether even as we most empathize with him. For if we were to lose ourselves in Strether totally, if we were confined within the perspective of his single consciousness, we would forfeit the self-reflexiveness (both of character and of story line) that allows us to discover how our experience can be shaped by the articulations of our consciousness, just as we perceive the character of our awareness to derive from contextual systems of speech, thought, feeling, and behavior that comprise our experiences. Because Jame's adherence to the "reversibility" of story is not unique to his art, but appears in diverse guises in other distinguished modern novelists (Mann and Proust and Conrad at once come to mind), it seems reasonable to suggest that the severest contestations of narrative in our century may be more a phenomenon of literary criticism than of literary art. Modern *criticism*, at any rate, has been most extreme in dismissing narrative, treating it as a primitive, rather than an elemental, mode of discourse. It is in critical commentaries that plot has been most exalted over story—appropriately enough so far as this century's criticism has tended toward rigorously abstract definitions of supposedly universal principles and conditions, turning away from story's fascinated engagement with contingencies as contingencies. Both the formalistic bias and the emphasis (most conspicuous in Marxist-influenced thought) on rationalistic, "scientific" explanations in twentieth-century criticism have distracted commentators from what interested the best modern storytellers: how the meaning of language is changed by the immediate context in which it is used, even though that context itself is the product of the language used in it. Much of the extraordinary impact of Bakhtin's criticism late in our century can be attributed to his concepts of dialogism and double-voicedness, which for the first time provide efficient forms for describing how utterances and their contexts are mutually constitutive. Yet, in thus looking beyond modernism to understand it, as nearly a century later we ought to do, we perceive that narrative, if making a comeback in criticism, seems perhaps a more problematic feature of contemporary art than it was eighty years ago.

Before glancing at the present situation of narrative, however, it will help to consider in a little more detail Henry James's narrative innovations and their functions as revealed by the art of *The Ambassadors*. The crux of that art, as all critics have recognized, lies in James's refusal, as he says in the "Preface to the New York Edition," to make Strether "at once hero and historian," to give himself "the large ease of 'autobiography,'" to avoid "the terrible *fluidity* of self-revelation" (45–46). To the specific functions of this decision in *The Ambassadors* we shall attend in a moment, but I want first to suggest that James's determination *not* to indulge in the monologic, stream-of-consciousness forms so popular in modern novels is rooted in his most fundamental conceptions of the nature and purposes of fiction. These were first cogently set forth in his essay of 1884, *The Art of Fiction,* one of the central passages of which provoked Robert Louis Stevenson's reply, *A Humble Remonstrance.* That initiated a close personal friendship between the novelists. The focus of Stevenson's remonstrance is James's claim that the novelist "competes with life," to which he was led by the following observations:

> I may venture to say that the air of reality (solidity of specification) seems to me to be the supreme virtue of the novel—the merit on which all its other merits . . . helplessly and submissively depend. If it be not there, they are all as nothing, and if these be there, they owe their effect

to the success with which the author has produced the illusion of life. The cultivation of this success, the study of
this exquisite process, form, to my taste, the beginning and
the end of the art of the novelist. . . . It is here, in very
truth, that he competes with life.[3]

To this Stevenson objected:

To "compete with life," whose sun we cannot look upon,
whose passions and diseases waste and slay us—to compete with the flavour of wine, the beauty of the dawn, the
scorching of fire, the bitterness of death and separation—
here is, indeed, a projected escalade of heaven. . . . No art
is true in this sense; none can "compete with life." . . .
What, then, is the object, what the method, of an art and
what the source of its power? The whole secret is that no
art does "compete with life." Man's one method, whether
he reasons or creates, is to half-shut his eyes against the
dazzle and confusion of reality. . . . Geometry will tell us of
a circle, a thing never seen in nature; asked about a green
circle or an iron cirlce, it lays its hand upon its mouth.
Literature, above all in its most typical mood, the mood of
narrative, similarly flees the direct challenge . . . so far as it
imitates at all, it imitates not life but speech; not the facts
of human destiny, but the emphasis and the suppressions
with which the human actor tells of them.[4]

Both James's subsequent comments on the art of fiction and
his practice as a novelist, not least in *The Ambassadors,* suggests
that with increasingly subtle success he absorbed his friend
Stevenson's amendment into his aesthetic creed, attaining that
"solidarity of specification" upon which depends "the air of reality" through "imitation" of the "emphasis and suppressions"
of *speech,* so that in his last novels story is almost entirely generated by conversational discourse, the language of his art rooted
in the language of social converse. This is why *The Ambassadors*
seems almost to have been written to illustrate Bahktin's views.
The following passage, for example, describes virtually every
conversation in James's novel:

When we seek to understand a word, what matters is not the direct meaning the word gives to objects and emotions—this is the false front of the word; what matters is rather the actual and always self-interested *use* to which this meaning is put and the way it is expressed by the speaker, a use determined by the speaker's position (profession, social class, etc.) and by the concrete situation. *Who* speaks and under what conditions he speaks: this is what determines the word's actual meaning.[5]

This describes precisely what Strether discovers about Bilham's phrase, "virtuous attachment."

Or consider how Bahktin's translators summarize his conception of heteroglossia: "[T]hat which insures the primacy of context over text. At any given time, in any given place, there will be a set of conditions—social, historical, meteorological, physiological—that will insure that a word uttered in that place and at that time will have a meaning different than it would have under any other conditions."[6] A commitment to a "Bakhtinian" conception of heteroglossia explains James's determination to avoid the *fluidity* of first-person, monologic forms. *The Ambassadors* is preeminently a story of changes, centrally Strether's transformations. These processes take shape in the developing meanings of conversations that themselves evolve under the pressures of the characters' articulations. This permits even silences to be meaningful. When Strether hesitates in responding to a question of Maria Gostry's, we are told, "Her comment on his hesitation was scarce the less marked for being mute" (99). The comprehensible if nuanced significance of a silence responsive to a pause can only occur because the context, the process of their conversing, is steadily developing, thereby facilitating changes in understanding, perception, and moral judgment—for in James's novel the focal site of moral judgment is situated in the psychic processes of the judge, not the object of judgment.

Such dialogic narrative, of course, is peculiarly appropriate because Strether is only an agent—both of Mrs. Newsome and, in a subtler fashion, of the novel's narrator. Our understanding of Strether's consciousness is more complete and exact than it could be were it represented directly, in the first person, because through the narrator we are enabled to see not only what Strether sees and knows but also what (and why) he doesn't see and has yet to discover: "Our friend took [Chad] in again—he was always taking him in and yet finding that parts of him still remained out" (289). Such small features of silence, of the yet undiscerned, of perceptions and revelations postponed, reflect analogous features in the macrostory, as gradually Strether learns truths he had not expected and arrives at new attitudes he (and we) had not thought possible for one of his age and experiences. So our response as readers is a steadily developing one of accepting new perspectives through which we understand his evolving encounters with new modes of perceiving and judging.

One might say that in *The Ambassadors* James makes the narrative itself double voiced, because it is a story of his protagonist's growing ability to articulate, complicate, and deepen perceptions, not merely into physical "facts," but more importantly into what others can and do, or could but don't, perceive and think, that is, what others *make* of such facts.[7] When Strether queries Little Bilham, for example, about the "virtuous attachment," the artist replies, "I can only tell you that it's what they pass for. But isn't that enough? What more than a vain appearance does the wisest of us know?" (204). In human society, in life that is cultural not natural, the primary reality is precisely what "passes," and therefore is impossible to define absolutely. This is why as Strether progresses, both in his perceptions and in his evaluations of what he perceives, his understanding is differential rather than syncretic. As Maria Gostrey observes to him, "[N]othing for you will ever come to the same as anything else" (104).

The larger, tragic aspect of this scrupulous regard for differentiations, above all, the partly verbal "metaverbal" context that determines what words mean and therefore what they do, is Strether's ultimate alienation from both Woollett and Paris. The final silence of Mrs. Newsome toward him is as portentously meaningful as Madame de Vionnet's last, sad observation to him that they *might* have been friends. Knowledge, something made concrete by language, the saying of what has been seen, is a loss, if only of innocent perception. Whatever Strether gains from his experience is at least a dissipation of possibilities unrealized, like the intimation of "innumerable and wonderful things" (468) lost "in the sharpest perception yet" that "a creature so fine could be, by mysterious forces, a creature so exploited, . . . the real coercion . . . to see a man ineffably adored" (482). Yet the point of the *The Ambassadors* is that Strether's story is not merely tragic, for it is a story with the profoundly modern lesson that, in Bakhtin's words, "in the act of understanding, a struggle occurs that results in mutual change and enrichment."[8]

Since *The Ambassadors* is, then, a story about storytellings, it is worth returning to the reasons why it is no accident that its crucial scenic confrontation, when Strether happens upon Chad and Madame de Vionnet on the river, is blatantly coincidental, that is, as overtly artificial as Jamesian contrivance can manage. The accidental meeting, furthermore, occurs "literally" within the imaginative "framing" of the little pre-Impressionist Lambinet that, years before, Strether had wanted to purchase in Tremont Street. Then the painting had enabled him to remember the French countryside; now the countryside enables him to recall the experience of imaginatively remembering it through the painting. When, therefore, Strether sees "exactly the right thing," which turns out to be Chad and Madame de Vionnet in the boat, what is challenged for him (and through him the reader) is not simply ignorance of the fact of their liaison. Were that the case *The Ambassadors* would not be worth rereading, whereas in fact it is one of the novels that most richly rewards the returning reader. The encounter forces him, and us, to recognize what would have been the case had he *not* happened upon the pair. Then his illusion of a technically "virtuous attachment" would have been unimpaired— the deliberately enjoyed illusion of the Lambinet would have persisted—whereas the painting disappears from the story the instant Chad and Madame de Vionnet float into the scene. The lovely illusion is superseded by the reality of another fiction, the "lie" that they are not enjoying a sexual relation at another country retreat.

Yet because Strether admits this fiction, waving his hat and stick, giving expression to "surprise" and "joy," the mere "violence" of a simple lie is "averted" (462). For to pretend not to have recognized the pair, demanding from them mutual pretense, would have been to make any relations between him and them permanently false. Whereas their "lie" Strether comes to realize is "after all such an inevitable tribute to good taste as he couldn't have wished them not to render" (477). Here we see clearly the functionality of the characteristic double negatives, both verbal and structural, endemic in James's story. They embody a superimposing of artifice upon artifice of which Woollett's discourse is incapable, pointing to conscious "deceit" that permits admission of the value to human intercourse of deliberate storytelling. The "good taste" of Chad's and Madame de Vionnet's fiction allows communication, the civilized interchange of evaluative understandings. This is the fictionalizing dependent upon and supportive of mutual trust, a fictionalizing inescapable to those willing to confront the difficulties of relationship as process, mutual understanding as continual discovering, not something ever definitive, conclusive, prepackaged—as Sarah Pocock would wish it to be.

The Ambassadors thus exemplifies what storytelling most essentially is—not fact but the telling of fact, the deliberately "artificial" display of experience that allows the mutually evaluative understandings upon which cultural—civilized—life depends. That life of speech, because it is cultural, is never simply conclusive or susceptible to formulaic definition, but is, instead, endlessly reassessible, because its significance is not merely multiple but reality-transforming.

Although the truths revealed by the artifice of storytelling cannot be absolute and definitive, they are none the less truths, as *The Ambassadors* by telling its story through Strether rather than simply by him or about him forcefully illustrates. One such personal truth is of Madame de Vionnet, captured in Strether's almost last vision of her, in an imagined context of the *ancien regime* being destroyed by revolution, literally "afraid" for "her life." It is, characteristically, a vision of a moment defined by its difference from his earlier view of her and from that which will succeed it.

> It was actually moreover as if he did n't think of her at all,
> as if he could think of nothing but the passion, mature,
> abysmal, pitiful, she represented, and the possibilities she

betrayed. She was older for him to-night, visibly less exempt from the touch of time; but she was as much as ever the finest and subtlest creature, the happiest apparition it had been given to him, in all his years, to meet; and yet he could see her there as vulgarly troubled, in very truth, as a maidservant crying for her young man. The only thing was that she judged herself as the maidservant would n't; the weakness of which wisdom too, the dishonor of such judgment, seemed but to sink her lower. (483)

The fearfully compassionate truth of this passage gives it full right to stand with Shakespeare's lines about Cleopatra, which surely it is meant to recall, that "Queen" who finally calls herself

No more but e'en a woman, and commanded
By such poor passions as the maid that milks
And does the meanest chores.

But James's story tells more than this truth through the personal story of Lambert Strether permitting us such sadly compassionate admiration of Madame de Vionnet. The truth of her physical intimacy with Chad revealed by the ostentatious artifices of Strether's day in the country is but one of many "physical" truths that provoke the complex discourse through which the protagonist strives to understand the complications of a society those whom he serves would, if they could, destroy by simplifications. Thus, fine as the relation of Chad and Madame de Vionnet is, the truth of it may fairly be termed "brutal," because Chad remains a "brute." His brutishness cannot be done away with even by Madame de Vionnet's charms because it is less a personal characteristic than a social commitment.

In the scene in the idyllic country, the fact of Chad and Madame de Vionnet's physical, sexual relation is unmistakably manifested, and from the emergence of that irrepressible reality arises in the final chapters the equally unmistakable awareness that Chad will be "a brute." That is to say, he will desert Madame de Vionnet, as he has already begun to do, as he will return to Woollett to administer the advertising of the family firm. What *The Ambassadors* as a whole displays are forces that cannot forever be evaded, postponed, repressed—above all the forces that are most dramatically embodied in the Newsome clan, the New World manufacturers and makers of money. The intense, even flagrant, artifices of the chapter describing Strether's excursion to the country force upon our attention (as well as his) how fragile are the artifices restraining "Newsome progress," most subtly epitomized in Chad's "brutishness," and most directly expressed by the hate-filled Sarah Pocock, speaking always proudly and only in the voice of her dictatorial mother.

As frankly as Waymarsh, Chad tells Strether that in opposing his mother the older man is giving up "a good deal of money" (433). And in the emerging world of the twentieth-century, a world to be dominated by American wealth based on manufacture, advertising will assure that dominance of financial motives, the language of advertising being the absolute antithesis of James's best language. A major revelation toward which *The Ambassadors* steadily moves in its final chapters is how much more than a personal matter is Strether's ambassadorship, how profoundly James understands the constitution of the society to whose superstructure his fiction itself contributes. His novel is a kind of climax and ending of the tradition of the bildungsroman, which, as Bakhtin has shown, is fiction tracing not merely the development of a protagonist but that personal development engaged with an evolving and changing society. At the beginning of the modern era James shows us a protagonist learning to be more tolerant and more humane as his society becomes more mechanized and cruelly oversimplified, less caring of individual sensibilities. The bildungsroman originated in more optimistic times, so that the development of the individual could be seen as an improvement meshing with society's progress. But by the end of the nineteenth century it appeared to writers such as James that the finest individual qualities that one could develop must separate one from the mainstream of society's evolution. Improvement of the individual as individual seemed only to guarantee alienation.

That is what makes Strether's return to Woollett so impressive. Strether is not a heroic figure, but he is capable of confronting what he has outgrown, of attempting to put to *use* the consciousness he has developed. Because he has perceived what can be made of the brute fact of physical sexuality, he would be untrue to what he has learned not to turn back against the source of the new brutishness, the "progress" that in fact wants no genuine change. For the commercialism of the Newsomes is offensive exactly because it would deny the possibility of real transformation, just as Mrs. Newsome carries on the business of her father and her husband without a name of her own, just as Chad can look forward to a career of advertising, that is, extolling the utility of an object that isn't even worthy of being named. Because he has learned that one need not be fixed in rigid fictions as constituents of a civilized person's life, Strether would be untrue to his European education by women did he not reject the possibilities of comfortable personal evasion offered to him in Paris. He is true not only to himself but to his ambassadorship in returning, not to combat, but consciously to confront the source of the false progressiveness that within a few decades, as we know, would inundate Europe, materialistically leveling the discriminating life for which Madame de Vionnet rightly feared, of which, one is tempted to say, Strether alone is returned to tell us.

Storytelling in a Postmodern/ Postcolonial World

Focus on contestations of narrative by modern art has led me to ignore many cross- and countercurrents within that complicated movement. David Perkins in his *History of Modern Poetry,* for example, devotes a chapter to the poetry of Rudyard Kipling, G. K. Chesterton, and John Masefield, who deliberately resisted the antinarrative impetus given to poetry by the aesthetes and symbolists.[1] More significant are some surprising contradictions at the very core of the modernist "revolution," one revealed in T. S. Eliot's praise of *Ulysses* as "the most important expression which the present age has found" because of its "mythical method," which "has the importance of a scientific discovery." That method, according to Eliot, consists in "manipulating a continuous parallel between contemporaneity and antiquity" as a way "of controlling, of ordering, of giving shape and significance to the immense panorama of futility and anarchy which is contemporary history." So far as myth *is* narrative, it is intriguing that Eliot defines the new artistic technique (which he associates with science and rational control) in opposition to storytelling: "Instead of narrative method we may now use the mythical method. It is, I seriously believe, a step toward making the modern world possible in art."[2] The dubiousness of Eliot's opposition of narrative and myth points to an ambivalence about story beneath modernism's ostentatious hostility to storytelling.

I am remiss, also, for failing to address modernism's impact upon nations or people marginalized by Western European–American culture. An impressive instance is the flowering of

Mexican mural paintings beginning in the 1920s. Diego Rivera, José Clemente Orozco, and David Siqueiros effectively adapted modernist methods to the demands of a popularly nationalistic, doubly revolutionary painting with strong narrative elements. Less well known but valuable to a student of storytelling is the work of Jacob Lawrence, an African-American painter from Harlem who in the 1930s created a series of impressive narrative sequences depicting the careers of Toussaint l'Overture, Harriet Tubman, and Frederick Douglass.

Such paintings prove that narrative need not be incompatible with the styles of modern art. Rivera, Orozco, and Lawrence demonstrate that some modernistic techniques may facilitate the painting of vivid and evocative stories.[3] Any modernist critique of narrativity is an "aesthetic" assertion inseparably entangled with ideological agendas. Orozco in his Hanover, New Hampshire, murals, for example, narratively represents modern Mexican history overcoming "futility and anarchy" engendered by colonialism. Rivera, likewise, depicts the violence of European exploitation by means of techniques learned through study of Cubism and other modern European art to celebrate the revolutionary triumph of a contemporary Mexican civilization over European colonialism. Rivera, indeed, is an artist who merits detailed attention by anyone who wants to get past clichés about modernism. I cite as illustration but one aspect of his work because of its relevance to both the contradictory forces I see revealed in Eliot's statement about "mythical method" and my analysis of the issues raised by William Holman Hunt's archaizing. Although passionately committed to, and an effective practitioner of, new and "revolutionary" painting styles, Rivera was also fascinated by the technical methods of Italian medieval fresco painters. His marriage of an "archaic" practical technique to new stylistic conceptions gives much of his work its special power—and illuminates a fundamental weakness in many archaizing or exoticizing artistic movements. These frequently cripple themselves by severing style from the history of technical competencies. Instead of merely exploiting stylistically some "primitive" or archaic motifs, as many painters exploited the forms and features of African masks, Rivera also took the trouble to master the ancient craft of fresco. This mastery enabled him, quite literally, to base his innovative painting on traditonal techniques and skills. That base helped him to become an enduringly "popular" artist.

That Rivera, along with Orozco, has consistently been ignored by leading commentators on modernism is further evidence of that movement's imbricating of aesthetics and ideology. The overlapping is also dramatized by attacks on modernism by officially sanctioned art movements, such as Socialist Realism in the Soviet Union, and Fascistic arts in Germany and Italy. These "reactionary" aesthetics proclaimed the virtues of popularly comprehensible story subjects, and thereby have wonderfully helped to give narrative a bad name. But in fact the "narrativity" favored by these viciously antimodern aesthetics is false. "Approved" Fascist and Soviet "stories" are propagandistic and authoritarian, not authentic interchanges of shared explorations into social and ethical problems. Enforced storytelling is an impossibility; propaganda offers a counterfeit display text.

For understandable reasons, students of narrative have paid too little attention to such pseudo-narratives—I myself have tried to sweeten the pill by focusing on Hunt. But both the motivations toward encouragement of pseudo-story and the inevitable failure of such storytelling can reveal much about the nature and function of genuine narrative in the twentieth-century world. Even some Mexican "official" revolutionary art would provide such insights.[4] The false narrativity of stories depending on official sanction, for example, proves how profoundly negotiational is genuine narrative; its "transaction" between teller and audience implies not just compliance and cooperation but a whole range of interactions, which may include discomfort, anger, repulsion. Any specific exchange, furthermore, is originated by a single individual. Stories are not told by committees. So, as I have observed, storytelling is intrinsically antiauthoritarian. Its deepest subversiveness is less in any expression of resistance to received doctrine than in the simple fact that even when loyally adhering to doctrine, when faithfully reinforcing tradition, a narrator necessarily tells in his own way. That opens a possibility of change and criticism, particularly since each member of his audience receives the story as an individual, in his or her own way, thereby permitting a complicity all the more dangerous because not deliberate, not plotted.

When we have noticed these facts, the uneasiness tyrannous and authoritarian powers often display toward popular storytelling becomes comprehensible. Yet, as the Soviet and Fascist examples demonstrate, there seems to be an equally strong compulsion in such powers to have "the right kind" of stories promulgated. This reveals narrative to be inseparable from its evocation of ethical responses. Storytelling cannot be regimented or commanded, but also it can never be ethically neutral. However oppressively dictatorial a power may be, it will feel strengthened if the "rightness" of what it enforces is recognized—as it will at least appear to be by an audience accepting an officially sanctioned narrative.

In a negative fashion, then, even the tyrannous recognize that to engage mutually, to share, to enter into the narrative transaction creatively, a story receiver must possess real freedom of response. Although this is not named as one of the "Four Freedoms," nor as one of the Rights of Man, I am inclined to regard it as a primal liberty, fundamental to being human. A story does not coerce me into judgment, it offers me an opportunity to make a judgment on my own. And this is why the possibility of retelling and rehearing or rereading is so important. When I reread I can reassess my own earlier judgment; I can call to account my earlier accounting. Therein lies a possibility of improving my judgment and enhancing my powers of evaluation. As I pointed out earlier, even the great sacred myths are narrative because as narratives they permit, even encourage, reinterpretations that keep the stories vital (that is, capable of transformation) through changing times and circumstances. And such reinterpretations *can* be improvements.

The foregoing should make plain why a core tenet in the ideology of modernism, namely, to excise ideology from art, to transcend the limitations inherent in any specific sociopolitical commitment, is so bound up with some contestation of narrative. Once again let me cite Kasimir Malevich: "[A]rt, at the turn of the century, divested itself of the ballast of religious and political ideas which had been imposed upon it and came into its own—attained, that is, the form suited to its intrinsic nature."[5] This anti-ideological ideology, this divestment of commitment to matters that form the basis of all ethical issues, not its formal innovations, is chiefly responsible for antinarrativism in modern art. Yet there appear implications in such hostility that have given thoughtful critics pause. As I suggested at the end of Chapter 6, implicit in this purification of art are potentialities for an absolutism finally as dehumanizing as some of the openly brutal political systems of our century, and the more dangerous because so easily self-disguising.[6] At the cost of raising some unpleasant questions about art of unquestionable beauty and interest, we need to penetrate that disguise.

As illustrative of this dehumanizing absolutism as the paintings of Mondrian or Malevich is the superlative sculpture of Constantin Brancusi, the Rumanian peasant who with difficulty made his way to Paris and single-mindedly labored to escape from the limitations of Rodin's influence, particularly as it intensified the tradition of sculpture as manufactured product. After the time of Giovanni Bernini, sculpture had become the most commercialized of the arts. Sculptors made clay models for statues that were then cut from marble blocks by pointing machines managed by laborers in marbleyards, cast in bronze by equally anonymous workmen at foundries, sometimes even finished by the workmen, too. Nathaniel Hawthorne in *The Marble Faun* wonders if under such circumstances sculptors had a right to the title of artist.[7] Some modern sculptors rejected such commercialized manufacturing, insisting on a return to methods of direct carving and hand-shaping. Even with works cast by a foundry Brancusi spent weeks, sometimes months, hand-polishing them to attain a perfected subtlety of curvatures and surface sheen. The irony is that the effect of his fanatical labor was totally to obliterate any impression of hand work. His hand labor produces what looks like the finest machine finish.

What Brancusi sought, and to a remarkable degree succeeded in creating, were forms purified of messy links to their constitutive contingencies, forms "dehistoricized," one might say. His works are truly autonomous in their elegant perfection. His *Prometheus*, for example, is only a head-like form so self-sufficient that it seldom occurs to a viewer to regard it as only a part of a body. Yet there is something almost obscene in thus obliterating the prolonged, intense suffering for humanity that is the core of Prometheus's story: Brancusi's dehumanizing is dramatized by the contrast of Orozco's fiery 1930 Prometheus painting at Pomona College. Perhaps an even more striking example of modernistic reductive essentialization is Brancusi's *The Beginning of the World,* an ovoid form resting on an oval surface. Any particular perspective, and thereby the possibility of imagining a truly alternative point of view toward the work, or the possibility of perceiving it as a process, as capable of self-transforming, is transcended by the sculpture's severe self-sufficiency, its detachment from any contingency.

Brancusi's intense reductiveness might be seen as an extreme form of "minimalizing": he has "left out" almost everything. This might illuminate Eliot's odd opposition of "myth" and "narrative." But what the storyteller subtracts *from* is complexity of being, a density of intersecting phenomena, the existence of which the audience is made imaginatively aware by the storyteller's lacunae; leaving out encourages apperceptive responses. So the storyteller does not essentialize in the fashion of a modern nonrepresentational artist. Even in myth, story in which we concentrate on the action as action, time is allowed for acts and their effects to unfold in their particularities. Or, to put the matter in terms of the Ricoeurian sentence model, narrative requires *both* singular agent and universal action, a requirement precluding the reduction to sheer essence for which Brancusian art strives. And to look at the same problem from the point of view of narrative effect, *The Beginning of the World* is not accessible to genuine revision. Perfect form assures stasis. When we return to look again, we see the same object. Change, as Plato said, implies imperfection, which is the realm of the storyteller.

Idealistic aestheticism such as Brancusi's, even when it would seem to incline toward narrative, moves away from story because its depersonalizing eliminates the imperfection of human experience. Brancusi strove to get rid of the "looseness or roughness" required of every kind of human discourse, the "imperfections" that Wittgenstein identified as essential to efficacious language use: "The *in*exactness, the impurity of our negotiations with language, is not . . . some secondary condition of a lapsed primary, not a quotidean deviation from some purer form of discourse or intelligence that we must always try to recover. 'Impurity' of this sort is on the contrary the working base of all our verbal experience."[8] Brancusi's purified visual language transcends both human sociality and individuality. Like the terrible beauty of some perfectly functioning machine, his accomplishments, specifically expressive of an idealism that would obliterate socialized heterogeneity, epitomize the power of human beings to dehumanize themselves. Such an aesthetic cannot be ideologically neutral, although one can understand why an artist like Brancusi could honestly believe he has transcended ideology. Art that seeks purely aesthetic response and denies the importance of singularity and imperfection is a condemnation of ordinary, "imperfect" people. It is sentimental self-deception not to recognize the relation of such aestheticism to absolutist and inhumane sociopolitical programs, whatever the artist's official allegiance.

The turn against modernism since about 1960 has drawn much of its force from a revulsion against such aesthetic self-mystification, a revulsion visible in celebrations of otherness, and assertions of the value of contingent forms, often along the Wittgensteinian lines of the citation just above.[9] Postmodernism, moreover, often strikes against the view of art that, in Richard Poirer's words, claims for art a "difficulty" beyond the capacity of the ordinary person, a difficulty "only the poet could confront *for* us, and . . . the reader should be selfless and humble and thankful for the poet's having done this." Such an elitist aesthetic, a natural concomitant to the drive to essentialize, produced critics who, in Robert Morris's words, operated under the metaphor "of preacher-moralist (if not high priest) who oversees, who separates the impure from the near transcendent."[10] It would seem natural, then, for postmodernism to revalorize storytelling. Narrative *has* been repopularized: even this essay reflects the growing critical interest in stories. Yet if postmodernism looks to narrative for alternatives to some unattractive tendencies in modernism, sociological obstacles to successful storytelling have become greater today than they were a century ago. This contradictory situation is illustrated in the work of pop artist Roy Lichtenstein, one of the best known—because of his "comic strip" canvases—of the postmoderns who seemed to utilize narrative to break with modernism. While exploitation of the most "popular" of mass culture genres would appear the ultimate inversion of the modernist anti-storytelling aesthetic, Lichtenstein's explicit denials that his pictures are narrative cannot be dismissed—if only because his later, frankly nonnarrative paintings support his assertions.[11]

Lichtenstein's claim that his works possess a "composition" lacking in actual comic strips is, one must admit, a kind of disclaimer necessary for an artist in a new style—Pop—who wants his work recognized as "serious art." But the claim should equally draw attention to his emphasis less on sequential action than on images in themselves. Lichtenstein, in fact, is obsessed with images. Many of his pictures are built upon a process of direct, mechanical transference of images, as he implies wittily in his *Mad Scientist,* whose words, after all, could be Lichtenstein's own: "What? Why do you ask that? What do you know about my image duplicator?" All his "comic strip" paintings are representations of what ostentatiously are not individuals but stereotypical images of people, although, unlike Tom Wolfe, Lichtenstein recognizes the horror of stereotypicality. The mordant commentary of his "romance" pictures turns upon such obvious stylization, perhaps most simply and acutely illustrated by *Him,* which displays a photograph of a young man held by a pair of female hands. Not only is Lichtenstein's picture of an image, a photograph, but he has presented it as representing a stereotypical handsomeness, so that this "photograph," valued as a portrait of a particular individual, shows an utterly conventionalized face.

It is interesting to compare what Lichtenstein is doing in this ingenious painting to how Thackeray describes George Osborne and Amelia Sedley. Thackeray's descriptions of George Osborne in both words and drawings produce very much the effect of the representation of the protagonist of *Him.* And we have no reason to doubt the "genuineness" of the feelings of the woman holding the picture in *Him,* any more than we doubt the "genuineness" of Amelia's feelings about George—indeed that is what most troubles us. We cannot know if she who holds the photograph admires "him" because of "his" stereotypicality, because he fits a predetermined "image" of what a lover "ought" to look like, rather as George does for Amelia. Yet the difference between Thackeray and Lichtenstein is even more revealing, because the latter works, and wishes us to be aware of his working, entirely in images, that is, secondary representations. Lichtenstein's picture (except for the woman's hands)

10. Roy Lichtenstein, *Him*, 1964. Graphite pencil and touche on paper, 21⅝ × 16⁵⁄₁₆″. The Saint Louis Art Museum, Museum Purchase: Eliza McMillan Fund and Friends of the Saint Louis Art Museum funds.

11. W. M. Thackeray, Illustration from *Vanity Fair*, 1848.

contains no "actuality" at all; the invisible woman is looking at a photograph. Amelia sees the "real" George Osborne, who is also an individual with a name and a history, not just a gender marker. Lichtenstein's painting is entirely without individuality, even the title is a pronoun, and in this respect is farther than Thackeray from Vermeer's young girl smiling, although a seed of Lichtenstein's representation may be discovered in the descriptiveness of the Renaissance picture.

Again we must remind ourselves that what we normally take as the "natural" individuality of persons is largely a socio-cultural construct.[12] Storytelling, as we've seen, requires some kind of singling out, just as sentences require "singular" subjects, because stories evoke evaluative responses to acts by people represented as responsible agents in specific circumstances. This singular responsibility is a magnified expression of narrative's focus on language as polysemic—using words "responsibly" is difficult but valuable just because words can mean more than one thing. I exemplified this conjunction with "Grasshopper in Love with Deer," in which reflexive inversions of names and story line enhance one another. If I interpret Lichtenstein's obsession with images rightly, he displays what he believes to be a historical fact: in contemporary society individuality in the traditional sense has vanished into a pure stereotypicality. From this perspective, Western civilization's insistence for the past two centuries on the autonomy of the individual can be seen as symptomatic of a reaction against our era's ever-greater threat to personal identity as we have conceived it.

In Lichtenstein's paintings there surfaces for our troubled contemplation a key tension in Western narratives that has operated since the time of the Renaissance. On the one hand, as we noted in relation to Vermeer's painting, an ideal of representational realism worked against narrative sequentiality, yet on the other this very "descriptive" realism—logically enough—excited intense interest in human individuality, the essential stuff of storytelling. Stories can evoke an actively participative response from an audience only by treating their characters as morally responsible agents. And the transactional sharing that is storytelling assumes an audience of individuals, *each* free to judge the right balance between personal and group interests, necessities, and aspirations.

Stories always, therefore, in some fashion single out, whether through the elaborate characterization of Anna Karenina or the simple designation of "a man killing fish" in "Why the Buzzard Is Bald." Just as stories are always told by individuals, so they are always interpreted by individuals. Narrative is an important mode of discourse because it permits shared evaluations among individually responsible persons.

Lichtenstein, then, is not only correct to deny that his "comic strip" paintings are simple narratives but also courageous to urge us to use such art to confront the difficulty of storytelling in a world whose reality has come to consist almost entirely of images. The sardonically jagged moral edge to Lichtenstein's work derives from its depicting how today we act and think according to formulas under the delusion that we are behaving independently. Perhaps worse, we have come to cherish as individual what is formulaic. We have come to treasure as most "real" the replicable and the stereotypical, rather than the mind-boggling peculiarity of the contingent. Lichtenstein's art allows us to realize that the images more and more constituting the major part of our experience are a seductively illusionary escape from intractably harsh uncertainties and accidentalities—the bedrock of storytelling.

An image, by definition a product, not a process, can be controlled, turned on and off, replayed, run backward. The same mechanical control is more difficult to exercise over authentic story, which exists by being transformed and by transforming itself. The retelling of narrative consists in making it anew: any telling, including any retelling, is unique, as is each rereading. Lichtenstein, with a kind of visualization of Benjamin's story of art in an age of mechanical reproduction, dramatizes how our world celebrates counternarrative, mechanical replicability. The reiterable, he suggests, appeals by seeming to eliminate the contingent. As demand for the security of a controllable reality (however delusory) grows, there will be less and less call for genuine narrative.

Lichtenstein shows us that once we accept the idea that pictures can tell stories, we are positioned to recognize an incompatibility of story and image. Although, as I have observed, storytelling involves several kinds of self-reflexive activity, and in the hands of a modernist such as Henry James this characteristic can be dominant, story self-destructs if it is made simply to image itself, if it becomes totally self-referential. This is quite distinct from story's use of repetition to expand, through the proliferation of episodic perspectives, the range and relevance of its evaluative affects, the kind of enrichment we observed in "Raw-Gums and White-Owl Woman." Self-referential imaging threatens narrative's existence as social negotiation, turning its process into a product, reifying its disturbingly nonsemiotic vitality, which depends on its being "about" something other than itself.

In effective storytelling the audience recognizes that a story is being told—its enjoyment is of the story as story. So far as an audience is engaged in a storytelling it is always consciously participating in the telling, acting imaginatively, in no danger of mistaking the representation for nonnarrative reality. Story receiving means deliberately committing oneself to something psychically very "real," but real only as an artifact. An adept story receiver is invariably conscious of pursuing the activity of imagining, just as when one is building a garage one is aware of doing carpentry. The pleasure of story receiving or of carpentry is inseparable from conscious engagement in the specific activity. This primary self-reflexive imaginative activity of story reception is reduced to mere admiration for an image by self-reflections of the narrative that are too simple, as when in the movie *Blazing Saddles* some of its characters ride into a showing of the movie *Blazing Saddles*.

The fondness of both contemporary artists and critics for such reified self-imaging testifies to the difficulties of any kind of imaginative sharing today—hazards foreshadowed as I have suggested by the insistence of Hunt's strained narrativity. Some desire to seek out shared grounds of imaginative experience would seem to attract postmodern artists to simple and broadly popular images—such as Lichtenstein's "comic strip" sources. Through their difference from genuine comic pictures, their intensified coloring, their simplified lines, their enormous size, Lichtenstein's paintings simultaneously distinguish themselves from and "remind" us of comic-book images. Reversing Joyce's parodic mythologizing so that his figures at once magnify and ridicule their popular (instead of mythic) prototypes, Lichtenstein ironically challenges "the modernist and avant-garde premises of the privileged nature of the artist's perspective." Lichtenstein does seem to wish to work from the same ground as his audience, reflecting to us so that we may together evaluate the significance of images equally familiar to him and us, images that have determined his and our understanding equally. But given his ironic attitude toward his sources, his technique may reflect as much uncertainty about his artistic situation as a conviction of his audience's "creative" capacities:

"No longer does the feeling of alienation suggest a compensat-
ing critical vantage point from which the artist can declare his
or her independence from the dominant culture. . . . There
can be no simple opposition to culture, no transcendent
language."[13]

The importance to postmodernism of the imagery of imagery is evidenced by frankly popular and commercial works.
One episode ("The Menagerie") in the *Star Trek* television series, for example, deals with inhabitants of a distant planet capable of creating illusions in the minds of others, who capture
some humans, hoping to use them to repopulate their devas-
tated planet. All this is shown through the display on a television screen the protagonists watch. So we see on our television
screen Mr. Spock watching on his screen images of himself vis-
iting the planet some years before. One scene shows "laser
guns" apparently failing to blast through a door. But we learn
that the guns did in fact destroy the door; the aliens had created in the minds of the humans the illusion that their weapons
were ineffective. Thus technology is used to dramatize the illusory nature of technological power. Since what the characters
"see" on the television screen (and we are as convinced as they)
turns out in fact to be itself illusions created in their minds
by these same aliens, *we* are forced to reflect on some of the
problematic aspects of our capacity to substitute images for
reality.

The peculiar effectiveness of this story derives from its being
part of a "popular" commercial television series. That is,
whereas "pop" art such as Lichtenstein's must present itself as a
challenge to sophisticated viewers and appear as a kind of deliberate trick, the *Star Trek* episode appears "natural," since the
viewers of *Star Trek* are presumed to enjoy it as "unsophisticated" fantasy. In our contemporary, image-dominated, mass-
culture world the ancient problems of illusion and reality are
most sharply focused by the technological modes of mass-cul-
ture storytelling. The point is not to assert that *Star Trek* is
"great art," whatever that might mean, but that postmodernism's relative hospitality (vis-à-vis modernism) to the popular
and commercial expresses a self-reflexivity now—thanks to the
effects of sophisticated modernism—deeply built into "popular" entertainments. Even our carnivals are no longer carni-
valesque. This self-reflexivity, however, is tinged with sinister

implications in so far as it testifies to lives dominated by imag-
ination-stultifying imagery, increasingly confined within stereotypicality. The frightening feature of TV sitcoms is the
possibility that they accurately reflect a *de*-realized quality in the
actual lives of most of their viewers.

Postmodernism arises in part from a broadening recognition
that our culture demands newly complex relations between
work and audience that require us to redefine most of the
terms by which we have traditionally thought about art and its
functions in society. This has often produced at least a superficial popularizing in recent art that makes modernism appear
rather stiff and limited. But the popular culture that modernists sought to separate themselves from has itself undergone
startling changes: mass culture isn't what it was when moderns
scorned it, thanks in part to the effects of modernist art. A very
simple, yet I think a highly revealing, example is provided by
the career of the cartoonist, Hergé, whose Tintin books have
become popular all over the world. But the difference between
his first books, published at the beginning of the thirties, and
his last, dating from 1976, is astounding in what it suggests
about the development of "mass" audiences. Leaving aside the
very early works, such as *Tintin in the Land of the Soviets, Tintin in
the Congo,* and *Tintin in America,* one might contrast the two
1950s volumes on an expedition to the moon with the penultimate *Flight 714* (1968), which deals with space travel in an entirely different fashion. Perhaps most revealing of the changes
is the difference in the ideological struggles involved in adventures dependent on new technology. In *Destination Moon* and
Explorers on the Moon of the 1950s the political issues concern
Graustarkian machinations of amusingly stupid Syldavian and
Bordurian pseudopoliticians, but in the later work at issue is
the deception by Western industrialists of a popular liberation
movement for "Sondenesian nationalism." This development is
paralleled by others. In *Flight 714* "truth" serum is used on the
international financiers, who, instead of revealing the number
of a private Swiss bank account, recount their personal histories, vying with one another over who is nastiest—a level of
both social criticism and satire of popular plot clichés impossible in the earlier books.

Even more revealing of the penetration of imagistic self-reflexivity into popular narrative is the contrast of the last book in the series, the intricately plotted *Tintin and the Picaros,* a kind of sequel to the early, loosely episodic *Tintin and the Broken Ear,* also set principally in Latin America. *The Picaros* in effect represents individual characters, such as General Alcazar, tribal groups, (though the Rhumbabas have vanished from an increasingly sophisticated world), and the entire Latin American social scene as now *not* exotic. What had been in the 1930s picturesquely different, *other,* now has been thoroughly penetrated by a contemporary "universal" technology and its accompanying life-styles—of which the Tintin books are, of course, profoundly representative. One reason that *The Picaros* is so Fellini-like is that it is self-consciously directed at an audience assumed to be not merely familiar with, but even expert in, and unsatisfied with anything less than, an intensely self-conscious art.[14]

The significance of these tendencies is illuminated by the writings of the late Italo Calvino, whose *If on a winter's night a traveller* conveniently summarizes many of the aims and difficulties of postmodern writers in reintroducing storytelling into literature.[15] Calvino's "novel" consists of ten first chapters of different novels in different languages linked by a story of "you," a reader trying to obtain later portions of these novels (mostly of the spy and mystery variety) and in the process becoming involved romantically with another reader, Ludmilla. The "you" who is the protagonist of the novel's frame story is what might be called a blank stereotype, an ideal reader from the point of view of a publisher of rather trashy fiction, "the sort of person who, on principle, no longer expects anything of anything" (4). Hence, part of the effect of Calvino's work is to complicate, or confuse, the actual reader's identification with the second-person protagonist, thereby assuring that nothing in the book can be "simply" read: everything I read addresses me but inaccurately, as somebody I may resemble but am not. In the terminology popularized by Wayne Booth, Calvino makes explicit the "implicit" reader to the consternation of any "real" reader.

Calvino poses thereby questions about how and to what end a contemporary reader "produces" a text. Calvino assumes, I should judge, that the contemporary reader usually vulgarizes if not perverts the participative sharing of authentic storytelling. The principal Reader, "you," is presented as naïve and passive. Ludmilla, the chief object of his desire and other principal "Reader," and the strange target of the translations of the elusive Ermes Marana (who is responsible for most of the incomplete texts we read), on the contrary, seems an innocent, rather than naïve and passive, reader. Her appetite is for stories driven only by the author's "desire to narrate, to pile stories upon stories, without trying to impose a philosophy of life on you" (92). Reading stories for Ludmilla "means stripping herself of every purpose, every foregone conclusion, to be ready to catch a voice that makes itself heard when you least expect it, a voice that comes . . . from the unsaid, from what the world has not yet said of itself and does not have the words to say" (239).

The importance of Ludmilla as a reader is dramatized by her sister Lotaria, who embodies everything that is atrocious about contemporary theoretical conceptions of readers' "producing" texts. We last see Lotaria turning stories into computerized word lists—for the benefit of the censors in "a prison society which stretches all over the planet" (215). This is an appropriate conclusion for someone whom we first meet organizing a seminar to transform reading into a deconstructive assembly line: "[T]here must be some who underline the reflections of production methods, others the processes of reification, others the sublimation of repression, others the sexual semantic codes, others the metalanguages of the body" (75).

Calvino's utilization of the second-person form ought not to be isolated from the international ambience of his novel, which is set in Japan and South America as well as most parts of Europe. The point being made is that when there is in essence but one worldwide culture, instead of a variety of "local" cultures, individual identity as we have been accustomed to conceive it becomes obsolete. The real and counterfeit become indistinguishable in homogeneous technological culture because roles are necessarily generalized, not distinguished by the contingent specifics of local circumstance. At one point in Calvino's book a character tries to explain the political complexity in which she is engaged.

"I'm an infiltrator, a real revolutionary infiltrated into the ranks of the false revolutionaries. But to avoid being discovered, I have to pretend to be a counterrevolutionary infiltrated among the true revolutionaries. And, in fact, I am, inasmuch as I take orders from the police; but not from the real ones, because I report to the revolutionaries infiltrated among the counterrevolutionary infiltrators." (Calvino, 214)

This kind of infinite regress, reinforced by the novel's plot turning on a problem of false translations, and echoed by numerous episodes, such as that in which an industrialist can believe he has masterminded his own kidnapping, is possible because in the postmodern world Calvino depicts the only things accepted as significant realities are the cultural constructs of images. Where primary reality is mass-produced simulation, the possibility of any authentic individuality in its traditional form disappears. In such a world we lose all means for testing "real" and "illusory," for the categories of true and false have disappeared, as in advertisements for "genuine simulated leather" and "authentic virgin vinyl." The amusing passage I've just quoted reminds us, therefore, that in this contemporary world no otherness can exist. So even alienation has become impossible, along with uniqueness. People are now exactly what Marx defined as commodities—which differ from *objects* by having lost their specificity, their individuality, what would make them less amenable to exchange and circulation, allowing them to become simultaneously agents and objects of consumption.

Quite simply, then, how does one write a novel in a such a single-culture world of self-multiplying simulacra? A basic formal solution, Fredric Jameson has astutely suggested, is the pastiche. Although pastiche like parody mimics, Jameson argues that parody imitates uniqueness while pastiche focuses on the generic. Modernism, in emphasizing the autonomy of the work of art, was strongly attracted to parody, which makes admiring fun of stylistic singularity that might be as distinctively identifiable as a fingerprint. Parody, therefore, implies that its object is worth being parodied, that its object does possess some kind of vital identity. Pastiche in Jameson's view differs because it is a mimicry of what is regarded as worthless or dead, as in Calvino's novel spy and mystery fictions are treated as aesthetically trivial, which makes the hunger of their readers for them that much more humorous—or bothersome.[16]

Pastiche also means a hodgepodge of elements, which *If on a winter's night* certainly is, for it describes the single worldwide culture of the affluent constituted of elements taken, more or less at random, from diverse sources with minimal reference to any local or historical significance they might retain. As does Lichtenstein, Calvino engages our attention through his reproductions of reproductions, with the equally strong implication that not only the characters in the representation but also those perceiving them (these categories overlapped by Calvino through the second-person form) exist only as utterly conventional beings. The banality of the novels whose pursuit makes up the plot of *If on a winter's night* images the minds of the readers of it and them, displaying the ultimate impotence of contemporary culture, the infinite regression of absolute self-reflexivity. This self-blockage is summed up by a reflection in the private journal of Silas Flannery, writer of James Bond–like thrillers whose works now can be mechanically fabricated: "I would like to be able to write a book that is only an *incipit*, that maintains for its whole duration the potentiality of the beginning, the expectation still not focused on an object. But how could such a book be constructed? Would it break off after the first paragraph? Would the preliminaries be prolonged indefinitely?" (177).

The perpetual *incipit* of Calvino's novel is founded on an original manufacturing defect. The source of the defect is later shown to be the enormous proliferation of books being published. Even a responsible publishing firm, like a contemporary hospital that can no longer keep track of its patients, is unable through the very efficiency of its technological productive processes to print books accurately reproducing what was written in the manuscripts in which they are supposed to have originated. Simultaneously, however, there appears a compensatory aesthetic use for books that has nothing to do with what is printed in them. One of Calvino's characters creates sculptures out of the physical substance of books, sculptures admired by contemporary art critics. This is, after all, a logical culmination of the aestheticizing of fiction, its dissassociation from any ethical functions.

If on a winter's night is principally about the production of novels, production in all senses, including of course the reader's production of the meaning of a text. What Calvino demonstrates is that this apparently "creative" act of "free play" is in fact merely the ultimate form of consumerism. In a technologically sterilized society *this* production completes the commodification of literature. Calvino perceives one root of this problem as the inability of modern society to sustain genuine stories, meaningful explorations into the social potencies of polysemism. *If on a winter's night* specifically dramatizes narrative impotence, stories begun but not concluded, stories so banal, so formulaic as to be no narratives at all, only story images—as is true of the frame "story," a perfectly Lichtensteinian romance between "you" and a female reader, "Her." Narrative is by its nature specific. A story that has lost its singularity, wherein resides its power to be retold differently, is no longer a genuine story. Story's uniqueness depends at the very least on one historical particularity, that of its reception, and at the most upon intrinsic qualities making the possibility of its retelling and rereading both attractive and feasible. In contemporary society as Calvino envisions it, there is no possibility of either singularity or making anew.

The chilliest aspect of *If on a winter's night,* (published in 1979) is its comedic treatment of what George Orwell in 1948 portrayed as horror in *1984.* Calvino can be lighthearted in his presentations of rigorous social conformity, novel-writing machines, and the subsumption of people and objects by images because Orwell's Big Brother, "newspeak," and torture by secret police have been internalized through economic and political "progress." The Orwellian shadows have not, however, totally disappeared. "Nobody these days," observes one of Calvino's characters, "holds the written word in such high esteem as police states do" (235). The implication in the novel, however, is that police states are culturally "backward" countries; in "advanced" societies external policing has become unnecessary, thanks to the hegemony of Lotaria-like theorists who have implanted their ideas in the minds of readers.

What the police take seriously, of course, are "plots," those hidden schemes that alone give deep meaning to superficial contingencies. And of course such police mentality, whether in law enforcers or criticism enforcers, logically moves toward the ideal of the deepest, universal master plot, the Moriarity who is the source of all London's crime. But the paradox of narrative is that its retellability derives from its engagement with the contingent quality of contingencies. A story is a unique telling of a singular set of events. This is the keystone of great myths: only once did Eve pluck and eat the apple, only once did Coyote reach out to touch his wife. But in a world in which a universal culture of simulacra prevails, narrative must disappear into mere repetitive imagings of narrative.

These imagings are unlike what I have called narrative allusions, because the latter refer always to other precedent or possibly subsequent stories and story relations. Calvino's work reinforces the lesson provided by the painful case of Tom Wolfe: the contemporary writer has no other stories to refer to but stereotyped versions of his own story. The point and resonance of narrative interconnectivity, therefore, disappears into the mere mimickry of pastiche, what can be no more than the pretense of a story in a denarrativized culture.

Calvino, nevertheless, turns toward story; his novel is a yearning for a Ludmilla. So far as that turn is representative of a direction in postmodern literature, it suggests at least the hope that narrative impotence may not be a definitive condition. It may be that such apparently self-defeating efforts to achieve narrative is the very matrix from which a more socially meaningful narrative artistry might emerge.[17] Calvino, one notices, is obsessed with what might be called the traditional written text, and he plainly believes that "reading is solitude" (147). Indisputably true, yet need we accept that as an ultimate truth? Calvino's aesthetic, like much of the critical theorizing that substitutes for acts of criticism today, may be misleading in its displaced transcendentalism, its inverted absolutism. Studying narrative, even when it is in desperate straits, may be a good corrective to faddish pessimism, if only in reminding us that throughout most of human history storytelling has worked to join people, to enable them to share without having to sacrifice their personal identities.

Change in the arts, moreover, is one of the most complex of cultural processes. It is not enough, as one of the few thoughtful analysts of the topic has observed, "for the comprehension of *change* to focus on a single sequence of events or on a single span of time regarded as a segment of a single temporal line," because what is involved is "a plurality of processes." These form "a relativity which implies a comparison not merely of the present with the past . . . but of the present with the present, of 'what arises' with 'what still is.'"[18] Yet however difficult it may be to judge the destiny of artistic narrative in the near future, it is possible to discern some of the strengths and weaknesses in current *critical* attitudes toward storytelling.

In the first place, however distinct the break of postmodernism from its predecessor, the influence of modernism remains powerful and pervasive. Much recent art extends or intensifies modernist ambitions and modernist solutions to aesthetic problems, rather than initiating new directions, and the same may be said of criticism. The more I read contemporary commentaries on story, the more justified I consider my premise that modernism's contestation of narrative is so deeply embedded in our preconceptions as still to be easily overlooked. The potency of this bias, moreover, is increased by the fact that many continuing social developments make ever more doubtful the traditional value of storytelling.

The world is becoming with accelerating swiftness a single culture, and narrative has always been rooted in localisms—the personal, the family, the tribe, even the nation. In a unitary worldwide civilization perhaps narrative discourse has little or no significant function.[19] Walter Benjamin thought that story was obsolete in societies in which mechanical reproduction is popular as well as feasible. But even he did not foresee the extent and rapidity with which reproductive technologies would spread. In a world capable of instant electronic transmissions and rapid and inexpensive reproduction of images, for example, the patience required of a narrative audience, its willingness to let a story unfold at its own pace, may not be a valuable attribute. Most significant is the question of repetition. I have stressed that retelling and rereading of stories permit transformations that keep narrative alive because everchanging. But the exact replicability of a film, now accessible everywhere through the VCR, would seem to threaten that vitality.

Modernism anticipated and foretold the impact of such developments. The depersonalizing of the addressee, the aiming of a work of art at an audience conceived "abstractly," as aesthetic respondents, leads all too naturally into postmodernism's stereotypical art. Both modern and postmodern art usually transcend culture-specific responses, appealing directly to some hypothesized panhuman element. Such an appeal cannot—as narrative does—encourage responses that transform the originating discursive stimulus: so far as a pure essentiality has been attained, it requires no modifying. The feedback crucial to authentic narrative art, what makes it a means for changing reality, has been rendered irrelevant.[20]

Yet I argue that modernism did not merely reject narrative but significantly transformed it—and our attention to those processes of transformation might free our critical awareness from adherence to overly simplified conceptions of art's function in the twentieth-century world. We do not make adequate use of our "belated" position; we are not critical enough of modernism—not because we need to destroy its pernicious influence, but because we need to understand its complexities more precisely. If we understand that storytelling did not simply disappear with the advent of the twentieth century, we open the way to different kinds of critical understanding that might enable us to break free from constrictive theoretical conceptions. One of these, to my mind, is the relentless insistence by contemporary critics on universalism, which may be a spin-off from some of the forces driving modernist resistance to narrative. I have even felt myself compelled to make this essay accommodate such expectations by stressing principles and fundamental characteristics of narrative. I would have preferred to give more detailed descriptions of a larger number of stories, as well as attention to the often laborious reconstruction of the particular social circumstances out of which they emerged. For me, the richest pleasure in critical practice is engaging my mind and emotions with a specific work of art and straining my imagination to recover something of the world it shaped and was shaped by. That makes me old-fashioned, if not something worse. But my fortune in being reared in a family that valued storytelling, and of having associated with peoples who still esteem narrative, gives me a vantage perhaps useful for assessing the paradoxes facing contemporary critics intuitively drawn, as so many now seem to be, toward the study of narrative.

Contemporary critics need to learn to respond with more sympathy to art that expresses fiercely held beliefs and moral convictions, alien as such intensity of commitment is to most present-day commentators. Or, to reverse the recommendation, more attention to narrative as narrative might assist in developing a responsiveness that does not flinch from art that is more than "aesthetically" interesting. Throughout human history, stories have been the preferred form for expression of moral commitments. But, as I have pointed out repeatedly, narrative is a primary means for testing with concrete particularizations the benefits and disadvantages of specific ethical decisions. Narrative retellability and rereadability ensure that such examinations will not too easily crystallize into mere dogma. Perhaps, then, our criticism will not fear becoming itself more narrative in form.

In any event, we critics should give up the marginalizing of peoples who do consciously practice, or have practiced, storytelling as a significant feature of their social life. Looking more respectfully to such "primitives" might help us challenge conceptions that seem to be leading us faster and faster into the formulaic. Such attention might also provide a basis for revaluing autonomous art. The assumption that art is irrelevant both to society and to our evolution produces a criticism ever more abstractly theoretical—perhaps most transcendental when most insistent on uncovering "ideological" substrata. Conceiving storytelling as a form of social negotiation is a possible model for resisting these tendencies.

The tendency in modern art to contest narrative is the foundation of contemporary abstract, universalizing criticism. This is epitomized by Ronald Paulson's complacent description of the debt American Abstract Expressionists such as Jackson Pollock and Mark Rothko in the 1940s and 1950s owed to earlier "social realists" in America and to the Mexican muralists. Pollock, Paulson observes, "discarded the content, then the figuration, but retained the forms, which in Orozco's angry attack were the gestures of the artist as activist." This process, discernible in Rothko, Willem De Kooning, and other Abstract Expressionists, "is to subtract the subject matter . . . the social realism, social protest—and to retain the angry, independent gesture by itself. The vehicle has in this sense become the painting, and this per se makes the painting an independent object in itself."[21] "Independent" in the rather frightening sense of meaningless, since, as I pointed out in Chapter 2, gesture without content can signify anything. Paulson's indifference to the moral dimension is hardly unusual. Much recent criticism seeks to empty all art of concrete meaning by reducing it to abstract gestures described in stereotypical terms such as "socially constructed reality," "family romance," "scene of reading," "aporia," and "hegemonic discourse." These are the metacultural absolutes by which contemporary critics conceal from themselves their desperate craving to transcend the risky, meaningful plane of phenomenal complexity and change.[22]

The two major antagonists of such critical totalizing, some contemporary anthropologists and many feminists critics, have with revealing frequency focused on narrative texts. Michael Taussig, for example, is representative of those ethnologists who, dissatisfied with glib chatter about "otherness," analyze how narrative is actually shaped by specific social beliefs and attitudes even as it evaluates the character of those beliefs and attitudes. Taussig's study of the "Putomayo Terror" (the genocidal torturing and killing of native peoples in South America by colonialist rubber plantation owners at the turn of this century) is founded on the presupposition that "people delineate their world, including its large as well as its micro-scale politics, in stories and story-like creations." His analysis of the reports of travelers, residents, journalists, and official investigators such as Roger Casement demonstrate how "colonists and rubber company employees not only feared but *also themselves created through narration fearful and confusing images of savagery* by which they justified to themselves their atrocities."[23]

Less sensational but equally useful are critical analyses by feminists of conventional judgments of romance and "romantic narratives." Leslie W. Rabine, to cite but one instance, argues that against the "totalizing" picture of romance presumed by George Lukács and Paul de Man, "feminine historicity" (operative both within romance narratives and among feminist critics of romance) seeks not synthesis but "invisible *interconnections* between domestic and sociopolitical, public and private, sexual and historical spheres." This approach does not attempt to "transcend history and is not a resolution of contradictions," but, instead, "an entry into history which women have been denied." Read from this perspective of the repressed feminine, "romantic love passion, which seems to epitomize private, self-enclosed relations, leads back into the network of social contradictions."[24]

Despite these attempts at revalorizing the nature and functions of storytelling, given the increased rationalizing and technologizing of social life, accompanied by appalling growth of population, any "return" to critical appreciation of narrative must remain doubtful. And storytelling is perhaps more precariously situated today than it was with our grandparents at the beginning of the century. I am moved toward that pessimism by the recent appearance of Derek Walcott's marvelous poem *Omeros*, perhaps the most important lengthy poem in English in more than half a century.[25] Utilizing an irregularly rhyming hexameter, Walcott describes with unparalleled evocativeness the sights, the sounds, the smells, the movements, the *feel* of the sea. With lucidly vivid metaphors he depicts the lives and emotions of both simple and highly sophisticated people. His poem includes brilliant recreations of historical events, and even a dazzling story of a dreamed return to Africa by a Carib fisherman. The interplay of realistic contemporary life in the Caribbean and New England with references to Homeric and Dantean prototypes are impressively unpretentious. Walcott, never far from laughter, does not strain for "mythic" significance, evidenced by his humorously direct deployment of Caribbean forms of classical names. His Black Helen in a yellow dress and her Homeric forerunner appear naturally and easily interilluminating, aided by the poet's compassionate insight into the confusions and uncertainties of day-to-day living.

The poem's one grave weakness, unfortunately underscored by its utilization of the Homeric parallel, is its lack of sustained narrative. Within the poem Walcott tells more than one inset story skillfully—and he possesses an enviable gift for historical reconstruction. But as his very title tells us, this splendid poet cannot fully get beyond the figure of the teller to the telling. We may refer to works of Homer by his name, but their titles properly are the stories he retold. That so courageous and gifted an artist as Walcott—and one so determined to restore to the realm of poetry the truth of the real lives of marginalized peoples—is least successful as a narrative poet suggests how difficult is artistic storytelling in our time.

How we live and how narrative operates are increasingly at odds. Story originates in representations of people functionally individualized through their relationships with others. Only thus, in MacIntyre's terms, can one be both "accountable" and call· others "to account." Only such accounts of responsible agents can animate the judgmental responsibility of those to whom they are recounted. The kind of responsibility of which narrative tells echoes the storytelling situation, because inter-subjective interchange between teller and audience constitutes narrative. This is why the "meaning" of authentic story can neither be predetermined nor abstractly summarized. Story's meaning is an evolution through complicated interweavings of anticipations and retrospections generated by continuous processes of cognitive, emotional, and ethical feedback through story between audience and teller. Through retelling and rereading this play of intersubjective forces—within the story between its characters and within the telling between teller and audience—takes on the potency to change, develop, and renew, in two words, stay alive.

Stories provide opportunities for us to bring into fruitful interaction our emotional and intellectual capacities for exploring ethical problems. Most of us, I believe, frequently find ourselves in moral uncertainty, and most of us believe that the cogency and precision of our judgments will be enhanced if we confront our doubts. This is what the display texts that are stories enable us to do without depending solely on dogmatic presuppositions and unchallenged prejudices. Storytelling is a social transaction requiring both in telling and receiving actively individualized participation; it modifies or reinforces received wisdom and traditional modes of behavior and belief by engaging our imaginations in an account of a singular sequence of events. From the "bewilderment," to use James's term, of thus confronting specific contingencies we may develop a skill for eliciting meaning from unexpected experience and for altering circumstances that would seem to control our destiny, even while defining the limits of our present effectiveness in both our practical or moral actions.

It seems to me, consequently, that recent critics who insist that there is no absolute truth ought to welcome renewed attention to the favored literary form of peoples whose fondness

for narrative testifies to their readiness to accept the precious-
ness of provisional modes of understanding and judging. Such
welcoming, however, would require that we bring home to our
hearts what we obscure with lip service: human beings are the
creations of particularized cultures they have themselves made,
primarily through the tool of a singular language. Narrative
teaches us that the thousands of different human languages are
equally valuable because all can polysemously sustain what is
most wonderful on this remarkable planet—and therefore are
never properly deployed to promote either metaphysical despair or moral nihilism.

Even today, most of us still tell stories to our children. The
deepest purpose of this book has been to induce readers to consider why we do that—thereby to suggest that storytelling may
be the best use to which we can put any language.

The Stories

COYOTE AND THE SHADOW PEOPLE

Coyote and his wife were dwelling there. His wife became ill. She died. Then Coyote became very, very lonely. He did nothing but weep for his wife. There the death spirit came to him and said, "Coyote, do you pine for your wife?"—"Yes, friend, I long for her. . . ." replied Coyote. "I could take you to the place where your wife has gone, but, I tell you, you must do everything just exactly as I say; not once are you to disregard my commands and do something else."—"Yes," replied Coyote, "yes, friend, and what else could I do? I will do everything you say." Then the ghost told him, "Yes. Now let us go." Coyote added, "Yes, let it be so that we are going."

They went. There he said to Coyote again, "You must do whatever I say. Do not disobey."—"Yes, yes, friend. I have been pining so deeply, and why should I not heed you?" Coyote could not see the spirit *clearly*. He appeared to be only a shadow. They started and went along over a plain. "Oh, there are many horses; it looks like a round-up," exclaimed the ghost. "Yes," replied Coyote, though he really saw none, "yes, there are many horses."

They had arrived now near the place of the dead. The ghost knew that Coyote could see nothing but he said, "Oh look, such quantities of service berries! Let us pick some to eat. Now when you see me reach up you too will reach up and when I bend the

Archie Phinney, *Nez Percé Texts*, vol. 25 of *Columbia University Contributions to Anthropology* (New York: Columbia University Press, 1934), 281–285.

limb down you too will pull your hands down."—"Yes," Coyote said to him, "so be it, thus I will do." The ghost reached up and bent the branch down and Coyote did the same. Although he could see no berries he imitated the ghost in putting his hand to and from his mouth in the manner of eating. Thus they picked and ate berries. Coyote watched him carefully and imitated every action. When the ghost would put his hand into his mouth Coyote would do the same. "Such good service berries these are," commented the ghost. "Yes, friend, it is good that we have found them," agreed Coyote. "Now let us go." And they went on.

"We are about to arrive," the ghost told him. "There is a long, very, very long lodge. Your wife is in there somewhere. Just wait and let me ask someone." In a little while the ghost returned and said to Coyote, "Yes, they have told me where your wife is. We are coming to a door through which we will enter. You will do in every way exactly what you see me do. I will take hold of the door flap, raise it up, and bending low, will enter. Then you too will take hold of the doorflap and do the same." They proceeded now in this manner to enter.

It happened that Coyote's wife was sitting right near the entrance. The ghost said to Coyote, "Sit here beside your wife." They both sat. The ghost added, "Your wife is now going to prepare food for us." Coyote could see nothing, except that he was sitting there on an open prairie where nothing was in sight; yet he could feel the presence of the shadow. "Now she has prepared our food. Let us eat." The ghost reached down and then brought his hand to his mouth. Coyote could see nothing but the prairie dust. They ate. Coyote imitated all the movements of his companion. When they had finished and the woman had apparently put the food away, the ghost said to Coyote, "You stay here. I must go around to see some people."

He went out but returned soon. "Here we have conditions different from those you have in the land of the living. When it gets dark here it has dawned in your land and when it dawns for us it is growing dark for you." And now it began to grow dark and Coyote seemed to hear people whispering, talking in faint tones, all around him. Then darkness set in. Oh, Coyote saw many fires in a long-house. He saw that he was in a very, very large lodge and there were many fires burning. He saw the various people. They seemed to have shadow-like forms but he was able to recognize different persons. He saw his wife sitting by his side.

He was overjoyed, and he joyfully greeted all his old friends who had died long ago. How happy he was! He would march down the aisles between the fires, going here and there, and talk with the people. He did this throughout the night. Now he could see the doorway through which he and his friend had entered. At last it began to dawn and his friend came to him and said, "Coyote, our night is falling and in a little while you will not see us. But you must stay right here. Do not go anywhere at all. Stay right here and then in the evening you will see all these people again."—"Yes, friend. Where could I possibly go? I will spend the day here."

The dawn came and Coyote found himself alone sitting there in the middle of a prairie. He spent the day there, just dying from the heat, parching from the heat, thirsting from the heat. Coyote stayed here several days. He would suffer through the day, but always at night he would make merry in the great lodge.

One day his ghost came to him and said, "Tomorrow you will go home. You will take you wife with you."—"Yes, friend, but I like it here so much, I am having a good time and I should like to remain here."—"Yes," the ghost replied; "nevertheless you will go tomorrow, and you must guard against your inclination to do foolish things. Do not yield to any queer notions. I will advise you now what you are to do. There are five mountains. You will travel for five days. Your wife will be with you but you must never, never touch her. Do not let any strange impulses possess you. You may talk to her but never touch her. Only after you have crossed and descended from the fifth mountain you may do whatever you like."—"Yes, friend," replied Coyote.

When dawn came again Coyote and his wife started. At first it seemed to him as if he were going alone, yet he was dimly aware of his wife's presence as she walked along behind. They crossed one mountain, and, now, Coyote could feel more definitely the presence of his wife; like a shadow she seemed. They went on and crossed the second mountain. They camped at night at the foot of each mountain. They had a little conical lodge which they would set up each time. Coyote's wife would sit on one side of the fire and he on the other. Her form appeared clearer and clearer.

The death spirit, who had sent them, now began to count the days and to figure the distance Coyote and his wife had covered. "I hope that he will do everything right and take his wife through to the world beyond," he kept saying to himself.

Here Coyote and his wife were spending their last night, their fourth camping, and on the morrow she would again assume fully the character of a living person. They were camping for the last time and Coyote could see her very clearly as if she were a real person who sat opposite him. He could see her face and body very clearly, but only looked and dared not touch her.

But suddenly a joyous impulse seized him; the joy of having his wife again overwhelmed him. He jumped to his feet, and rushed over to embrace her. His wife cried out, "Stop! Stop! Coyote! Do not touch me. Stop!" Her warning had no effect. Coyote rushed over to his wife and just as he touched her body she vanished. She disappeared—returned to the shadow-land.

When the death-spirit learned of Coyote's folly he became deeply angry. "You inveterate doer of this kind of thing! I told you not to do anything foolish. You, Coyote, were about to establish the practice of returning from death. Only a short time away the human race is coming, but you have spoiled everything and established for them death as it is."

Here Coyote wept and wept. He decided, "Tomorrow I shall return to see them again." He started back the following morning and as he went along he began to recognize the places where he and his spirit friend had passed before. He found the place where the ghost had seen the herd of horses, and now he began to do the same things they had done on their way to the shadow-land."Oh, look at the horses; it looks like a round-up." He went on until he came to the place where the ghost had found the service berries. "Oh, such choice service berries! Let us pick and eat some." He went through the motions of picking and eating berries.

He went on and finally came to the place where the lodge had stood. He said to himself, "Now when I take hold of the door flap and raise it up you must do the same." Coyote remembered all the little things his friend had done. He saw the spot where he had sat before. He went there, sat down, and said, "Now, your wife has brought us food. Let us eat." He went through the motions of eating again. Darkness fell, and now Coyote listened for the voices, and he looked all around, he looked here and there, but nothing appeared. Coyote sat there in the middle of the prairie. He sat there all night but the lodge didn't appear again nor did the ghost ever return to him.

ORPHEUS AND EURYDICE

Thence through the boundless air Hymen, clad in a saffron mantle, departed and took his way to the country of the Ciconians, and was summoned by the voice of Orpheus, though all in vain. He was present, it is true; but he brought neither the hallowed words, nor joyous faces, nor lucky omen. The torch also which he held kept sputtering and filled the eyes with smoke, nor would it catch fire for any brandishing. The outcome of the wedding was worse than the beginning; for while the bride was strolling through the grass with a group of naiads in attendance, she fell dead, smitten in the ankle by a serpent's tooth. When the bard of Rhodope had mourned her to the full in the upper world, that he might try the shades as well he dared to go down to the Stygian world through the gate of Taenarus. And through the unsubstantial throngs and the ghosts who had received burial, he came to Persephone and him who rules those unlovely realms, lord of the shades. Then, singing to the music of his lyre, he said: "O ye divinities who rule the world which lies beneath the earth, to which we all fall back who are born mortal, if it is lawful and you permit me to lay aside all false and doubtful speech and tell the simple truth: I have not come down hither to see dark Tartara, nor yet to bind the three necks of Medusa's monstrous offspring, rough with serpents. The cause of my journey is my wife, into whose body a trodden serpent shot his poison and so snatched away her budding years. I have desired strength to endure, and I will not deny that I have tried to bear it. But Love has overcome me, a god well-known in the upper world, but whether here or not I do not know; and

Ovid, *Metamorphoses*, translated by Frank Justus Miller, 2 vols. (Cambridge, Mass.: Harvard University Press, Loeb Classical Library, 1916), 2:64–69.

yet I surmise that he is known here as well, and if the story of
that old-time ravishment is not false, you too, were joined by
love. By these fearsome places, by this huge void and these vast
and silent realms, I beg of you unravel the fates of my Eu-
rydice, too quickly run. We are in all things due to you, and
though we tarry on earth a little while, slow or swift we speed to
one abode. Hither we all make our way; this is our final home;
yours is the longest sway over the human race. She also shall be
yours to rule when of ripe age she shall have lived out her allot-
ted years. I ask the enjoyment of her as a boon; but if the fates
deny this privilege for my wife, I am resolved not to return.
Rejoice in the death of two."

As he spoke thus, accompanying his words with the music of
his lyre, the bloodless spirits wept; Tantalus did not catch at the
fleeing wave; Ixion's wheel stopped in wonder; the vultures did
not pluck at the liver [of Tityus]; the Belides rested from their
urns, and thou, O Sisyphus, didst sit upon thy stone. Then first,
tradition says, conquered by the song, the cheeks of the Eu-
menides were wet with tears; nor could the queen nor he who
rules the lower world refuse the suppliant. They called Eu-
rydice. She was among the new shades and came with steps
halting from her wound. Orpheus, the Thracian, then received
his wife and with her this condition, that he should not turn his
eyes backward until he had gone forth from the valley of
Avernus, or else the gift would be in vain. They took the up-
sloping path through places of utter silence, a steep path, in-
distinct and clouded in pitchy darkness. And now they were
nearing the margin of the upper earth, when he, afraid that she
might fail him, eager for sight of her, turned back his longing
eyes; and instantly she slipped into the depths. He stretched
out his arms, eager to catch her or to feel her clasp; but, un-
happy one, he clasped nothing but the yielding air. And now,
dying a second time, she made no complaint against her husband; for of what could she complain save that she was beloved? She spake one last "farewell" which scarcely reached her
husband's ears, and fell back again to the place whence she had
come.

By his wife's double death Orpheus was stunned. . . . Orpheus prayed and wished in vain to cross the Styx a second
time, but the keeper drove him back. Seven days he sat there on

the bank in filthy rags and with no taste of food. Care, anguish of soul, and tears were his nourishment. Complaining that the gods of Erebus were cruel, he betook himself to high Rhodope and wind-swept Haemus.

Three times had the sun finished the year and come to wattery Pisces; and Orpheus had shunned all love of womankind, whether because of his ill success in love, or whether he had given his troth once for all. Still, many women felt a passion for the bard; many grieved for their love repulsed. He set the example for the people of Thrace of giving his love to tender boys, and enjoying the springtime and first flower of their youth.

RAW-GUMS AND WHITE-OWL WOMAN

There was a camp-circle near the river. The ground was covered with snow and there prevailed sharp winds.

In a family there was a young baby just born. Both parents were very fond of the new baby. As is the custom, this baby was nicely wrapped up with buffalo chips, remnants of buffalo hide and other pieces of skin of animals.

The young baby was growing fast and was plump, and at times very noisy, especially in the fore part of the night. Of course the parents would do all they could to calm him, but he would cry freely until perfectly exhausted and then go to sleep. Early in the morning, when the old folks got up, they saw their baby nearly out of his cradle, but still sound asleep. "Well, well; I am so surprised to see our baby so lively. Surely he is doing well and you can see that he has tried to get out," said the wife, smiling as she began to unwrap him. The child was gentle of disposition during the day and slept most of the time. When the night came on, the mother again wrapped the baby as usual and placed him to sleep. Finally, the parents retired, lying on each side of their child.

Some time during the night this child got out of his cradle

Traditions of the Arapaho, compiled and edited by George A. Dorsey and A. L. Kroeber, vol. 81 of *Field Columbia Museum Publications,* Anthropology Series no. 5 (Chicago, 1903), 231–236.

and wandered off. Towards dawn he would come back to his cradle without disturbing his parents. In the morning when the parents got up again they saw their child nearly out of the cradle, but still sound asleep. "Oh! my dear child is so active and thriving. Just look at his broad breast and arms," said the wife, as she at this time started the fire. "Yes, he is quite a boy now," said the husband. The young baby was still asleep. Late in the day he awoke and began to cry, but closed his lips tightly. After the mother had unwrapped him he moved his hands and feet continually and gazed out of the top of the tipi into the deep atmosphere. Early at night the mother again wrapped the child comfortably and placed it to sleep. After the parents had spent some time chatting and telling stories they both retired.

After they had gone to sleep the baby got out of his cradle and wandered off. Again, in the morning, they found it partly in the cradle, still sound asleep.

Before leaving their breakfast they heard across the camp-circle much weeping and wondered. Another chief had died early in the morning.

Since this baby was born frequent deaths occurred at night among the good classes of people. The people began to wonder at it, and prayed for the discontinuance of lamentations. During the day this young baby was exceedingly joyful, but closed his lips most of the time. The parents began to suspect the child at this time, because he would be sleeping yet, when people were stirring about. They decided to watch him during the night, but somehow they could not keep awake.

The next night the mother wrapped the baby and placed it to sleep. Both the father and the mother lay on each side of their child, so as to find out its strange ways. For a long time they kept awake, watching their child. Towards midnight they went to sleep; the young child, hearing his parents snoring away, worked himself gradually out of his cradle and wandered off. In the morning when the parents go up this young baby was snoring with elevated head and mouth closed.

While they were eating their breakfast, and occasionally glancing at the child, the mother saw him open his mouth, and she saw in his teeth fresh morsels of human flesh. "Say, man, turn and look at those teeth with morsels of human flesh. There is the identical person who kills those chiefs. The baby, though human in form, must be a mystery," said the mother to her husband. After the mother unwrapped the child it began to stretch itself and work its limbs all day long. Of course he would go to sleep at intervals.

At this time the parents both slept during the day, in order to find out the strange disposition of the child. Night came and the mother wrapped the baby rather tightly and placed it in the center of the bed to sleep. When all the people had gone to sleep and all the lights in the camp were out, the parents pretended to go to sleep, laying on each side of their child. Late in the night this young baby, Raw-Gums, woke up and fretted and cried loudly, but these parents both snored. Raw-Gums, believing they were both sound asleep, went his way, slowly leaving the cradle. At times he would look to see if they were really sound asleep. Raw-Gums then took his pieced buffalo robe and went out toward a chief's tipi. This chief was the only surviving ruler of the tribe, and there was much lamentation among the people on account of the recent losses.

Shortly after Raw-Gums had gone, the parents peeped through the breastpin holes of their tipi and watched their child. "Just look at him, will you? He is such a mysterious being, and we have got to do something to prevent him from doing his wrong deeds," said the wife with a deep breath. "Well, yes, we shall plan to get rid of him soon, before he kills any more," said the husband. Raw-Gums walked briskly to the chief's tipi and entered it. At this time of night there was a deep calm in the camp; even the dogs were sound asleep. The parents watched the child closely until he came out, carrying the chief in his arms toward the river. "Say, look at him, with that big man in his arms!" said the wife. "Yes, I think he is a dreadful being; watch him closely, to see what he will do with the man," said the husband.

Raw-Gums ate this chief's flesh and left only the bones. How Raw-Gums killed the chiefs was a mystery. The parents saw him climbing the cottonwood snag, which had square edges at the top, and drop the remnant of the chief into the body of the snag. This snag was hollow from top to bottom. After they had seen what their child was doing at that time of night, they both went to sleep. About twilight Raw-Gums went back to the tipi and entered. Walking slowly toward the bed, and breathing easily, he managed to get back to his cradle without disturbing the parents; but they both heard him entering the tipi, and lay awake.

After the parents had noticed the child's deed with the chief, they were so afraid that they slept in bed watching the child for fear of being injured. Just as soon as the sun had risen, they got up from bed, and the wife made the fire.

"While the child is still sleeping, please boil enough beef this morning and clean out the tipi and spread some mats for seats," said the husband to his wife. So his wife hurried in preparing the food, and soon got it ready. Raw-Gums was still sleeping, all wrapped up, when the invitation was announced to the men to assemble in this tipi. When the men had seated themselves they were somewhat gloomy in spirits, because another chief had recently died. This invitation was an unusual thing, because in the camp they were still mourning.

"Well, young men, I have this day called you together in order to decide on the best plan to get rid of this child. Our chiefs have been taken away by this cruel child. How he kills them is a mystery. But we have good proof, for we saw pieces of human flesh remaining in his teeth. Until lately, while he has slept, his mouth has always been closed, but yesterday, while we were eating our breakfast, my wife called me to look at his teeth, and to my surprise I saw that some time he had eaten human flesh. Then my wife and I slept all day and watched him last night until he got out of his cradle and went to that chief's tipi. After he had done some act inside, he came out, carrying the remnant of the man to the river. Reaching a cottonwood snag, he climbed it with the body and dropped the body in the hole in the snag. When we both saw him doing this we began to be afraid of him. Now, since you men are supposed to correct the evils and suppress disorder and violence in the tribe and camp-circle, I want you to consider and devise a plan to get rid of this cannibal child," said the husband.

After the man had informed the men who had killed the chiefs, they were very much amazed and said nothing for some time. Finally they left it all entirely with the father, and told him to punish his child in the best way. So after the men had eaten the feast provided and had gone back to their respective tipis in despair, the father told his wife to provide him with fat from the tripe and unwrap the child. Without much conversation with his wife, in order to prevent the child from knowing, he then carefully wrapped this baby with fat, and with all his might threw it out of doors, and at the same time he called the dogs to plunge for it.

When Raw-Gums lighted on the ground, he became a young man, wearing his remnant buffalo robe, and began to dance around the circle, singing thus: "A skeleton! A skeleton!"

When the bereaved families heard about Raw-Gums's conduct and the disposition of the chiefs' bodies, they went to the cottonwood and cut it down. At the foot of this hollow snag they found the skeletons of their chiefs. The people, seeing that Raw-Gums was an extraordinary man, and on account of the recent mourning among the people, broke camp and left the locality.

When the people had deserted the place, an old woman, White-Owl Woman, came to the place. "Well, I am so glad to see you; did you see me coming?" said White-Owl Woman. "Yes, I am enjoying myself on this old camp-ground," said Raw-Gums. "Let us challenge each other to an exhibition of power. We will erect a blue stem (grass) and burn it at the bottom. If this blade of grass falls toward you, then you will have to seek for good food," said old White-Owl Woman. "All right, I am up to all kinds of fun," said Raw-Gums. So old White-Owl Woman made the fire and staked the blue stem and started it to burn at the bottom. The blue stem burned and fell toward Raw-Gums. He then at once got up and went to the deserted camping place and brought in a good dried beef, with some tenderloin fat and gave it to old White-Owl Woman, who ate it. After she had eaten the beef, she staked another blue stem by the fire and started to burn it, and it fell toward her. She then got up and went to the deserted place, and in a short time brought in tenderloin and dried beef with thick fat, and gave it to Raw-Gums, who at once ate it. Again she staked a blue stem by the fire and it burned at the bottom, falling towards the young man. Raw-Gums then got up and went away to a deserted place and soon brought in a nice fat roll of pemmican, mixed with berries, and gave it to old White-Owl Woman, who at once ate it. "You are a good one, grandchild," said old White-Owl Woman, who at the same time broke off another blue stem, staked it and burned it at the bottom. This stem fell toward old White-Owl Woman. "Well, I cannot help it, the blue stem burned and fell over to me. So I have to go out and provide the food," said she. So she went about the deserted places and soon brought in a delicious roll of pemmican, mixed with berries, and delivered it to Raw-Gums. Raw-Gums received it and ate it with much relish.

"Now, dear grandchild, I shall ask some more questions, and if you can answer them I then shall consider that you are a powerful man with intelligence. In the first place, can you tell me what is the most essential article?" said old White-Owl Woman. "Well, there is only one article which I consider to be essential for all purposes, and that is a moccasin," sad Raw-Gums. "That is very good, dear grandchild," said old White-Owl Woman. Raw-Gums was impatient. "Say, dear grandchild, what is it that never gets tired motioning people to come over?" said White-Owl Woman hastily. "Let me see—oh! It is the ear-flaps of the tipi that wave people to come," said Raw-Gums, clearing his throat. "Now, can you tell me what it is that never gets tired of standing in an upright position, and is very attentive on all occasions?" said old White-Owl Woman. "Well, old woman, I cannot think of any but tipi pins, and they never get tired of listening, and always are waiting to hear more," said Raw-Gums. "Well, dear grandchild, what is it that has two paths?" "Ha! Ha! It is the nose; there is no other thing that bears two holes," said Raw-Gums.

"Which travels fastest?" said old White-Owl Woman lazily. "It is the brain (thought) that travels swiftly and at a great distance," said Raw-Gums. "What animal is harmless to all?" said old White-Owl Woman. "Well, the most harmless creature is a rabbit, and its color signifies purity and benevolence," said Raw-Gums, with a louder voice. "Which of the two hands is the most useful?" asked old White-Owl Woman. "Let me see—oh, yes, it is the left hand, because it is harmless, pure and holy," said Raw-Gums.

"Well, grandchild, you have answered my questions readily, and so this day is a glory to you. You may now strike my head at the top," said old White-Owl Woman, stooping down. Raw-Gums then struck her head with a stone sledge and burst her skull, and so scattered the brains, which was the snow, melting away gradually. That is why there is a season of vegetation.

BLOOD-CLOT BOY

1. A rabbit lived happily until a bear and his young came and took possession of his home, driving him out. So he was obliged to dwell in a makeshift hut near by. 2. And each morning the bear stood outside his door and said, "You Rabbit with the ragged muzzle, come out. Your buffalo-surround is full." Then Rabbit came out with his magic arrow and, with one shot, sent it piercing through each buffalo in turn till all were killed. Then the bear would rush up with his young, and take all the meat home. 3. They never gave the rabbit any meat, and the result was that he was now very thin. Once again they were cutting up the meat; so he came and stood to one side, but before he even asked for a piece, they ordered him off, so he turned to leave. Somewhat removed from the scene was a blood clot on the ground. So, as he went over it, he pretended to stumble, and picked it up, thrusting it under his belt. 4. And the bear called out, "Hey, there, you worthless wretch, you aren't taking anything, are you?" So the rabbit answered, "No, I only stagger because I am weak from hunger." Then he came home. Immediately he made a sweat-bath over the blood clot. He was busy pouring water over the hot stones when someone within heaved a deep sigh, and then said, "Whoever you are who are thus kind, open the door for me." So he opened the door, and a young man, red (from the heat), stepped outside. Rabbit was very happy. 5. "Oh, would that my grandson had such and such things," he would say, and instantly they would appear, so that all in the same day, he had everything desirable. Everything he wished for him was his. But Rabbit couldn't offer him food, for he had none. Then Blood-Clot Boy said, "Grandfather, how is it that you starve while a rich man lives near by?" So Rabbit related everything to him. 6. "Alas, grandson, what do you mean? Why, the fact is that it is I who shoot all the game, and then when I am through, the bear comes with his young and they take the meat all away. They always call me by saying, 'Say, you Rabbit with the ragged muzzle, come out; your surround is full.' So I come out, and do the shooting for them." On hearing this, Blood-Clot Boy was very angry. He took a piece of ash and

Ella Deloria, *Dakota Texts*, vol. 14 of *American Ethnological Society Publications* (Washington, D.C., 1932), 113–120.

burned it here and there, and made a club, and sat ready with it. 7. As usual, the bear stood outside very early in the morning and, "Hey, you Rabbit with the ragged muzzle, come on out; your surround is full," he said, so he answered as his grandson had taught him, "*Hoh!* Get out, what are you talking about? I suppose you'll be claiming all the meat again!" And he didn't come out. The angry bear came in, thinking to force him out, but Blood-Clot Boy was ready for him, and killed him with one blow of his club. 8. Then he sent his grandfather to the bear's wife, telling him what to say. He said, "Bear sends for extra help." And the wife called out, "Is that so? How many is he carrying?"—"He is carrying two buffaloes."—"That's funny. I never knew him to carry so few!" 9. So the rabbit tried again. "He is carrying three buffaloes," he said. "How funny. He used to carry more than that," she said. So Rabbit said, "He is carrying four buffaloes." And this time the wife said, "It that so? Well, wait, then." And she started to come out of the tipi but Blood-Clot Boy was ready for her and the moment her head appeared, he struck her with a resounding blow and killed her. 10. Then he entered the bear's home, and found all the bear children sitting in a circle, eating their meal. So he said to them, "Now, if anyone here has been kind to my grandfather, let him say, I," and they all yelled, "I." And then one said, "Do they think that, simply by saying the world 'I,' they will be spared? He who was kind to your grandfather sits over here!" he said. And in the corner they saw him sitting, the very youngest little bear wearing his very brown coat. 11. The rabbit spoke up, "Grandson, he speaks true. Ever so often, he dragged a piece of meat over to me, and pushed it with his snout into my hut." So Blood-Clot Boy said, "In that case, step outside; you shall live." After he had gone out, the boy killed all the other cubs. The rabbit now moved into his old home and as he still had his magic arrow, he provided meat in abundance so that the three, including the little bear, lived without want.

12. And then one day Blood-Clot Boy declared his plans. "Grandfather, in what direction do the people live?" he asked; so he told him they lived in the west. Then he said he planned to go there on a visit. The rabbit advised against it vigorously. "No, grandson, I dread it for you. Something very deceptive lives on the way." But that made him all the more eager to be

off, and he started. 13. He hadn't gone far before he saw a man shooting at something. "Ah! This must be what grandfather warned me of as not to be trusted," he thought, and tried to go around him, but he called, "My younger brother, come over here and shoot this for me before you go."—"Impossible! I am on a rush trip, I haven't time to loiter and shoot your game for you!" he said. 14. But he begged so earnestly that he persuaded the boy to turn and come back to him. The boy sent an arrow which pierced the bird; and then he started to go on. But he called again, "That's a fine arrow, younger brother; who would discard it this way?" He shouted back, "Well then, take it and own it," and would go on, but, "My younger brother, please climb the tree and get it for me," he pleaded; so, as the best way to get rid of him, the boy came and prepared to climb the tree. 15. But the man said again, "My younger brother, you better take off your clothes. They are very beautiful; it would be a pity to tear them on the branches." With that he persuaded the boy further, until he removed all his clothes and started to climb the tree in his naked state. He got the arrow and was coming down when he heard the one below saying something under his breath. "Are you saying something?" he called out. "I just said, Hurry down, brother!" he answered. 16. So, "Oh, all right!" he called and continued down. Then, just as he was about to step to the ground, the man called in a great voice, "Stick to the tree!" And at once Blood-Clot Boy became glued to the tree. It was Ikto who had thus deceived him, and now he hurriedly dressed himself in the boy's finery and flung his old garments at him saying, "There, Blood-Clot Boy, put those on!" Then he went towards the village. 17. In that village was a young woman, the eldest child of her parents, and greatly loved by them. "She-dwells-within-the-Circle" was what her name meant. He was going to her. As soon as he entered the tribal camp, the cry went up, "Blood-Clot Boy comes on a journey, and C⁽ᶜ⁾oka'p T⁽ᶜ⁾i'wį is the one he comes for!" The parents immediately gave their daughter to him and placed their tipi within the circle. So Ikto, all in a day, settled into the rôle of the son-in-law. 18. The next morning he proceeded to demonstrate his supernatural powers. "Let all the young men remove the hair from a buffalo-hide and scatter it about in the bend of the river, beyond the hill." It was done accordingly. Next day he told them to send scouts to see the result. They went; but came back to report that nothing had happened. 19. Now, *C̓oka'p T̓̓i'wį* had a young sister who stayed around her tipi. She didn't like her around, and ordered her off each time, saying, "Go on away! I don't want her to even look upon my husband!" Finally the girl went crying into the woods and gathered firewood. There she came upon a youth, very handsome, stuck fast to a tree. He said to her, "Young girl, if you have pity, free me from this tree. Ikto has dealt thus badly with me and gone into camp leaving me to my fate." So the girl took her ax and peeled the man off from the tree; and then, sharing her blanket with him, she took him home. 20. And then he said, "Now go to the one who is living inside the circle and bring my clothes to me; Ikto has worn them long enough." So the girl stood at the door of her sister's tipi and said, "Ikto, you have worn certain clothes long enough; I have come after them for their owner." But her sister said, "Go away. I don't want you to look upon my husband!" But all the while Ikto repeated without a pause, "Hand them out, hand them out." At last then, the young woman realized that Ikto himself had duped her; so she began to cry. 21. Now Blood-Clot Boy put on his own clothes and sat looking very handsome, and said, "Let all the young men remove the hair from a buffalo-hide and scatter it about in the bend of the river beyond the hill." They did so; and the next morning when they went to see, the bend was packed with buffalo, so the people had a real killing, for this young man had true supernatural power. 22. That evening everyone took part of his killing to the council tent where men sat about and feasted and talked; and they say all Ikto took was a shoulder-piece; it was all he managed to secure (from some hunter). Soon after, Blood-Clot Boy announced that he was going home, taking with him the girl who saved him. So they made preparations. And the once-proud elder sister who had been so mean to her younger sister, now rejected Ikto and went following the girl and her young husband. 23. They in turn ordered her back, but she did not have any ears. And so they came on until they neared Blood-Clot Boy's home. The little bear who was sitting on a hilltop saw them. He had been sitting there alone, viewing the country round about. He started up, evidently having seen them, and disappeared downhill in the other direction. Breathlessly he arrived home and said, "Grandson is now returning; but he brings a woman home." 24. Immediately the rabbit, very happy, ran hopping out to meet them; and taking his grandson on his back he carried him the remainder of the way. The little bear also came to meet them, and he took the daughter-in-law on his back; but she was so heavy (for him) that he could not lift her entirely off the ground; so her feet dragged behind. As for the proud elder sister, nobody took any notice of her, so she came along behind them, and lived with them there. They kept her to take out the ashes for them. 25. That is all.

GRASSHOPPER IN LOVE WITH DEER

A man had two wives, Djahdjai (Grasshopper) and Djihens (Ant). When it came root-digging time, the two women went out every morning to dig roots, but they went in different directions; they didn't dig on the same flat.

At midday Djihens always went home with a basketful of nice white roots. Djahdjai never went home till it was getting dark, and then she had only a few roots in the bottom of her basket. Each night she took Djihens's basket and picked out all the longest and best roots, and when her husband came from hunting deer, she said: "I dug these."

The man loved Djahdjai better than he did Djihens, but Djahdjai didn't love him; she loved Wies (deer).

Each morning as soon as she got to the flat she began to dance and chirp her love song. Her song said: "Come this way, Big Head! Come this way; I want to see you!"

Wies listened, and as soon as he heard the song, he came up on the rocks and looked down on the flat. He looked all around, as if counting the trees and bushes to see that everything was right, that there was nobody around, then he went to Djahdjai.

Each evening the husband asked his wives if their moccasins were worn out. Djihens always answered: "No, I don't kick the

Jeremiah Curtin, *Myths of the Modocs* (Boston: Little, Brown, 1912), 355–58.

ground all the time and wear my moccasins out." Djahdjai always had holes in her moccasins.

Her husband scolded, and asked: "How do you wear out your moccasins so? I haven't made moccasins for Djihens since we came here."

"I can't stand still when I dig; I have to jump around and stand hard on the ground. I dig roots among the rocks, where they are long and sweet. Djihens digs on the flat, and her roots are not as long as mine, or as nice."

"Well," said the man, "I don't know how you can wear out a pair of moccasins every day. your feet eat up moccasins as stones do."

One morning, when Djahdjai started off with her basket and digging stick, Djihens thought she would watch and see where she went. So she followed her. Every little while Djahdjai turned around to find out if anybody was looking at her. Djihens was hiding in the grass; she couldn't see her. When Djahdjai got near the mountain, she stopped and began to sing her love song. The song drew Wies to the rocks. Djihens hid under the grass, so he couldn't see her. He looked all around, then he started toward Djahdjai.

The Wies people had two trails up the mountain, one for men, the other for women. Djahdjai always waited for him at the end of the men's trail.

Djihens thought: "Now I know why she comes home with an empty basket. She comes here to see Wies; she draws him to her with her love song. How nice it sounds!"

After a while Djihens crept away, went off to the flat to dig roots. The next morning she followed Djahdjai again. She listened to her love song and saw Wies come to meet her. That night she said to her husband: "Don't make new moccasins for Djahdjai; she doesn't care for you." The man didn't believe her; he thought she was jealous of Djahdjai.

Djihens always knew what he thought. She said, "If you don't believe me, go and listen to her love song." Then she told him how Djahdjai stole her roots and said she had dug them herself.

The next day, after Djihens had carried her roots home, she went to watch Djahdjai. The woman spent the whole day with Wies, then she dug a few roots and went home.

The man had been a good hunter, but after Djahdjai fell in

love with Wies, he couldn't find a deer, couldn't find even a fresh track. One day he went home early and asked Djihens: "Where does Wies come from when he comes to meet Djahdjai?"

"I don't know," said Djihens. "I see him first on the rocks. He looks around, then he comes straight down the mountain."

When Djahdjai came home and found her husband there, she said to Djihens: "Why did you leave and come to the house? I hunted a long time for you."

The man said nothing. He made believe he loved Djahdjai more than ever. But he said to Djihens: "Tomorrow I will watch her myself." The next morning Djahdjai said: "I am going to dig roots tomorrow; today I will stay home and rest." When she didn't see her husband, she asked where he had gone. Djihens said: "He can't find any deer on this side of the mountain. He is going to the other side. That is why he started so early."

Djahdjai said she was going to stay at home, but as soon as Djihens was gone, she started off toward the mountain. The man was hidden by the side of the trail Wies came on. He hunted for his most poisonous arrow and was going to shoot him. Then he thought: "No, I will just watch them today." Soon he heard Djahdjai singing. Then he saw a big man stand on the rocks and look down at her, and he was so jealous that he cried. After a while he went home.

That day Djahdjai said to Wies: "My husband hunts all the time. I am afraid he will see you."

The next morning the man got up early and went to the mountain. As he went, he talked to the mountain and to the earth; said: "Draw him toward me. You, Earth, see everything; you know everything; you know what Wies has done. I want to punish him. Draw him to me."

That day Djahdjai wanted to stay at home. She didn't know why her husband went off so early in the morning, but Djihens said: "I am sick. One of us must dig roots; you had better go." The man tracked Wies, then sat down to watch him and see where his life was. As Wies went toward the top of the mountain, the man saw that he kept his life in his neck. He shot at him. Wies ran off northeast and fell among the trees. The man found him, cut up his body, and carried home some of the flesh. Djahdjai looked up at the mountain and sang her love song; she sang a long time, but Wies didn't come. When she got home, she said to her husband: "You have killed a deer. Why don't you cook some meat for me?"

He gave her a plateful. She ate it all; she liked it. Then he said: "That was Wies's flesh. Did you like it?" The woman was scared. When she tried to run away, the man shot her through the body. The arrow went in under one arm and came out under the other; it left a hole in each side. Then he said: "Hereafter you will be nothing but a grasshopper, but your name will be what it is now, Djahdjai. I hope that in later times a man will never have such a wife as you were."

To this day grasshoppers have a hole in each side.

Notes

CHAPTER ONE
Storytelling and Modern Criticism

1. Kwame Anthony Appiah, "Is the Post- in Postmodernism the Post- in Postcolonial?" *Critical Inquiry* 17 (1991): 336–357, is very cogent on this topic. Appiah focuses on the difficulties faced by postmodern critics, who cannot legitimate "primitive art" by the "culture- and history-transcending standards" of modernism, because according to the tenets of modernism, "primitive art was to be judged by putatively *universal* aesthetic criteria" (347). As David Simpson observes:

> [I]t seems fair to say that . . . we live in a "theoretical" time. If this commitment to theory has assumed a hegemonic form . . . then it is one often characterized by an aspiration toward *totality;* something that can pronounce upon all poetry, all language, all criticism. The totalizing aspiration remains latent even within the antagonistic but still canonical celebrations of relativism, or agnosticism, of which poststructuralism provides the best-known examples. (*Wordsworth's Historical Imagination* [London: Methuen, 1987], 12.)

2. Gérard Genette, "Boundaries of Narrative," *New Literary History* 8, no. 1 (1976): 1–13, aptly observes that in the last quarter of our century it is with "shock" that we realize "the extent to which modern literature . . . made itself . . . a contestation of . . . narrative" (1). I take Genette's point to be that *only* through comprehension of this fundamental "contestation of narrative"—comprehension impossible unless we correctly understand what narrative is and to what ends it shapes itself—can we hope to grasp the common driving force in different expressions of modernism. Such a view is exactly congruent with the efforts of Hayden White (to be cited again subsequently) to define what constitutes, and what may be the significance of, the "story" in "history." Twenty years ago, J. H. Plumb wrote eloquently of the paradox of "a past that is in ruins and a proliferating world of historical studies" (*The Death of the Past* [Boston: Houghton-Mifflin, 1970], 108) to encourage recognition that beneath rather sterile debates about "history as art" and "history as science" lay the enduring fact that there are diverse stories of diverse cultures. In differ-

ent ways all these scholars urge us to recover, against the grain of currently dominant intellectual systems, sympathetic appreciation of the elemental nature of narrative and its social purposes, for without that we cannot hope to build a satisfactory historical awareness of cultural phenomena either of our own era or of other times.

3. James Phelan, *Reading Plots, Reading People* (Chicago: University of Chicago Press, 1989). My remarks on this work are also applicable to another excellent study, which in fact is complementary to Phelan's work, Peter Rabinowitz, *Before Reading: Narrative Conventions and the Politics of Interpretation* (Ithaca: Cornell University Press, 1987). Both books exemplify an encouraging trend of recent criticism to insist upon the importance of understanding the contexts of reception as determinants of literary structures.

I may observe here that a charge that much of my comment on story could apply, *mutatis mutandis,* to literature that is not narrative would not upset me. I have come to believe that story is one of the originating matrixes for literary art. But arguing for that position will require an entirely different line of research and mode of presentation from that employed in this volume. Here I will only remark on the obvious fact that hermeneutic criticism, which begins in an understanding of the history of reinterpretations, assumes as a given retelling and rereading. I do not find hermeneuticists, from Friedrich Schleiermacher to Hans-Georg Gadamer, scrutinizing narrative retellability; they take it for granted. Modernism compels us to rethink that assumption.

4. Keith H. Basso, "'Stalking with Stories': Names, Places, and Moral Narratives among the Western Apache," in *Text, Play, and Story: The Construction and Reconstruction of Self and Society,* 1983 Proceedings of the American Ethnological Society, edited by Stuart Plainer and Edward M. Bruner (Washington, D. C.: The American Ethnological Society, 1984), 19—55. Basso's essay ought to be required reading for all narratologists (who have universally overlooked it), especially for his description of the Western Apache explanations of how story enables individual "replacing of oneself," *replacing* meaning both renewing one's personality and resituating oneself within one's culture. In the light of my subsequent discrimination of narrative from conversational and scientific discourse, it is interesting that the Western Apache, like several other Native American peoples, formally distinguish "narrative," "prayer," and "ordinary talk."

5. Granted world enough and time, I should like to devote a volume to the detailed "reception contexts" of diverse narratives. A critical challenge that has long piqued me, for example, is the possibility of using the evidence of "internalized context" (how the reception situation appears within the form of a story) to enrich our comprehension of the situation in which it was "performed." We tend to overlook how much of our understanding of the context of any particular narrative is determined by the story itself, even though it is plain in some instances, such as that of the Homeric epics, that a significant proportion of what we know about the situations in which they were recited is derived from the stories themselves.

6. E. M. Forster, *Aspects of the Novel* (New York: Harcourt, Brace, 1927), 46—47; Forster consistently treats Scott as a cheerful scribbler for profit whose

appeal is to immature minds, or those whose brains have decayed. It interests me that the "simple devices" of story, in Forster's view, are unworthy of the analysis demanded by "plot," but require only "paraphrase" (54), that is, re-telling. Andrew Lewis shrewdly suggested to me that Forster might have spoken more appreciatively of stories had his culture allowed him to tell his own personal story.

7. Torgovnick provides an extended and fiery critique of the centrality of "primitivism" in modern aesthetics in *Gone Primitive: Savage Intellects and Modern Lives* (Chicago: University of Chicago Press, 1990).

8. See "Introduction to the Structural Analysis of Narrative," in Roland Barthes, *Image, Music, Text,* translated by Stephen Heath (New York: Hill and Wang, 1977), 79–124. In Chapter 5 I suggest why such use of "popular" contemporary fiction is almost guaranteed to confuse theoretical definitions of narrativity. It should be observed that Barthes's essay, though frequently cited by subsequent commentators, is seldom mentioned in the history of his intellectual development. The essay was first published in 1966 and marks, I should judge, an important effort by Barthes to break free of the most rigid structuralist influences, and its very awkwardnesses and inconsistency point toward his later more sophisticated and interesting ideas about narrative.

9. Revaluation of such prejudices is characteristic of much contemporary feminist criticism such as Ann Ardis's *New Women, New Novels: Feminism and Early Modernism* (New Brunswick: Rutgers University Press, 1990). Ardis addresses the question, "Why might it have been important for modernists *not* to acknowledge either turn-of-the-century New Women writers' experimentations with the form of the novel or the 'gate-keeping' stance of those writers' harshest critics?" (5). Among the rapidly growing body of work by feminists challenging such traditional gatekeepers to which my study is indebted are Gayatri Spivak, *In Other Worlds: Essays in Cultural Politics* (London: Methuen, 1987); Elaine Showalter, *A Literature of Their Own* (Princeton: Princeton University Press, 1977); Rachel Blau DuPlessis, *Writing Beyond the Ending: Narrative Strategies of Twentieth-Century Women Writers* (Bloomington: Indiana University Press, 1985; Patricia Meyer Spacks, *The Female Imagination* (New York: Knopf, 1975); and Nancy Armstrong, *Desire and Domestic Fiction* (London: Oxford University Press, 1987), who is especially cogent in her analysis of the "psychoanalytic fables of desire" underlying many recent narratological analyses by men. Other feminist studies of which I have made specific use, such as those of Carol Gilligan and Susan Winnett, are cited subsequently.

10. Fredric Jameson, "Postmodernism and Consumer Society," in *The Anti-Aesthetic,* edited by Hal Foster (Port Townsend, Wa.: Bay Press, 1983), 112. Another view is articulated by Gianni Vattimo, *The End of Modernity* (Oxford: Polity, 1988), who defines the modern as running from Descartes to Nietzsche, so that everything after the late nineteenth century is for him "postmodernity."

11. Andreas Huyssen, *After the Great Divide* (Bloomington: University of Indiana Press, 1986), 53–54.

12. Clement Greenberg, *The Collected Essays and Criticism,* edited by John O'Brian, 2 vols. (Chicago: University of Chicago Press, 1986), 1:9.

13. Charles Jencks, *What is Post-Modernism?* (New York: St. Martin's Press, 1986), although muddying already dirty waters with distinctions such as "late Modernism," rightly observes that "Post-modernism, like Modernism, varies within each art both in its motives and time-frame," but is in all arts best distinguished by its "double coding," that is, functioning both as "the continuation of Modernism and its transcendence" (14).

14. Susan Winnett, "Coming Unstrung: Women, Men, Narrative, and Principles of Pleasure," *PMLA* 105, no. 3 (May 1990): 505—518. Her principal target is, of course, Peter Brooks, though she cites also D. A. Miller and Robert Scholes, all of whom I refer to later in this study. Winnett builds persuasively on the earlier feminist work of Margaret Homans, *Bearing the Word: Language and Female Experience in Nineteenth-Century Women's Writing* (Chicago: University of Chicago Press, 1986); Nancy K. Miller, *Subject of Change: Reading Feminist Writing* (New York: Columbia University Press, 1988); and Marianne Hirsch, "Ideology, Form, and *Allerleihrauh:* Reflections on *Reading for the Plot,*" *Children's Literature* 14 (1986): 163—68—this last, to my mind, containing one of the most convincing demonstrations of the presence of gender-prejudice in criticism—how in the world can those male critics misperceive what is going on with spunky "All-Kinds-Of-Fur"?

Bakhtin is discussed at length in Chapter 3.

15. One of the most fascinating reports of rereading (though of course in this case by the writer considering revision) is Henry James's "Preface to the New York Edition" of *The Golden Bowl,* available in *The Art of the Novel: Critical Prefaces,* introduction by R. P. Blackmur (New York: Charles Scribner's Sons, 1934), 327—348. J. Hillis Miller has commented in detail on James's self-analysis in *The Ethics of Reading* (New York: Columbia University Press, 1987), 105—122.

16. A Marxian analysis of this phenomenon in contemporary life is to be found in Wolfgang Fritz Haug's *Critique of Commodity Aesthetics,* translated by Robert Bock, 8th ed. (Minneapolis: University of Minnesota Press, 1986); the book was originally published in German in 1971. The linkage of this commodification to the emergent independence of the "fine arts" (see note 20 below) is obvious, but no more important than the concomitant rise of consumerism.

17. The importance of J.M.W. Turner in the socioeconomic history of European art remains to be described adequately. Turner, like has contemporary Sir Walter Scott, achieved enormous financial success through "popular" sales, but, unlike Scott, Turner came from an impoverished background and had little formal education. Although he had a few rich patrons, his success was essentially professionally based, first through the support of the principal organization of painters, the Royal Society, then through tapping into a profitable consumer market for engraved reproductions. William Hogarth, of course, was his forerunner—a change in the copyright law enabling him to profit, enormously, from the sale of reproductions. Yet, Turner is the more significant figure in the rise of commodified consumerist art, for he was more a professional in the specifically modern sense, and his means of success are more directly exemplary of the peculiar interplay of "high" aesthetic purpose

and practical commercial marketing central to the history of art during the past two centuries.

18. Colin Campbell, *The Romantic Ethic and the Spirit of Modern Consumerism* (Oxford: Blackwell, 1987), 90. Campbell's book, although not entirely satisfactory, at least escapes the lecture-hall-Marxist banalities afflicting most "new historicist" discussion of these problems. Campbell, like most who have tackled this problem seriously, relies heavily on Neil McKendrick, John Brewer, and J. H. Plumb, *The Birth of a Consumer Society: The Commercialization of Eighteenth-Century England* (London: Europa Publications, 1981). In my *British Romantic Art* (Berkeley: University of California Press, 1986) I draw attention to the absolute centrality in Romantic aesthetics of art as a source of personal pleasure and some of the implications in such focus, implications further elucidated in the discussion of William Holman Hunt in Chapter 6.

19. Greenberg in his 1940 essay "Towards a Newer Laocoon" justly observes: "The dogmatism and intransigence of the 'non-objective' or 'abstract' purists of painting today cannot be dismissed as symptoms merely of a cultist attitude towards art. Purists make extravagant claims for art, because usually they value it much more than anyone else does" (*Collected Essays* 2:23).

20. The origins of this separation of the moral from the artistic are clearly identifiable in the emergence of the concept of the "fine arts" in the eighteenth century: see Paul Oskar Kristeller, "The Modern System of the Arts: A Study in the History of Aesthetics," *The Journal of the History of Ideas* 12 (1951): 496–527, and 13 (1952): 17–46.

21. Jonathan Arac, "Rhetoric and Realism, or Marxism, Deconstruction, and the Novel," in *Criticism without Boundaries*, edited by Joseph A. Buttgeig (Notre Dame: University of Notre Dame Press, 1987), 173.

CHAPTER TWO
Narrativity and Landscape Art

1. "Plastic Art and Pure Plastic Art," in *Modern Artists on Art*, edited by Robert L. Herbert (Englewood Cliffs, N.J.: Prentice-Hall, 1964), 120. The essay, which originally appeared in 1937, like all of Mondrian's writing rewards careful scrutiny. Here I notice only the emphasis on "progress" and the style of insistent superlatives. Mondrian is of peculiar relevance to my argument because of his early indebtedness to such artists as Caspar David Friedrich—for which see the important study by Robert Rosenblum, *Modern Painting and the Northern Romantic Tradition* (New York: Harper and Row, 1975), 173–194. Mondrian was, as Clement Greenberg said in his obituary, "the only artist to carry to their ultimate and inevitable conclusions those basic tendencies of recent Western painting which cubism defined and isolated" *The Collected Essays and Criticism*, edited by John O'Brian, 2 vols. [Chicago: University of Chicago Press, 1986], 2:187).

2. Wendy Steiner, *Pictures of Romance: Form against Context in Painting and Literature* (Chicago: University of Chicago Press, 1988). Subsequent refer-

ences to this work are given in the text. The principal source for Steiner's theoretical positions is Gerald Prince, two of whose essays she cites, "Narrativity," in *Axia: Davis Symposium on Literary Evaluation,* edited by Karl Menges and Daniel Rancour-Leferriere (Stuttgart: Akademischer Verlag Hans-Dieter Heinz, 1981); and "Aspects of a Grammar of Narrative," *Poetics Today* 1, no. 3 (1979): 45–52. More important than these is Prince's *Narratology: The Form and Function of Narrative* (Berlin: Mouton, 1982).

3. Jacques Derrida's most important work on visual art is probably *The Truth in Painting,* translated by Geoff Bennington and Ian McLeod (Chicago: University of Chicago Press, 1987). To my mind, even the elaborate narrative semiotics of A. J. Greimas, with its adaptations of Chomskian "deep" and "surface" structures, is weakened by its failure to value properly narrative omissions.

4. Steiner of course realizes that the repetition of figures cannot be separated from problems of sequentiality. But the problems of pictorial narrative are not easily evaded. As I have pointed out in relation to the Jonah and the Whale mosaic, knowing that one is seeing a narrative is of small help in understanding the story if one does not know which way to read it. The assumption, moreover, that a repeated figure implies temporal succession needs to be carefully specified by cultural context. Whether or not a sequence of repeated figures exists, for example, is a central issue of debate about the cave art at Lascaux and Altamira, to cite one well-known instance.

5. See Irene J. Winter's fascinating essay, "After the Battle Is Over: The *Stele of the Vultures* and the Beginning of Historical Narrative in the Art of the Ancient Near East," in *Pictorial Narrative in Antiquity and the Middle Ages,* edited by Herbert L. Kessler and Marianna Shreve Simpson (Washington, D.C.: National Gallery of Art, 1985), 11–34. To me, Winter is persuasive that the stele was probably sited in a temple as a formalized "treaty" monument, but its utilization as an actual boundary marker cannot definitively be dismissed.

6. Rosalind Krauss, "Sculpture in an Expanded Field," in *The Anti-Aesthetic,* edited by Hal Foster (Port Townsend, Wa.: Bay Press, 1983), 35.

7. Richard Brilliant, *Visual Narrative: Storytelling in Etruscan and Roman Art* (Ithaca: Cornell University Press, 1984), 90–123, extensively analyzes Trajan's Column and asserts its significance. Marilyn Aronberg Lavin, "Computers and Art History: Piero della Francesca and the Problem of Visual Order," *New Literary History* 20, no. 2 (1989): 483–504, provides a systematic study of fresco disposition, noting "that the majority of cycles, far from following what might be considered normal and consecutive reading traced paths . . . that varied greatly . . . a number of repeated patterns that, once observed, were obvious and yet did not seem to be known to art historians" 494–495). What I call the "ploughed field" order, Lavin more learnedly terms "boustrophedon," but refers to that pattern slightly misleadingly as "zig-zag," since the "turns" in fresco cycles (or ox-ploughed fields) are rarely sharp.

8. On the Arena Chapel frescoes one may consult the collection of essays *Giotto: The Arena Chapel Frescoes,* edited by J. Stubblebine (New York: W. W. Norton, 1969), which reprints what remains the best study of the vertical relation of the frescoes, that of M. A. Alpatoff, "The Parallelism of Giotto's Paduan Frescoes," which originally appeared in *The Art Bulletin* 29 (1947): 149–159. An older study, that of Friedrich Rintelen, *Giotto und die Giotto-*

Apokryphen, 2d ed. (Basel: Benno Schwabe, 1923) 11–89, discusses the Arena Chapel in terms relevant to my observations. There is an excellent essay by Hans Belting, "The New Role of Narrative in Public Painting of the *Trecento: Historia* and Allegory," in Kessler and Simpson's *Pictorial Narrative,* 151–170, with a useful bibliography (see note 5). Bruce Cole's *Giotto and Florentine Painting 1280–1375* (New York: Harper and Row, 1976) is unpretentious but based on a thorough command of the scholarship and lucid in its presentation of Giotto's achievements and the problems posed by his art.

9. Hugh Witemeyer makes the claim for Hogarth's originality in *George Eliot and the Visual Arts* (New Haven: Yale University Press, 1979), 120. It is important that Hogarth aimed at a "mass" audience—his substantial income from the series derived from inexpensive reproductions. In his work one sees the union of narrative and the "popular" that some modernists decried. In *British Romantic Art* (Berkeley: University of California Press, 1986), I discuss Hogarth's awareness of the stories he was unable to tell through his art (see especially Chapter 1), a visual illustration of what D. A. Miller has discussed illuminatingly as the "unnarratable" in *Narrative and Its Discontents* (Princeton: Princeton University Press, 1981). Curiosity about "what will happen next" is E. M. Forster's characterization of the "primitive" appeal of story, also discussed in Chapter 1.

10. Michael Riffaterre in his elegant *Fictional Truth* (Baltimore: Johns Hopkins University Press, 1990), analyzes one of the most interesting of these disjunctive features, what he calls a "subtext" (see especially his third chapter). By *subtext* Riffaterre refers to a dispersed unit of recurrent meaning, not a theme or a subject, that refers metalinguistically to the whole novel in which it appears, or to some aspect of the whole novel's significance.

11. "Causality," Hannah Arendt caustically observed, "is an altogether alien and falsifying category in the historical sciences" ("Understanding and Politics," *Parisan Review* 20, no. 4 [1953]: 388). On a less philosophical level, Seymour Chatman, *Story and Discourse: Narrative Structure in Fiction and Film* (Ithaca: Cornell University Press, 1978) provocatively poses a problem of the relation of causality and sequentiality in story: "Is the relation between sequence and causality one of necessity or probability?" (47). Recently Philip J. M. Sturgess, "A Logic of Narrativity," *New Literary History* 20, no. 3 (1989): 763–784, attempted an elaborate development of Chatman's question by utilizing some Bakhtinian concepts.

12. Ann Bermingham, *Landscape and Ideology: The English Rustic Tradition, 1740–1860* (Berkeley: University of California Press, 1986), 96.

13. Cited by Lawrence Gowing, *Turner: Imagination and Reality* (New York: The Museum of Modern Art, 1966), 10. My overschematized sketch of Constable's career is especially indebted to the scholarly work of Michael Rosenthal, *Constable: The Painter and His Landscape* (New Haven: Yale University Press, 1983), and Ann Bermingham's *Landscape and Ideology,* as well as her forthcoming essay "Reading Constable," in which she justifies at length the term "fictionality" for Constable's "six-footers." My commentary has also been influenced by the admirable studies of John Barrell and of course Graham Reynolds, *The Later Paintings and Drawings of John Constable,* 2 vol. (New Haven: Yale University Press, 1984). So far as Ronald Paulson makes no

distinction between the narrative features in early and late Constable (in good measure because he regards visual and verbal structurings as antithetical), my interpretations differ from his in *Literary Landscape: Turner and Constable* (New Haven: Yale University Press, 1982). Yet Paulson perceives that Constable seldom depicts "simple landscape," preferring "farming, milling, canal transport," that is, events, not scenes (118). My remark a few sentences on that *The Leaping Horse* represents a climax of Constable's move into narrativity derives from my discussion of the transformation in that painting of static scene into dynamic event in *Romantic Landscape Vision: Constable and Wordsworth* (Madison: University of Wisconsin Press, 1975), 112−115.

14. Rosenthal, *Constable,* 192.

15. Bermingham, *Landscape and Ideology,* 128.

16. Rosenthal, *Constable,* 117.

17. Ibid., 158; Bermingham, *Landscape and Ideology,* 119−123.

18. "Unenriched by strange events" appears in Wordsworth's "Michael," and the adjuration to the reader to "make" a story comes from his poem of "An Incident" concerning "Simon Lee" in *Lyrical Ballads.* The implication of this lyric, as in Wordsworth's insistence in the preface to *Lyrical Ballads* that in his poems feeling gives importance to actions, rather than the reverse, is that narrativizing is inseparable from perceiving, that what we see or hear we partly create. This is why Wordsworthian "landscapes," as in "Tintern Abbey," are always also stories. Chapter 2 of my *British Romantic Art* contains a detailed comparison of Wordsworth's and Constable's uses of narrative. It is worth noting that there is a tendency even among the English Romantic poets to emphasize narrative as they come to artistic maturity. The most impressive exemplar of this tendency is William Blake, who in his prophetic works narrativizes his early representations of rigid and simply antithetical "States of the Human Soul" in the *Songs of Innocence and Experience,* the manifesto-like *Marriage of Heaven and Hell,* and even the satiric *Island in the Moon.*

19. Bermingham, *Landscape and Ideology,* 145.

20. Merle E. Brown, *Double Lyric* (New York: Columbia University Press, 1980), 156.

21. "In modeling an infinite object (reality) by means of a finite text, a work of art substitutes it own space . . . not only for a part but also for the whole of that reality" (Yurij Lotman, *The Structure of the Artistic Text,* translated by Gail Lenhoff and Ronald Vroon [Ann Arbor: University of Michigan Press, 1977], 211). Lotman here is of course concerned with verbal art, but his comments, central to his argument, are equally applicable to painting, as when he describes the "dual likeness" of realistic representation: "[I]t is like . . . that part of the universe which it depicts, and it is like the whole of that universe" (250).

22. Renarrativizing of landscape is but one aspect of the English Romantics' adventurous rethinking of narrative functions in art—literary manifestations of which I analyze in *British Romantic Art* (Berkeley: University of California Press, 1986). An acute analysis of the metaphysical crises provoking such reassessments of narrative forms will be found in Andrew M. Cooper, *Doubt and Identity in Romantic Poetry* (New Haven: Yale University Press, 1988).

23. A point insisted upon by Steiner, *Pictures of Romance*, 11, drawing on William Labov, *Language in the Inner City* (Philadelphia: University of Pennsylvania Press, 1972), who introduced "evaluation" into American analyses of narrative form—and about whom I have more to say in Chapter 4. One of the most valuable recent studies of narrative, Ross Chambers, *Story and Situation* (Minneapolis: University of Minnesota Press, 1984), works out in careful detail, using for examples nineteenth-century "art" texts, implications of Labov's observations, demonstrating how the "point" of narrative texts, the focus of their evaluative ordering, can constitute the situation created by their impinging upon the circumstances giving rise to the storytelling act itself (4, *passim*). In subsequent discussions of this matter I try to make clear the need to avoid the temptation simplistically to reduce narrative "point" to "moralizing"—an error that even Hayden White may have made in his important essay "The Value of Narrativity in the Representation of Reality," now in *The Content of the Form* (Baltimore: Johns Hopkins University Press, 1987), 1–25. See also White's "Introduction: The Poetics of History" in his *Metahistory* (Baltimore: Johns Hopkins University Press, 1973), 1–38.

24. Central passages in *The Republic* bearing on these issues will be found in the Penguin edition, translated by Desmond Lee (Harmondsworth, 2d ed. 1974), part 3, pp. 129–157, and part 10, pp. 421–439.

25. A more formal statement of this quality of story that is essential to history is provided by W. Wolfgang Holdheim, who observes that "historical understanding is an active, hermeneutic appropriation by an interpretive mind," and that "the putative discovery of objective laws or patterns that deserve universal application is itself merely a type of interpretation—a concealed and distorted one that does not recognize itself as such." And he goes on to point out that "the basis of this conception of historicity is given in the theological tradition of the Old Testament, which cannot be grasped by ideal systematic constructs but only through narrative re-creation and reinterpretation" (*The Hermeneutic Mode* [Ithaca: Cornell University Press, 1984], 220–221). Holdheim appropriately cites as authority for his last statement the work of scholars such as Gerhard von Rad, but Gerald Bruns, commenting on the function of Midrash in a very different context makes much the same point: "[T]he function of the Oral Torah is precisely to maintain the openness of what is written to that which is unforeseen or which is yet to come—new situations of human life and new understanding which will require what is written to be fulfilled in ways that cannot be accounted for by the letter alone" (*Inventions* [New Haven: Yale University Press, 1982], 29).

26. Meyer Schapiro, *Modern Art: Nineteenth and Twentieth Centuries* (New York: George Braziller, 1982), 223. Schapiro is one of the most valuable commentators on modernism because his extensive knowledge of other periods and styles makes his defense of twentieth-century tendencies both cogent and persuasive. Exemplary is his essay on Mondrian in the volume just cited (233–261). All critics of modern art have noted its emphasis on immediate sensation, but Adrian Stokes is one of the few to connect this "matter-of-factness" to what Cézanne called his "hatred of the imaginative," the linkage leading to works lacking "parts or pieces," the discrete units necessary to narrative (*Three*

Essays on the Painting of our Time [London: Tavistock, 1961], 54–55, 58–61). The most succinct formulation of modernism's rejection of moral purposiveness is Wilde's, "the sphere of Art and the sphere of Ethics are absolutely distinct and separate," which appears in "The Critic as Artist," *The Complete Works of Oscar Wilde* 10 vols. (New York: Doubleday, 1923), 5: 226.

27. "Art, at the turn of the century, divested itself of the ballast of religious and political ideas which had been imposed upon it and came into its own— attained, that is, the form suited to its intrinsic nature" (Kasimir Malevich, "Suprematism," translated by Howard Dearstyne, in *Modern Artists on Art*, edited by Robert L. Herbert [Englewood Cliffs: Prentice-Hall, 1964], 100). There are critics, such as Clement Greenberg in his celebrated essay "Avant-Garde and Kitsch" (now available in *Collected Essays and Criticism*, edited by John O'Brian, 1:3–41), who suggest that modern artists sought only a moral high ground from which to criticize inadequate ideological positions. While this is doubtless true of some artists much of the time and many artists some of the time, I think it loses sight of the intensity of the idealism at the heart of modernism, the idealism, finally, that gives the movement its uniquely powerful impact.

28. There have been few judiciously sympathetic discussions of issues posed by the modernist separation of aesthetics and ethics, one of the earliest being that of Eugene Goodheart, "The Failure of Criticism," *New Literary History*, 7, no. 2 (1976): 377–392; and the most significant recent example being Tobin Siebers, *The Ethics of Criticism* (Ithaca: Cornell University Press, 1988). Both Goodheart and Siebers have found it politic to approach the problems of art divested of ethical significance through discussion of critical responses.

29. *Pablo Picasso: A Retrospective*, edited by William Rubin, chronology by James Fluegel (New York: The Museum of Modern Art, 1980), 120.

30. Sharply focused by changes in art are analogous shifts at least as important in the sciences, as is persuasively demonstrated by David Bleich, *Subjective Criticism* (Baltimore: Johns Hopkins University Press, 1978). He quotes Heisenberg's famous observation that "the object of research is no longer nature itself, but man's investigation of nature," which the German physicist explicitly linked to Eddington's assertion that "we have found that where science has progressed the farthest, the mind has but regained from nature that which mind has put into nature" (17). One item of value in Bleich's work is its elucidation of how intensified emphasis on subjectivity may simultaneously encourage attention to essential and universal principles.

CHAPTER THREE
Social Foundations of Narrative

1. Paul Ricoeur, *Interpretation Theory: Discourse and the Surplus of Meaning* (Fort Worth: University of Texas Christian Press, 1976), 7. Subsequent references to this work are given in the text. I cite chiefly from this little volume because in succinct fashion it articulates most of the basic principles under-

lying Ricoeur's analyses of narrative. Ricoeur's *magnum opus* on this topic is of course his three-volume *Time and Narrative*, translated by Kathleen McLaughlin and David Pellauer (Chicago: University of Chicago Press, 1984–1987). There is a superb discussion of the first two volumes of this work by Hayden White, now in his *The Content of Form* (Baltimore: Johns Hopkins University Press, 1987), 169–184. Two earlier, very significant essays by Ricoeur are cited in notes below. Roland Barthes's principal contribution to my topic is his "Introduction to the Structural Analysis of Narratives," *Image, Music, Text*, translated by Stephen Heath (New York: Hill and Wang, 1977), 79–124; on the "homological relation" between sentence and narrative structure, 83–84. Barthes recognizes without being able to resolve a central problem of narrative as the ambiguity between chronological succession and total form (84–85), which Bakhtin explains by the "chronotope."

2. The relativity of such distinctions and their primary applicability to the practical circumstances of life rather than as philosophical profundities makes them critically useful. As Geoffrey Strickland observes, "[W]e cannot read a text, that is, we cannot 'make sense of it' . . . unless we read it *as if* we understand to some extent, at least, the intentions of the author" (*Structuralism or Criticism?* [Cambridge: Cambridge University Press, 1981] 38). In "face-to-face" discourse normally that "as if" does not immediately arise. But, of course, one of the fascinations of drama is watching a display of the dubiety of our ordinary assumptions about the clear intentionality in speech.

3. Walter Benn Michaels, "Against Formalism: The Autonomous Text in Legal and Literary Interpretation," *Poetics Today* 1, no. 1–2 (1979): 23–34, articulates forcefully the principles that underlie contemporary dissatisfaction with the limitations of "anti-intentionalist" criticism, principles whose implications Michaels has spelled out in later essays in collaboration with Steven Knapp. The crux of this approach is to recognize that the artifacts we call "texts" have meaningful existence only within the contexts in which they are received. In Michaels's phrasing, it is not that words "have no plain meanings but those plain meanings are functions not of texts but of the situations in which we read them" (33).

4. Paul Ricoeur, "The Hermeneutical Function of Distanciation," *Philosophy Today* 17 (Summer, 1973): 132–134. Part of what Ricoeur is getting at is indicated by Ernst Cassirir's observation that where immediate relation to sensory experience ends, language begins: "[T]he aim of linguistic designation lies in difference. . . . [T]he more the sound resembles what it expresses the more it continues to 'be' the other" (*The Philosophy of Literary Form*, translated by Ralph Mannheim, 2 vols. [New Haven: Yale University Press, 1953] 1:189). It is curious that the development of methods of audial recording and reproduction have gone virtually unnoticed in all the recent discussions about the relation of speech to writing. The phonograph record, the cassette, or even the audio portion of the videotape allows "spoken discourse" to be preserved and disseminated in a fashion similar to that which has been possible with writing for a long time—and with the concomitant dependency upon some material form of the recording. When this development is taken into account, the spuriousness of some common distinctions between speech

and writing becomes apparent. One of the few scholars to address this issue seriously is Dennis Tedlock, particularly notable being his essay "Phonography and the Problem of Time in Oral Narrative Events," now in his important book *The Spoken Word and the Work of Interpretation* (Philadelphia: University of Pennsylvania Press, 1983), 194–215.

5. Vladimir Propp, *The Morphology of the Folktale,* translated by Laurence Scott, 2d ed. (Austin: University of Texas Press, 1968): "[D]efinition should in no case depend on the personage who carries out the function [action]" (21).

6. Yurij Lotman, *The Structure of the Artistic Text,* translated by Gail Lenhoff and Ronald Vroon (Ann Arbor: University of Michigan Press, 1977), speaks with cogency on the paradoxical uniqueness of the literary work of art, observing, for example: "[E]ach artistic text is created as a unique sign with a particular content, constructed ad hoc. . . . [Yet] the 'unique' sign turns out to be 'assembled' from standard elements, and on a certain level is 'read' according to traditional guidelines. Every innovative work is constructed of traditional material. If a text does not sustain the memory of traditional construction, its innovativeness will no longer be perceived" (22). Bakhtin's dialogical view, of course, treats *every* utterance as unique: "[T]he word is expressive, but, we repeat, expression does not inhere in the word itself. It originates in the point of contact between the word and actual reality, under the conditions of that real situation articulated by the individual utterance . . . the word appears as an expression of some evaluative position of an individual person. . . . This is why the unique speech experience of each individual is shaped and developed in continuous and constant interaction with others' individualized utterances" (M. M. Bakhtin, *Speech Genres and Other Late Essays,* translated by Vern W. McGee, edited by Caryl Emerson and Michael Holquist [Austin: University of Texas Press, 1986], 88–89).

7. Adapted from the translation of J.P.B. De Josselin de Jong, "Original Ojibwe Texts," *Baessler-Archiv* (Leipzig/Berlin) 5 (1913): 30, which includes a transcription of the original language; I am grateful to John Nichols for suggestions concerning the probable meaning of some of the original Ojibwa.

8. René Girard, *Violence and the Sacred* (Baltimore: Johns Hopkins University Press, 1977).

9. Jarold Ramsey, "From 'Mythic' to 'Fictive' in a Nez Percé Orpheus Myth," in *Traditional Literatures of the American Indian,* edited by Karl Kroeber (Lincoln: University of Nebraska Press, 1981), 32.

10. Perhaps his most specific discussions of this cluster of issues are to be found in "The Problem of Speech Genres" and "The Problem of the Text," at 60–102 and 103–131, respectively, in Bakhtin, *Speech Genres and Other Late Essays.* This work is cited in the text as Bakhtin, 1986.

11. M. M. Bakhtin and P. M. Medvedev, *The Formal Method in Literary Scholarship,* translated by Albert J. Wehrle (Cambridge, Mass.: Harvard University Press, 1985), 120; cited in this text as Bakhtin, 1985.

12. Michael Holquist, "The Surd Heard: Bakhtin and Derrida," in *Literature and History,* edited by Gary Saul Morson (Stanford: Stanford University Press, 1986), 150–151.

13. Judith Fetterley, *The Resisting Reader: A Feminist Approach to American*

Fiction (Bloomington: Indiana University Press, 1978), illuminates the importance of various conflictual aspects of utterer-audience relation. Fetterley's analyses, like much recent feminist criticism, are especially helpful in centering attention on how significant diversity of audience response may be, a fact undervalued by many earlier "reception theorists."

14. Holquist, "The Surd Heard," 148–153, makes clear the significance of Bakhtin's preference for the psychological theories of Vygotsky, drawing attention to the importance of his *Freudianism: A Marxist Critique,* published under the name of Voloshinov in 1927. A good deal of the recent comment on Bakhtin in this country, and France, is vitiated by a failure to take into account this psychological orientation. Worth consulting is L. S. Vygotsky, *Mind in Society,* edited by Michael Cole et al. (Cambridge, Mass.: Harvard University Press, 1978). I would observe that Friedrich Schleiermacher in his "Outline for the 1819 Lectures" emphasized that every act of understanding is the obverse of an act of discourse, so Bakhtin's interpenetrating of hermeneutics and rhetoric could also be attached to a longstanding critical tradition in the West.

15. The importance of evaluation to narrative I discuss at length subsequently, but here I will simply observe that Bakhtin's view of dynamic judgmentalism is congruent with some of the most sophisticated recent philosophic analyses of literature's moral function. For example, Hilary Putnam, "Literature, Science, Reflection," *New Literary History* 7, no. 3 (Spring 1976): 483–491, using Lady Murasaki's *Tale of the Genji* as illustrative text, points out that "[l]iterature does not, or does not often, depict *solutions.* What especially the novel does is aid us in the imaginative re-creation of moral perplexities" (485). Noting how difficult it is "to imagine *any* way of life which is both at all ideal and reasonable," Putnam observes that "literature often puts before us both extremely vividly and in extremely rich emotional detail why and how this seems to be so in different societies, in different times, and from different perspectives" (486).

16. Frank Kermode, *The Genesis of Secrecy* (Cambridge, Mass.: Harvard University Press, 1979), elegantly articulates this important feature of narrative on what might be called the macroscopic level. Yurij Lotman, more aware of the concurrence in fine stories of the "structurally heterogeneous," calls attention to the "continual violation" of "definite perceptible structural sequences" by "the imposition of other structures and their 'disruptive' influence. This leads to the creation of an extremely flexible mechanism [the story] with incalculable semantic energy" (Lotman, *Structure of the Artistic Text,* 280). Some recent narratological studies have unfortunately ignored the semantic effects of macrostructures, plot, character, and so on, since they have not been focused on story as a system for making the most of the polysemic potential of words.

17. I have summarized from two essays by Gunther Buck, "The Structure of Hermeneutic Experience and the Problem of Tradition," *New Literary History* 10, no. 1 (Autumn 1978): 31–48, and "Hermeneutics of Texts and Hermeneutics of Actions," *New Literary History* 12, no. 1 (Autumn 1980): 87–96. This intrinsic implicitness does not, of course, exclude the possible relevance

of repression *also* being operative in and determinative of a text. Some contemporary psychoanalysts are very interested in this problem. Roy Schafer, for instance, discussing the psychoanalytic concept of "overdetermination" (multiple definitions of a single action) points out the need for analysts to recognize that "there is far more to an[y] action than could have entered into its creation at the moment of its execution" (*Language and Insight* [New Haven: Yale University Press, 1978], 21). Schafer is intensely aware of the mutual illuminations possible from joint study of literature, especially narrative, and psychoanalysis, and all his work is of interest to literary critics.

18. I discuss William Labov's work in the following chapter. W. B. Gallie, *Philosophy and the Philosophical Understanding*, 2d ed. (New York: Schocken, 1968), especially 22–50. I cite Louis O. Mink's important essay "History and Fiction as Modes of Comprehension" as it appears in Louis O. Mink, *Historical Understanding*, edited by Brian Fay, Eugene O. Golub, and Richard T. Vann (Ithaca: Cornell University Press, 1987), 42–60. This volume includes other valuable essays by Mink, notably "Narrative Form as a Cognitive Instrument."

19. As I indicate below, Gallie's description fails to take account of rereading or rehearing, but his game analogy has the virtue of exposing the crucial flaw in narrative analyses that make a story's ending wholly determinative of its meaning. D. A. Miller, cited again in the next chapter, has most cogently demonstrated the need to avoid this weakness (visible in commentators as diverse as Barthes, Kermode, and Peter Brooks) in *Narrative and Its Discontents* (Princeton: Princeton University Press, 1981).

20. Mink, "History and Fiction," 47.

21. Yurij Lotman, differentiating artistic from nonartistic repetition (which I treat in the next chapter) stresses that "in art, equating or contrasting takes place at the cost of some—occasionally considerable—effort which includes emotional effort" (*Semiotics of Cinema*, translated by Mark E. Suino [Ann Arbor: University of Michigan Press, 1976], 57). Eugene Goodheart, "The Failure of Criticism," *New Literary History* 7, no. 2 (1976): 377–392, has demonstrated the reductiveness of the exclusively rationalistic criticism favored in this century, which subverts "all tacit, unexamined acceptances and beliefs" *except* the faith of rationalistic critics in the validity of their method" (382). The openness and looseness of narrative, which I discuss subsequently, make it an excellent vehicle for thinking sceptically about one's own scepticism. I agree with Goodheart that *this* is the thinking most lacking from modern criticism.

22. Mary Louise Pratt, *Toward a Speech Act Theory of Literary Discourse* (Bloomington: Indiana University Press, 1977), defines display texts at 136–148. The conception that underlies the definition of "display texts" is of language as dialogic, as exchange, not mere transmission. That conception enables Pratt to define elegantly the fallacy of the concept of "poetic language" popularized by Roman Jakobson (3–37). In "The Wolf Comes: Indian Poetry and Linguistic Criticism," in *Smoothing the Ground*, edited by Brian Swann (Berkeley: University of California Press, 1983), 98–111 (see especially 100), I point out some logical difficulties in Jakobson's most celebrated essay on poetic language.

23. Mink, "History and Fiction," 48. Subsequent references to this work are given in the text.

24. Walter Benjamin, "The Storyteller," in *Illuminations,* translated by Harry Zohn, edited by Hannah Arendt (New York: Schocken, 1969), 91.

25. Mink's term "play" neatly recalls Gallie's analogy between story and game, and reminds us of the relevance of storytelling to playing, a connection I believe best analyzed not by Johan Huizinga but by Yurij Lotman in his *The Structure of the Artistic Text,* especially 59–69. For Lotman, "[T]he art of play consists in the mastery of biplanar behavior," in which the player "must remember that he is participating in a conventional (not a real) situation . . . but simultaneously *not* remember that fact" (62). This skill at sustaining the simultaneously contradictory is the basis on which the audience of storytelling can maintain not merely the "static simultaneous coexistence of different meanings" in the story, but even the "constant recognition that there may be other meanings besides those perceived at the moment" (67). Among recent critics who emphasize the need to understand narrative in narrative (rather than in reductively philosophical) terms one of the most interesting is Michel Serres. He, for example, deliberately begins his study *Les Cinq Sens* (Paris: Grasset, 1985) with a parable because one of his major purposes is to demonstrate the value of language forms responsive to the full range of human capacities and needs, not merely to our intellectual powers.

26. Narrative's capacity to provoke an understanding of interrelations of events without reducing such connectivity to some abstract system such as cause and effect has made it essential to historians. Few commentators on this point have been as vigorous as Hannah Arendt.

> Whoever in the historical sciences honestly believes in causality actually denies the subject matter of his own science. Such a belief can be concealed in the application of general categories to the whole course of happenings, such as challenge and response, or in the search for general trends which supposedly are the deeper strata from which events spring and whose accessory symptoms they are. Such generalizations and categorizations extinguish the "natural" light history itself offers and, by the same token, destroy the actual story with its unique distinction and eternal meaning. ("Understanding Politics," *Partisan Review* 20, no. 4 [1953]: 388–389).

CHAPTER FOUR
How Stories Are Constructed

1. Barbara Herrenstein Smith, "Narrative Versions, Narrative Theories," *Critical Inquiry* 7, no. 1 (Autumn 1980): 222. As I emphasize throughout this essay, I think Mrs. Smith's minimal definition of narrative as "someone telling somebody about something" (221) requires the additional phrase "evoking evaluative responses" if the vigorous specificity of narrative transaction is to

be appreciated. A intelligent survey of some contemporary commentaries on narrative, although it ignores Smith and Gallie, and doesn't do justice to Seymour Chatman, *Story and Discourse* (Ithaca: Cornell University Press, 1978), is Wallace Martin, *Recent Theories of Narrative* (Ithaca: Cornell University Press, 1986).

2. Robert Georges, "Toward an Understanding of Storytelling Events," *Journal of American Folklore* 82 (1969): 318−319.

3. *Biographia Literaria,* edited by John Shawcross 2 vols. (1907; corrected edition, London: Oxford University Press, 1962) vol. 2, chap. 14, p. 11. Full references to Mink's contributions will be found in the preceding chapter.

4. A brilliant description of the uniqueness of each retelling of the "same" story is provided by Balzac at the beginning of his "Christ in Flanders."

5. An excellent analysis of Ricoeur's description (indebted to Heidegger) of how in narrative a "recounted past is made present out of concern for the future," and how through eliciting "a structure from a sequence" narrative "organizes and transforms culture," can be found in Geoffrey Harpham, *The Ascetic Imperative in Culture and Criticism* (Chicago: University of Chicago Press, 1987), 82−84.

6. Wolfgang Iser, *The Act of Reading* (Baltimore: Johns Hopkins University Press, 1978), 109.

7. René Wellek and Austin Warren, *Theory of Literature,* 3d ed. (New York: Harcourt Brace, 1977), 22−28; Jean-François Lyotard, *The Postmodern Condition* (Minneapolis: University of Minnesota Press, 1984), 25. Aldous Huxley makes the same distinctions: "As a medium of literary expression, common language is inadequate. It is no less inadequate as a medium of scientific expression. . . . [The scientist] uses the vocabulary and syntax of common speech in such a way that each phrase is susceptible of only one interpretation. . . . The scientist's aim . . . is to say one thing and only one thing . . . [but] the literary artist undertakes . . . creating a language capable of conveying . . . the multiple significance of human experience" (*Literature and Science* [New York: Harper and Row, 1963], 12−13). Non-Western peoples seem often to make analogous distinctions, as do the Western Apache, whose discriminations among "ordinary talk," "prayer," and "story" I referred to in Chapter 1.

8. Paul Ricoeur, "Structure, Word, Event," *Philosophy Today* 12, no. 2/4 (Summer 1968): 114−129: "Words have more than one meaning, but they do not have an infinity of meanings" (127). Words cannot mean anything because they belong to a language system. This point deserves emphasis because so many recent critics, particularly among the French, have missed it in oversimplifying the "arbitrariness" of words. Saussure, who popularized the idea of that arbitrariness, does not so oversimplify, because *he* never lost sight of the dialectical relation between language and speech acts.

9. Geoffrey Hartman, *Criticism in the Wilderness: The Study of Literature Today* (New Haven: Yale University Press, 1980), 5 and 299.

10. I cite "Why the Buzzard Is Bald" from James Owen Dorsey and John R. Swanton, *A Dictionary of the Biloxi and Ofo Languages,* Bulletin 47 of the Bureau of American Ethnology in Washington, D.C., 1912, 33−36. Since I

refer to the native text with interlinear analyses, it is necessary to call attention to the observations of Mary R. Haas on the linguistic shortcomings of some of the Dorsey-Swanton material in "Swanton and the Biloxi and Ofo dictionaries," *The International Journal of American Linguistics* 1969, no. 4: 286–290.

11. "Interpretation" may be thought of simply as this processing of narrative by the addressee, which is essential to what Louis O. Mink describes in "Narrative Form as a Cognitive Instrument," in *Historical Understanding*, edited by Brian Fay, Eugene O. Golub, and Richard T. Vann (Ithaca: Cornell University Press), 181–210. D. A. Miller's enlightening discussion of what he calls "the narratable" in fiction is centered on the same issues—see his *Narrative and Its Discontents* (Princeton: Princeton University Press, 1981). Fascinating proof of the active part played by the reader of narrative appears in the report of a failed experiment by Janos Lazlo, "Understanding and Enjoying," in *Literary Discourse*, edited by Lazlo Halasz (Berlin: de Gruyter, 1987), 113–124. Lazlo, using a technique that had been successful with expository prose, asked subject-readers to mark certain features in short stories. But "the first subject read more slowly than the normal speed . . . instead of checking adjectives [as he read] he just read the passage. . . . Another subject . . . stopped checking adjectives after a couple of lines and plunged into reading. . . . [T]he subjects were reading with apparent joy" (121). Even the promise of extra money failed to make readers conform to instructions. A finer exemplification of the value of negative results would be hard to imagine.

12. "Semantic saturation" is the phrase Lotman, *The Structure of the Artistic Text*, translated by Gail Lenhoff and Ronald Vroon (Ann Arbor: University of Michigan Press, 1977), uses to define the unparaphraseability of discourse that falls outside the bounds of the "conversational" or "scientific." A subtle form of reductive intellectualized interpreting is that which identifies the ultimate discovery about a story to be an irresolvable perplexity, an aporia. Narrative perplexities are productive, encouraging purposeful rethinking. They are the foci for particularized affective and ethical effects. Adequate interpretation of story demands specification of the consequences (sociological as well as psychological) for feeling and moral judgment of its aporias. So accurate and comprehensive delineation of these requires, not scientific analysis, but something at the least very like narrative discourse.

13. Lotman, confessedly building on Bakhtin's analyses, observes that a word in such a text as "Why the Buzzard Is Bald" can be semantically complicated because it simultaneously belongs to more than one semantic system (which systems would include perhaps most significantly sociolects)—as is plainly illustrated by "home" in this story. Since the "semantics" of the story consists in a relating of multiple subsystems, "that which negates does not annul that which is negated; rather they enter into a relation of contrast and opposition" (*The Structure of the Artistic Text*, 248). To put the matter simply, "home" for a fish in this tale is simultaneously the same as *and* absolutely different from "home" for a man. "Scientific truth exists in one semantic field," Lotman goes on to point out, while in a well-told story "truth exists simultaneously in several fields within their mutual correlation. This circumstance greatly increases the number of meaningful features of each element"

(Lotman, 249). And, of course, the elements of story range from words and sentences up to characters, episodes, even an entire story, for a story audience is treated by the story as a heterogenous unity.

14. William Labov, *A Study of the Non-Standard English of Negro and Puerto Rican Speakers in New York City*, Research Report for the Department of Health, Education and Welfare (New York, Columbia University, 1968), 297, 301. On this report is based Labov's book, *Language in the Inner City* (Philadelphia: University of Pennsylvania Press, 1972). Ross Chambers's important study, *Story and Situation: Narrative Seduction and the Power of Fiction* (Minneapolis: University of Minnesota Press, 1984), develops the significance of Labov's observation through analyses of nineteenth-century short stories, in the process advancing our understanding of how storytelling works upon and is shaped by its addresses, what, in Labov's terms, a story can *do*. Chambers is particularly helpful in demonstrating that, because the act of storytelling "constitutes the historical situation in which assessment is made" (Chambers, 22), retellings and rehearings of narratives provide wonderful insight into the processes of history, the processes by which what Bakhtin would call ideological environments are generated.

15. One of the most valuable studies of such variability in response is to be found in David Bleich, *Subjective Criticism* (Baltimore: Johns Hopkins University Press, 1978). Bleich's critique of what he calls the "objective paradigm" upon which much narratology is in fact based is cogent, and his suggestion that we conceive interpretation as a resymbolization of response is a fruitful one. The hermeneutic tradition, especially in the line of Wilhelm Dilthey, has consistently treated understanding (*Verstehen*) as a kind of personal living-through not describable in conventional subject-object terms. And Hans-Georg Gadamer treats understanding as a myriad-faceted dialogue with no privileged position.

16. George Poulet's description of the reading process, "Phenomenology of Reading," *New Literary History* 1, no. 1 (1969): 54–68, with its emphasis on the sharing of different consciousnesses *through* a text, is the best modern discussion I know of the psychology of reading stories. It is remarkable how closely Poulet's description fits with Walter Benjamin's imagining of how oral tales were heard: "[S]torytelling is always the art of repeating stories. . . . The more self-forgetful the listener is, the more deeply is what he listens to impressed upon his memory. . . . [H]e listens to the tales in such a way that the gift of retelling them comes to him all by itself" ("The Storyteller," in *Illuminations,* translated by Harry Zohn [New York: Schocken, 1969], 91). Poulet's analysis, of course, is congruent with Benjamin's observation that the conditions of modern life are hostile to storytelling because they inhibit retelling, not least by destroying our capacity to receive self-forgetfully and patiently.

17. Louis O. Mink, *Historical Understanding* (Ithaca: Cornell University Press, 1987), 199. On the same page Mink observes that "there is something incompatible about our concept of 'event' and our concept of 'narrative,'" and the essay from which the quotations are taken, "Narrative Form as a Cognitive Instrument," is addressed to elucidating how this paradoxical circum-

stance establishes narrative as an invaluable rival to "theoretical explanation and understanding," even though, for reasons I have described above, he believes that "narratives . . . contain indefinitely many ordering relations, and indefinitely many ways of *combining* these relations" (198). A major tendency of modernism was to reduce through essentializing this multiplicity of orderings, hence what Joseph Frank described as "Spatial Form in Modern Literature." That essay is now reprinted in his book *The Idea of Spatial Form* (New Brunswick, N.J.: Rutgers University Press, 1991), which includes Frank's assessments of the many critiques his original article has provoked.

18. Analysis of the collection from which the story is taken suggests that there is also a strong convention of beginning certain kinds of story with such a camp circle: "Raw-Gums and White-Owl Woman," translated by George A. Dorsey, text 102, 231−236, in *Traditions of the Arapaho*, edited by George A. Dorsey and A. L. Kroeber, Field Columbia Museum Publication 81, Anthropological Series 5 (Chicago, 1903).

19. Yurij Lotman, *Semiotics of Cinema*, translated by Mark E. Suino (Ann Arbor: University of Michigan Press, 1976), 68−69. For a fuller discussion of wandering viewpoint, see Wolfgang Iser, *The Act of Reading* (Baltimore: Johns Hopkins University Press, 1978), especially 108−109 and 196−199.

20. Albert B. Lord, *The Singer of Tales* (Cambridge, Mass.: Harvard University Press, 1960), provides the most accessible introduction to the use of exact repetitive elements, notably, of course, verbal formulas, in epic narrative— though he also considers macrolevel reiterations. In a recent essay, "Oral Performance in a World of Mechanical Reproduction," in *Narrative Chance*, edited by Gerald Vizenor (Albuquerque: University of New Mexico Press, 1989), 175−191, I discuss some related issues raised by a remarkable five-hour, heavily repetitive retelling of a European fairytale by a contemporary Colville Indian.

21. Mink, "Narrative Form," 185.

22. As has now often been remarked, a root difficulty with structuralist analyses of linguistic texts, especially narrative ones, is the simplistic "scientific" model from which their analyses are derived. The depicting of structure, for example, in terms of binary oppositions, a practice that has become so deeply embedded in structuralist thinking that it is now often taken for granted, inevitably leads to reductive analyses even of uncomplicated literary texts. More promising for critics determined to adapt their discipline to scientific models would be recent studies of "chaos," which rigorously describe complex physical phenomena open to "unpredictable" variations. And the concept of "fractals" enables one to describe the forms of shifting and variable entities, clouds, for example, in terms of the operation of self-similar, reiterative structures. Appropriate "scientific" models for literary analyses are to be sought, if such are desired, in sophisticated studies of complex phenomena such as turbulence, which Heisenberg identified as more baffling than relativity. My own view is that literary criticism does best when it does not try to imitate scientific procedures, especially when treating narrative.

23. In "The Structural Study of Myth," which was first published in the

Journal of American Folklore 78 (1955): 428–444, Lévi-Strauss provided the formula which I cite from the Doubleday Anchor reprint, *Structural Anthropology* (Garden City, 1967), 225:

$$F (a): F (b) = F (b): F (y)$$

Vladimir Propp, *Morphology of the Folktale,* translated by Laurence Scott, 2d ed. (Austin: University of Texas Press, 1968), was originally published in Russian in 1928. The second edition I cite is preferable to the first because of the editing and new preface by Louis A. Wagner and the introduction by Alan Dundes, which provides a summary but lucid distinction between the "paradigmatic" structuralism of Lévi-Strauss and the "syntagmatic" structuralism of Propp. On pages 22 and 23 of this edition will be found the basic discussion of the invariant order of the segments or episodes according to Propp under the heading "The sequence of functions is always the same."

24. Elaine Jahner, "Cognitive Style in Oral Narrative" *Language and Style* 16, no. 1 (Winter 1983): 32–51, provides a detailed analysis, taking into account especially the function of key Dakota words referring to spatial arrangements and movements, as well as defining the story's "genre," that of the *ohunkakan.*

25. Ibid., 44–45.

26. On the basis of storytelling experience with my own children, I judge that part of children's insistence on exact repetition in the telling of a familiar story springs from their finding the "meaning" of the tale embodied in its structure; they perceive correctly that a story told in a different *way* becomes a different story.

27. Marie Maclean, *Narrative as Performance* (London: Routledge, 1988), develops some of the suggestions of Michel Serres concerning the functionality of repetition in making what information theorists call "noise" or "interference," such noise, she understands, being productive in storytelling (166–168). One of Serres's contributions to the understanding of narrative lies in his emphasis on how repetition and parallelism are means by which change and innovation *evolve:* grit in the oyster without which there could be no pearl. Implicit in his approach is recognition that narrative episodes and macrostructures function in a fashion that can be equated with the polysemism of words—of which we become aware when these are employed in an unusual fashion, as in punning. Serres's chief work available in English is *The Parasite,* originally published in 1980, translated by L. R. Scher (Baltimore: Johns Hopkins University Press, 1982).

28. The source of the story printed in the appendix is Jeremiah Curtin, *Myths of the Modocs* (Boston: Little, Brown, 1912), 355–358. There are a substantial number of Native American stories parodying or ringing changes on the European Ant and Grasshopper tale.

29. Mink, "Narrative Form," 188.

30. Lotman, *Semiotics of Cinema,* 67.

31. See Morse Peckham's collection of essays, *Romanticism and Ideology* (Greenwood, Fla.: Penkeville Publishing, 1985).

32. Ross Chambers, *Story and Situation* (Minneapolis: University of Minnesota Press, 1984), 214. Chambers, it seems to me rightly, focuses on the "seductive" qualities of the nineteenth-century stories that are his principal illustrations, since, as I suggest in the next chapter, the power of traditional storytelling was then coming into question. Previously, the storyteller's role had been recognized in most societies by various formal devices. In preliterate societies especially, a teller was normally "authored" by the story, for which she or he supposedly was a mere vehicle of re-presentation, so that "seduction" need not be so prominent. The crucial fact is that storytelling is a mutual transaction in which the audience is as empowered as the teller. Peter Brooks, therefore, appears to me wrong to claim tellers always try to "subjugate the listener" (*Reading for the Plot* [New York: Knopf, 1984], 61).

33. Mink, "Narrative Form," 186.

34. Gerald Bruns, *Inventions* (New Haven: Yale University Press, 1982), 117.

35. Hannah Arendt, *Men in Dark Times* (New York: Harcourt, Brace, and World, 1968), 105.

CHAPTER FIVE

Syntagmatic and Paradigmatic Fiction

1. Wolfe's novel was published by Farrar, Straus, Giroux, New York, in 1987. In an interview with John Taylor, *New York Times Magazine*, March 21, 1988, 47–58, Wolfe's observation I have cited appears on page 50. *The New York Times* quoted Wolfe, March 11, 1988, page B 4, as saying "he wanted to write 'an honest book of and about the city' as Thackeray did in *Vanity Fair*, Mr. Wolfe's original inspiration. 'The subtitle of *Vanity Fair* is "A Novel without a Hero," and there are very few heroic figures in the book,' he said. 'And I don't see many heroic figures in New York City just now, to tell you God's honest truth.'" The final phrase and the inability to distinguish between "not many" and "none" are characteristic of Wolfe's prose.

2. On the size of the novel's "cast," one may consult my *Styles in Fictional Structure* (Princeton: Princeton University Press, 1970). All citations from *Vanity Fair* are to the superb Riverside edition, edited by Geoffrey and Kathleen Tillotson (Boston: Houghton Mifflin, 1963) by chapter number and page. My understanding of *Vanity Fair* is probably most indebted to the following critics: Kathleen Tillotson, *Novels of the Eighteen-Forties* (Oxford: Clarendon, 1954), 224–256; Gordon Ray, *The Buried Life* (London: Oxford, 1957), and "*Vanity Fair:* One Version of the Novelist's Responsibility," *Essays by Divers Hands: Transactions of the Royal Society of Literature*, n. s., 25 (1950): 87–101; Jack P. Rawlins, *A Fiction That Is True* (Berkeley: University of California Press, 1974); K. C. Phillips, *The Language of Thackeray* (London: Andre Deutsch, 1978); J. A. Sutherland, *Thackeray at Work* (London: Athlone Press, 1974), especially 11–44; John Loofburrow, *Thackeray and the Forms of Fiction* (Princeton: Princeton University Press, 1964); Juliet McMaster, *Thackeray: The*

Major Novels (Toronto: University of Toronto Press, 1971); George Levine, *The Realistic Imagination* (Chicago: University of Chicago Press, 1981), especially 131–160; Michael Lund, *Reading Thackeray* (Detroit: Wayne State University Press, 1988); Martin Meisel, *Realizations* (Princeton: Princeton University Press, 1983), especially 334–339.

3. Harry Levin, *James Joyce: A Critical Introduction,* 2d ed. (London: Faber and Faber, 1960), 116. My comments on *Ulysses* may be most deeply indebted to the commentaries of Hugh Kenner, whose delight in his subject is infectious. Besides *Ulysses,* rev. ed. (Baltimore: Johns Hopkins University Press, 1987), I have found Kenner's *The Stoic Comedians: Flaubert, Joyce, Beckett* (1962; reprint, Berkeley: University of California Press, 1974) helpful in explaining the origins and results of the central Joycean achievement: "as long as we adhere to the commonsense view that a novel tells a story, *Ulysses* is simply impossible" (97). I owe much to David Hayman's *Ulysses: The Mechanics of Meaning* (1972; new, rev. and expanded ed., Madison: University of Wisconsin Press, 1982). Hayman's most celebrated contribution to *Ulysses* criticism was the identification of what he called "the arranger," who "should be seen as something between a persona and a function, somewhere between the narrator and the implied author. . . . Perhaps it would be best to see the arranger as a significant, felt absence in the text, an unstated but inescapable source of control" (122–123). This articulates exactly how modernists replace narrator with invisible author. In *Re-forming the Narrative* (Ithaca: Cornell University Press, 1987), Hayman's excellent analysis of Joyce's use of paratactic forms, 153–164, shows its centrality to most modernist fiction. Finally, I have profited enormously from Karen Lawrence, *The Odyssey of Style in Ulysses* (Princeton: Princeton University Press, 1981), which builds on earlier criticism in its penetrating analyses of diverse Joycean styles.

4. Jospeh Frank is the critic who first concretized the significance of Joycean technique in his famous essay, now reproduced along with later reflections on the topic and critiques of his work in *The Idea of Spatial Form* (New Brunswick: Rutgers University Press, 1991). While insisting on the importance of Joyce's technique, "unbelievable laborious fragmentation of narrative structure . . . on the assumption that a unified spatial apprehension of his work would ultimately be possible," Frank insists that "in a far more subtle manner than in either Joyce or Flaubert, the same principle is at work in Marcel Proust" (21).

5. Levin, *James Joyce,* 69.

6. Kenner, *Ulysses,* 33.

7. Ibid., 41.

8. A footnote in the first edition explained: "It was the author's intention, faithful to history, to depict all the characters of this tale in their proper costumes, as they wore them at the commencement of the century. But when I remember the appearance of people in those days . . . I have not the heart to disfigure my heroes and heroines by costumes so hideous; and have, on the contrary, engaged a model of rank dressed according to the present fashion" (6:65). The loveliest touch in this explanation, besides the accompanying drawing, is that "model of rank."

12. W. M. Thackeray, Illustration from *Vanity Fair*, 1848.

The inefficacy of Wolfe's "realism" (which strikes me as representative of many current bestsellers celebrated as "readable" that I find boring) is perhaps best understood in terms of Michael Riffaterre's demonstration in *Fictional Truth* (Baltimore: Johns Hopkins University Press, 1990) that good fiction advertises its fictionality, depending for its existence on a rejection of naïve verisimilitude.

9. Georg Lukacs, "The Intellectual Physiognomy in Characterization," *Writer and Critic*, translated by Arthur D. Kahn (New York: Grosset and Dunlap, 1974), 149–188, especially 158–159. Because Joyce's characters participate in a paradigmatic story, they are less dependent, paradoxical as it may first appear, on prototypes than Luckasian "typical individuals." The latter are readily associated with preexisting patterns, especially literary ones, because their individuality articulates specific forces of social pressure and change in social traditions. Thus Don Quixote deliberately models himself on Amadis, but undergoes quite different adventures. Becky as a woman has less

freedom of choice, is more forced into her roles, and therefore more consciously attends to disjunctions between the pattern she both realizes and "distorts"—symbolized by her flinging Johnson's dictionary (source of traditional definitions) in the direction of her schoomistress-employer. Leopold Bloom's unconscious paradigmatic relation to Odysseus is realized, to the contrary, through the absolute uniqueness of his sensual and psychic experiences.

10. Joseph Frank, analyzing Philip Rahv's critique of his argument, accepts responsibility for seeing in modernist writers not "'workings of the mythic imagination but an aesthetic simulacrum of it'" (79). The strength of Frank's argument is exactly what opens it to misunderstanding: the synchronicity of modern literature produces effects *like* those of some myths. But myths are stories. A novelist such as Joyce would be less original, and less "modern," if he did not create mythic simulacra, images of myths. Frank rightly denies that he ever claimed that modern writers "have *literally* reverted to the condition of primitives, to have forgotten all about time and history, and to be truly living in—and writing out of—a mythical imagination untouched by their situations as moderns. Of course no such absurd idea had even entered my head" (80). In my final chapter I suggest some of the problems posed by the deep penetration into our literature of this imaging of narrative.

11. I again refer the reader to the important essay by Keith Basso (cited in Chapter 1), "'Stalking with Stories': Names, Places, and Moral Narratives among the Western Apache," in *Text, Play, and Story: The Construction and Reconstruction of Self and Society,* 1983 Proceedings of the American Ethnological Society, edited by Stuart Plainer and Edward M. Bruner (Washington, D.C.: American Ethnological Society, 1984), 19–55. Another essay in this volume, by Bruner and Phyllis Gorfain, "Dialogic Narration and the Paradoxes of Masada," 56–79, starting from recognition that "recurrent tellings not only define and empower storytellers but also help to constitute and reshape . . . society," illustrates through the Masada narrative how stories, provoking "an inherent versatility in interpretation," open the way to "conflicting readings and dissident, challenging voices" (56).

12. Michael Peled Ginsburg, "Pseudonym, Epigraphs, and Narrative Voice: *Middlemarch* and the Problem of Authorship," *ELH* 47 (1980): 542–558, points to George Eliot's equivalent creation of "a mixture of fiction and reality" through the use of a narrator who moves into and out of the narration, observing that a variety of stylistic techniques characteristic of Victorian fiction, such as free indirect discourse, "create, on a different level, a structure similar to that of the intrusive narrator." Ginsburg goes on to insist that Eliot's deployment of such devices, as I argue for Thackeray's parallel use, reveals the novelist's express refusal to claim "a truth which lies outside and independent of the text which the text simply expresses," but, instead, a "truth" that is "a product of the text, which therefore necessarily remains complex, contradictory, and 'diffusive'" (555–556). "Diffusive" suggests how much this limited, provisional, "story-truth" depends not merely on the novelistic text in itself but that text as processed in diverse fashions by various readers.

13. Gustave Flaubert, *Madame Bovary,* edited and translated by Paul De Man (New York: W. W. Norton, 1965), 106.

14. Wolfgang Iser, *The Act of Reading* (Baltimore: John Hopkins University Press, 1978), 108–109, 196–199. Several critics, of whom perhaps the most notable is Dorrit Cohn, *Transparent Minds* (Princeton: Princeton University Press, 1978), in discussing "free indirect discourse" and associated devices unwittingly touch on effects of the "wandering viewpoint," but make surprisingly little of them, perhaps because their attention is concentrated upon writer or text rather than audience.

15. Jonathan Arac, "Rhetoric and Realism, or Marxism, Deconstruction, and the Novel," in *Criticism without Boundaries,* edited by Jospeh Buttigeig (Notre Dame: University of Notre Dame Press, 1987), 160–176.

16. An impressive exception is the presentation of Bute Crawley's son James on his visit to Miss Crawley's home in chapter 34.

17. Narrative allusiveness can become "displacement" when applied by the storyteller to parts of his own story. *Beowulf* uses an interlaced structure masterfully for such displacing self-allusiveness. Thackeray's representation of Sedley's bankruptcy works in a somewhat analogous fashion, since, as I've pointed out, the account of his default follows accounts of its results. These examples of self-reflexive displacement belong to the teller's repertoire of reconfigurative devices by which the sequential progress of a tale is enriched by being complicated through self-interruptions. Perhaps the most spectacular example in *Vanity Fair* is the illustration entitled "Becky's second appearance in the character of Clytemnestra" (67:663), which presents a visual development of the verbal description of Becky's triumph acting in the charade of *Agamemnon* sixteen chapters before. But the crux of this visual representation is that it does *not* correspond to what the verbal narrative of the later chapter tells us. This is, however, merely a sensational exploitation by Thackeray of his "dual media" novel to achieve narrative displacement, which elsewhere he carries out just as assiduously but in a quieter, and therefore perhaps more effective, manner: see Meisel, *Realizations,* 335–338.

18. Fredric Jameson has articulated with impressive cogency the development of emphasis on the sensory as fundamental to literary modernism, perceivable, for example, in the contrast between Flaubert and Balzac: see his essay "Baudelaire as Modernist and Postmodernist: The Dissolution of the Referent and the Artificial 'Sublime,'" in *Lyric Poetry beyond New Criticism,* edited by Clavira Hosek and Patricia Parker (Ithaca: Cornell University Press, 1985), 247–263. Until the middle of the nineteenth century "bodily perception was not . . . felt to be a proper content for literary language. . . . [T]he older rhetoric was somehow fundamentally nonperceptual . . . [Balzac's] apparently perceptual notations, on closer examination, prove to be so many *signs*. . . . Perceptual language only emerges in the ruins of that older system of signs" (253).

19. James Joyce, *Ulysses* (1934; New York: Random House, 1946), 115.

20. From the preface to *The Tragic Muse, The Art of the Novel,* edited by R. P. Blackmur (New York: Charles Scribner's Sons, 1934), 84. Revealing in this passage is James's metaphorizing, as in much of his best criticism, of story into painting by referring to narrative as image. The significance of this critical transmutation of the dynamic into the static, the diachronic into the synchronic, becomes clear when one contrasts it with Romantic commentators

such as Coleridge and Scott, whose regular simile for narrative was the journey. But in making such distinctions, we must not lose sight of the essential
Modernist thrust of James's critique. As Donald Kuspit phrases it, "Modernism is in large part an attempt to become conscious of the rules that give art its
existence, and to use them self-consciously to make art" "Archaelogism: Postmodernism as Excavation, in (*The New Subjectivism: Art in the 1980s*" [Ann
Arbor: University of Michigan Press, 1988], 531).

21. Levine, *The Realistic Imagination*, 142.

22. John Carlos Rowe, *The Theatrical Dimensions of Henry James* (Madison:
University of Wisconsin Press, 1984).

23. McMaster, *Thackeray: The Major Novels*, 23. With these words she describes Thackeray's accomplishment of what Mary Louise Pratt, *Toward a
Speech Act Theory of Literary Discourse* (Bloomington: University of Indiana
Press, 1977), identifies as the primary value of fictional stories, a "doubling"
of experience through the creation of a recognizedly alternative world to the
real one—an achievement only possible if the artificiality of the alternative is
firmly kept in mind (174).

24. McMaster, *Thackeray: The Major Novels*, 8.

25. Yurij Lotman, *Semiotics of Cinema*, translated by Mark E. Suino (Ann
Arbor: University of Michigan Press, 1976), 73. This definition of narrative
event as a challenge to regularity of either experience or textual pattern Lotman illustrates with two sentences, calling the first nonnarrative, "Ivan is
walking about in the field," the second narrative, "Ivan is walking on the
ceiling." Lotman observes, however, that the narrativity or nonnarrativity of
such sentences, or larger units, depends on the contextual patterns within
which they occur: in a proper context the first sentence could be narrative.
Lotman's claim needs to be qualified by recognition that many stories will
consist principally of "positive" reworkings of familiar narrative patterns.
Transformation need not mean only challenge or subversion but can function
as effectively as reaffirmation through demonstration of a new way of realizing an old system. One of the most exciting examples of this process in
Homer is provided by Richard Sacks in a book that should be required reading for all those interested in the history of narrative: *The Traditional Phrase in
Homer* (Leiden, Netherlands: E. J. Brill, 1987).

26. Loofburrow, *Thackeray and the Forms of Fiction*, 44–45.

27. Leo Bersani, "The Other Freud," *Humanities in Society* 1, no. 1 (Winter
1978): 35.

28. Flaubert, as he was so famously the first to observe, identified himself
with "romantic" Emma, and this can be seen as a necessary identification,
since Flaubert appeals to his readers in terms of a conflict between actual
experience and a mind that "works" in terms of internalized structures of
expectation and desire that seem inappropriate to the facts of the social existence to which Emma is confined. Thackeray never would think of saying,
"Amelia, c'est moi," because he always consciously and ostentatiously speaks
of her from the role of storyteller. This distinction illuminates why modern
storytelling privileges author over teller.

29. Ray, "*Vanity Fair*: One Version of the Novelist's Responsibility," 87–
101. H. M. Daleski's chapter, "Strategies in *Vanity Fair*," in his *Unities: Studies*

in the English Novel (Athens: University of Georgia Press, 1985), illuminates what I have focused on as skewings of narrative schemata through description of Thackeray's "outrageous transformations of the convention of 'omniscient' narration." Although it is not his primary concern, Daleski, I suspect, shares my view that Thackeray's "illicit border crossings" of conventions are symptomatic of increasingly difficult circumstances for storytelling. Many critics of George Eliot have drawn attention to her parallel manipulations of conventional story patterns. Now both Trollope's and Dickens's fiction have been subjected to similar, and similarly revealing, analyses. Larry J. Swingle's *Trollope and Romantic Literature* (Ann Arbor: University of Michigan Press, 1990) is a major revaluation along these lines, and Jon Reed, in "Astrophil and Estella: A Defense of Poetry," *Studies in English Literature* 30, no. 4 (1990): 655–678, building on Iain Crawford's "Pip and the Monster," *Studies in English Literature* 28 (1988): 625–648, demonstrates how *Great Expectations* is constructed to reject the confinement of narrative form by what seemed to Dickens socially regressive narrative models, such as the pattern of chivalric romance.

30. The argument for Cervantes's importance is made in Erich Kahler's fine book, *The Inward Turn of Narrative*, translated by Richard and Clara Winston (Princeton: Princeton University Press, 1983). I develop this line of thought through a discussion of Vermeer's painting in the next chapter. It ought to be observed, however, that Thackeray's prefatory remarks on his traveling show are interestingly complicated. While the "Becky puppet," is purely his invention, his "Wicked Nobleman" in fact owes much to a traditional figure, and it is by using that conventionalized conception as a foil that Thackeray so brilliantly and economically creates the distinctively "original" character of Lord Steyne. I don't mean to imply that the loss of a common imaginative, narrative heritage is due solely to the practice of "inwardly turning" novelists, but that practice inevitably did contribute to the destruction of shared patterns of pretense, a destruction wrought chiefly by social developments outside the sphere of literature.

31. Pierre Bordieu. "Flaubert's Point of View", translated by Priscilla Parkhurst Ferguson, *Critical Inquiry* 14, no. 3 (Spring 1988): 560–561.

32. Todorov's essay appeared in the *Times Literary Supplement*, June 17–23, 1988, pp. 676 and 684, one of several dealing with the De Man case.

33. Michel Foucault, "What Is an Author?" in *Language, Counter-Memory, Practice*, translated by Donald F. Bouchard and Sherry Simon (Ithaca: Cornell University Press, 1977), 113–138.

CHAPTER SIX
The Aesthetics of Contingency

1. The placing of the *Bribe* has been discussed, for instance, by Mosche Barasch, *Giotto and the Language of Gesture* (Cambridge: Cambridge University Press, 1987), 157, where he suggests it functions as a contrast to the *Cleansing of the Temple* to its left. But I have not encountered in the critical literature any

discussion of the "double" Judas. A matter I should like to pursue is the deployment of full-front, profile, angled, and reversed representations of figures in narrative paintings—to develop suggestive observations by Meyer Schapiro, *Words and Pictures* (The Hague: Mouton, 1973), 37ff.

2. Barasch, for example, although he discusses at length the hands of the priest giving Judas the sack of silver, says nothing of the jerked-thumb gesture.

3. "Low narrativity" is Wendy Steiner's phrase, *Pictures of Romance* (Chicago: University of Chicago Press, 1988), 11; she classes all such works as this of Vermeer's as "genre" painting, rightly stressing that the subject matter is "commonplace, run-of-the-mill," unextraordinary. But my comments are indebted mainly to the work of Svetlana Alpers, an example of which is "Describe or Narrate? A Problem in Realistic Representation," *New Literary History* 8, no. 1 (1976): 15–40. My focus on narrative leads me to different emphases, exacerbated by my attention to the backward-looking Pre-Raphaelitism of the nineteenth century rather than to Courbet and Manet, her exemplary figures of nineteenth-century realism. Yet I think my comments on Vermeer are congruent with her argument for "a displacement in the subtle balance, the assumed partnership, between imitation and narration" in which "representation and narration pull away, though not apart, from each other" (26). Alpers is correct in suggesting that the "hybrid" seventeenth-century narrativity she and I are concerned with was often for its practitioners seen as linking their art to antiquity while distinguishing it from medieval art (17). Odd as it may at first seem, then, my discussion of narrative in Vermeer's painting is deeply dependent on Alpers's book, *The Art of Describing* (Chicago: University of Chicago Press, 1983), because her discussion both of the antinarrative impetus of descriptive realism and of the significance of detail in such realism underlies the differentiation between Giotto and Vermeer I stress.

4. A work to which I, like others studying Vermeer, am indebted is Lawrence Gowing, *Vermeer* (New York: Harper and Row, 1953), which includes visual evidence of Vermeer's utilization of common topics and conventional motifs and poses. Equally valuable to me has been Edward A. Snow, *A Study of Vermeer* (Berkeley: University of California Press, 1979). I may here mention as specially helpful, besides Alpers's work, the essay by Harry Berger, "Conspicuous Exclusion in Vermeer: An Essay in Renaissance Pastoral," *Yale French Studies* 47 (1972):241–275. Since these scholars refer to Vermeer's painting as *Soldier and Young Girl Smiling*, I use that title, although the Frick Collection calls it *Officer and Laughing Girl*.

5. Erich Kahler, *The Inward Turn of Narrative*, translated by Richard and Clara Winston (Princeton: Princeton University Press, 1981).

6. Snow, *A Study of Vermeer*, 72.

7. Ibid., 79.

8. Ibid., 162. Snow cites this description from John J. Walsh, Jr., "Vermeer," *The Metropolitan Museum of Art Bulletin* 31 (1973): sec. 2.

9. My comments on Hunt ought to be balanced by a reading of Michael Fried's "Thomas Couture and the Theatricalization of Action in 19th Century French Painting," *Artforum* 8, no. 10 (1970):42–45, which brilliantly analyzes

the strategy of avant-garde painters such as Courbet and Manet to create "a new paradigm for ambitious painting that no longer *essentially* comprised the representation of an action" (44), this being the genesis of graphic modernism—rather as Flaubert's resistance to narrative became a foundation of literary modernism. Some modification of Fried's view seems required, however, in the light of Robert L. Herbert's *Impressionism: Art, Leisure and Parisian Society* (New Haven: Yale University Press, 1988), which demonstrates persuasively the presence of significant narrative elements in paintings by Manet, Monet, and Renoir where they have been overlooked previously. Herbert's analyses of Manet's canvases, for instance, suggest that it is precisely the unobtrusiveness of narrative elements that permit them to function so effectively as disturbing commentaries on what seems so "simply" described. Herbert's study thus appears to "justify" Alpers's contrastive juxtaposition of seventeenth-century Dutch painters with nineteenth-century French realists.

10. A thoughtful analysis of *The Awakening Conscience*, which uses the term "hyperrealism," is that of Martin Meisel, *Realizations* (Princeton: Princeton University Press, 1983), 365–368. John Ruskin's famous defense and explanation of the painting appeared originally in a letter to the London *Times* (25 May 1854), and can be found in *The Works of John Ruskin*, edited by E. T. Cook and Alexander Wedderburn (London: 1903–12), 12:333–334. The most valuable essay of revisionary criticism is that of Kate Flint, "Reading *The Awakening Conscience* Rightly," in *The Pre-Raphaelites Re-assessed,* edited by Marcia Pointon (Manchester: Manchester University Press, 1989), 45–65, emphasizing Hunt's confronting of Victorian stereotypes of fallen women. This entire volume is a valuable corrective to the conventionalized understanding of Pre-Raphaelitism.

11. Robert Weimann, *Structure and Society in Literary History* (1978; expanded ed., Baltimore: Johns Hopkins University Press, 1984), 288–289.

12. Ruskin, *Works*, 333.

13. Ibid., 334.

14. I have discussed nineteenth-century reactions to Lessing's view of "the moment" in *British Romantic Art* (Berkeley: University of California Press, 1986), especially 96–99; in *Realizations* Meisel has depicted Victorian attitudes toward Lessing, emphasizing Hunt's originality.

15. On Pre-Raphaelite "proto-modernism" see Robert Rosenblum's review of an exhibition of Pre-Raphaelite painting at the Museum of Modern Art in 1957, *Partisan Review* 24 (1957):95–100.

16. Erwin Panofsky, *Early Netherlandish Painting* (1953; New York: Harper and Row, 1971), 201–203. Subsequent references to this work are found in the text.

17. Alastair MacIntyre, *After Virtue*, 2d ed. (Notre Dame: University of Notre Dame Press, 1984). Subsequent references to this work are found in the text.

18. E. M. Forster, *Aspects of the Novel* (New York: Harcourt Brace, 1927), 130.

19. Nelson Goodman, "The Telling and the Told," *Critical Inquiry* 7, no. 4 (1981): 799–801. Subsequent references to this work are found in the text.

CHAPTER SEVEN
Modern Dialogic Narrative

1. Henry James, *The Ambassadors* (London: Penguin, 1986), 63. I cite from this edition because of its ready availability and because it conveniently includes the "Preface to the New York Edition." Subsequent references to this work will be found in the text.

2. Carol Gilligan, *In a Different Voice* (Cambridge, Mass.: Harvard University Press, 1982), 63.

3. *Henry James and Robert Louis Stevenson: A Record of Friendship and Criticism*, edited by Janet Adam Smith (London: Rupert Hart-Davis, 1948), 67–68. This volume conveniently brings together not only the two key essays but also more than forty letters exchanged by the novelists, as well as two striking reviews of Stevenson's work by James.

4. Ibid., 90–91.

5. *The Dialogic Imagination: Four Essays by M. M. Bakhtin*, edited by Michael Holquist, translated by Michael Holquist and Caryl Emerson (Austin: University of Texas Press, 1981), 263.

6. Ibid., 428.

7. At issue throughout *The Ambassadors* (for both Strether and the reader) is not so much seeing through dissimulations of others as of perceiving defects in one's own mode of perception and evaluation. Analogously, then, both Strether and the reader must discover modes of rearticulating what the inadequacies of their powers of expression have disguised for them.

8. M. M. Bakhtin, *Speech Genres and Other Late Essays*, translated by Vern W. McGee, edited by Caryl Emerson and Michael Holquist (Austin: University of Texas Press, 1986), 142.

CHAPTER EIGHT
Storytelling in a Postmodern/ Postcolonial World

1. David Perkins, "The Narrative Protest," in *A History of Modern Poetry* (Cambridge, Mass.: Harvard University Press, 1976), 60–83. American poets such as Edwin Arlington Robinson also wrote significant narrative poems during the height of modernism.

2. T. S. Eliot's review of *Ulysses* appeared originally in his "London Letter" in *The Dial* 75 (November 1923): 480–483, and many commentators have pointed to the relevance of his remarks to *The Waste Land*, already published and already attacked. To appreciate the significance of Eliot's contrastive representation of "mythical method" one should read his "London Letter" of the previous year in *The Dial*, (September 1922): 329–331, which discusses contemporary novels, beginning with an analysis of the "old narrative method . . . traditional in English fiction," for which Eliot shows affection and respect. Eliot's remarks precipitated the writing of this study by leading me to meditate on the validity of, and the causes for, his belief that cultural conditions in

the twentieth-century required new modes of representation—to be defined so paradoxically. I take it for granted (as I've already observed that Joseph Frank did in putting forward his idea of "spatial form") that Eliot's observation derives from his underlying assumption of the impossibility of any direct recovery of unselfconscious mythic imagining. A useful collection of studies, informatively edited by Alan Dundas, *Sacred Narrative: Readings in the Theory of Myth* (Berkeley: University of California Press, 1984) begins with Dundas's statement that "A myth is a sacred narrative," and the other twenty-one commentators concur. Modernist universalizing theories of myth are well illustrated by Joseph Campbell, probably the century's most widely read mythologist, whose key "monomyth" derived from *Finnegans Wake*, and whose data is notably eurocentric.

3. To formalistic narratologists like Wendy Steiner, *Pictures of Romance* (Chicago: University of Chicago Press, 1988), the absence of narrative in modern art is puzzling, since she observes that the break with Renaissance illusionary realism *should* have made graphic storytelling an attractive option. With modernism the representation of different moments of time in the same canvas, for instance, once again became acceptable: "Now, seemingly, nothing stood in the way of strong pictorial narrativity" (Steiner, 144). If one looks at the history of art in purely formalistic terms, with attention focused solely on conventionally defined mainstream practitioners, modernism's bias against narrative does seem odd. The oddness vanishes, however, as soon as one recognizes that storytelling is a social activity, its waxing and waning depending in good part on sociohistorical circumstances. An adequate history of storytelling must take into account the ideological dimensions of any stylistic changes. These dimensions are unmistakable when marginalized peoples seize upon new techniques to affirm through popular narrative the integrity of their history and cultural aspirations—asserting these against the oppressive and colonialist powers in which the stylistic innovations originated.

4. The "true narrativity" of Rivera and Orozco is suggested by their unpopularity with the more politically orthodox: Rivera was more violently attacked by Siqueiros and other doctrinaire communists than by Rockefeller, and some of Orozco's work was defaced by politically inspired "revolutionary" mobs. Ronald Paulson, *Figure and Abstraction in Contemporary Painting* (New Brunswick, N.J.: Rutgers University Press, 1990), argues that Orozco's importance lies in the "unresolved quality" with which he represents the faltering and reviving of the revolutionary spirit" (23). Commitments of personal passion, the source of Orozco's power, should not be confused with ideological conformity. Although Jacob Lawrence's narrative paintings are animated by passionate social and political convictions, they are impressive as narratives because they never become mere vehicles for ideology. Indeed, much of their efficacy derives from the fashion in which the paintings lure one into the vividness of the visual story so that Lawrence's powerful moral/social "message" is absorbed, as it were, subliminally, "assimilated," not enforced, to use Bakhtinian terms. More interesting, but beyond the scope of this essay, is a tendency in Lawrence's later work away from narrative toward "series," sets of related images lacking a story line. An analogous tendency is visible in a more complicated fashion in the later works of Orozco and Rivera. The lat-

ter's "Dream of a Sunday Afternoon on the Alameda" (1947), for example, creates an overall image constituted of a variety of subnarratives. Yet other late murals of Rivera, such as the *Disembarkation at Vera Cruz* (1951) are as profoundly and pervasively narrative as his earlier frescoes.

5. I quote from "Suprematism" of 1927 as translated by Howard Dearstyne in *Modern Artists on Art,* edited by Robert L. Herbert (Englewood Cliffs, N.J.: Prentice-Hall, 1964), 100. It is worth remembering that Malevich's best known painting, now called *Red Square and Black Square* (Figure 5) originally bore the combatively ironic title: *Painterly Realism: Boy with Knapsack: Color Masses in the Fourth Dimension.*

6. Of course, some elements of modernism, Futurism, for example, were consciously and overtly ideological, and there is no question that a bias of some modernists tended toward the totalitarian rather than the democratic. But I believe it to be true that the effort to supersede all ideology, the ultimate absolutism, is the most significant driving force in modern art, not least because "concealed" from its proponents by their genuinely idealistic fervor, their authentic faith in an aesthetic "purity."

7. For a history of sculpture, see Rudolph Wittkower, *Sculpture: Processes and Principles* (New York: Harper and Row, 1977), on pointing machines, 30–32, *passim.* Most of the Roman figure sculpture one sees is the product of pointing machines. Thanks to the "dark ages," which abandoned this kind of progress, Renaissance sculptors such as Donatello and Michelangelo learned to do their own carving. In his early years in Paris Brancusi was briefly employed by Rodin, but not surprisingly found uncongenial the factory atmosphere created by a master who was so spectacular a commercializer. Henry Moore has since surpassed Rodin, becoming one of the wealthiest men in England by utilizing in his later years as many as forty full-time assistants to produce a vast number of works to which his personal contribution was minimal. Moore's case is of special interest, because he began his career in the modern tradition as a direct carver, and because the brilliance and originality of his early work owes much to his hands-on knowledge of materials and cutting techniques.

8. James Guetti, "Wittgenstein and Literary Theory," *Raritan* 3, no. 1 (1985): 73.

9. Since postmodernism attained coherency of style first in architecture, it is appropriate that still possibly the clearest statement of the grounds for its antimodernism appears in one of the earliest books on the subject, Robert Venturi's impressive *Complexity and Contradictions in Architecture* (New York: The Museum of Modern Art, 1966).

10. Richard Poirier, "The Difficulties of Modernism and the Modernism of Difficulty," *Humanities in Society* 1, no. 4 (Fall 1978): 275. Robert Morris, "Words and Images in Modernism and Postmodernism," *Critical Inquiry* 15, no. 2 (Winter 1989): 343. Morris goes on to observe that postmodernism, for all its "delegitimizing" of modernism, has been careful to leave "untouched the institutions that support the dissemination" of their enterprise (346)—a telling point.

Ronald Paulson rightly observes that the "parallel to the small political elite led by Lenin was an elite of avant-garde painters, innovators who, in Wassily Kandinsky and others, produced the first totally non-representational paintings" (*Figure and Abstraction in Contemporary Painting* [New Brunswick, N.J.: Rutgers University Press, 1990], 23). The linkage between elitism in politics and art is *purity,* which is antithetical to genuine narrativity.

11. Typical comments are cited by Lawrence Alloway, *American Pop Art* (New York: Collier/Macmillan, 1974), 7; and Robert Rosenblum, "Pop Art and Non-Pop Art," in *Pop Art Redefined,* edited by John Russell and Suzi Gablik (London: Thames and Hudson, 1969), 93. See also G. R. Swenson, "Roy Lichtenstein: An Interview," in the valuable book *Roy Lichtenstein,* edited by John Coplans (San Diego: Pasadena Art Museum, 1916), 15. The most useful book on Lichtenstein is Lawrence Alloway, *Roy Lichtenstein* (New York: Cross River Press, 1983).

12. Two lucid and complementary treatments of recent philosophical discussions of the problem of identity are Kathleen V. Wilkes, *Real People: Personal Identity without Thought Experiments* (Oxford: Clarendon Press, 1988), and Jonathan Glover, *I: The Philosophy and Psychology of Personal Identity* (New York: Viking, 1988).

13. This and the quotation just above are from Charles Russell, *Poets, Prophets, and Revolutionaries* (New York: Oxford University Press, 1985), 245. It is worth remembering that Manet's *Dejeuner sur l'herbe* of 1863 is partially based on Marcantonio Raimondi's engraving of a painting by Raphael. Lichtenstein is not interesting because he uses images created by others but because he utilizes images deriving from popular, mass culture in a fashion that is neither purely celebratory nor derisive. The complex effect of his intense stylizations is possible precisely because he does not separate himself—quite the contrary—from the culture that produces the basic images. Because he does not take the "superior" position of the modernist, Lichtenstein can make scarifying use of familiar yet anonymous comic-book images: we do not have to know the originals he reworks because we share his familiarity with the style of this popular art, and he makes us think about the significance of that familiarity.

14. My principal interest, obviously, is in the variety of ways the Tintin books reveal cultural history—not least because they themselves were transformed from the creation of a single artist to an industry exploiting technological innovations in order to reach mass markets worldwide. But as a critic I cannot refrain from remarking on the qualitative falling off of the final volume—which is not solely the result of taking Tintin himself out of knickers. Although the deterioration doubtless owes most to conditions in Hergé's personal life, it reflects also the debilitating effects of constructing a story on too simple self-imaging—equivalent effects being visible, for example, in the later *Oz* books.

15. The novel was originally published in 1979. My in-text citations are from the translation of William Weaver (New York: Harcourt Brace Jovanovich, 1981). Among the best commentaries on the novel are Barbara Orr, "Beginning the Middle: The Story of Reading in Calvino's *If on a winter night a traveler,*" *Papers on Language and Literature* 21 (1985): 210−219, and James Phelan, *Reading People, Reading Plots* (Chicago: University of Chicago Press, 1989), 133−164.

16. Fredric Jameson, "Postmodernism and Consumer Society," in *The Anti-*

Aesthetic, edited Hal Foster (Port Townsend, Wa.: Bay Press, 1983), 111–125, 114–115.

17. Any thorough analysis of Calvino's novel would have to include comment on his indebtedness to Borges, whose works also would illustrate several of the points I have made in this chapter.

18. Claudio Guillén, "Literary Change and Multiple Duration," *Comparative Literature Studies* 14, no. 2 (1977): 115.

19. Countertendencies to this universalizing currently appear most impressively in so-called postcolonial literatures. I find intriguing, for example, the fiction of Naguib Mahfouz, notably *The Cairo Trilogy,* because there the European novel form is challenged by the introduction of elements deriving from traditional indigenous storytelling and poetry. Even more interesting in this respect are the novels of Chinua Achebe, all of which describe various functions of traditional storytellings in the confusions of evolving African postcolonialism, including their role in contemporary fiction in English about oral cultures. In *Things Fall Apart,* to cite a small but telling instance, Achebe shows native children drawn to Christianity by their fascination with biblical parables, because these recover something of the enchantment created by stories they heard in their mother's hut.

20. Various participative devices, painting on mirrors, signs urging spectators to manipulate works, live TV, and the like, now rather common in art galleries, are in fact powerful testimony to how small a part is today available to serious audience response, response that would truly transform the original artistic stimulus. And, as Calvino makes clear, critical emphasis on readers' "production" of textual meaning may disguise how modern conceptions of literature reduce processes of interchange between work and audience to a fixed pattern, making supposed "producers" complicit in what is actually only enhanced consumerism.

21. Paulson, *Figure and Abstraction,* 50, 65.

22. See Hilary Putnam, "The Craving for Objectivity," in *Realism with a Human Face,* edited by James Conant (Cambridge, Mass.: Harvard University Press, 1990), 120–131.

23. Michael Taussig, "Culture of Terror, Space of Death. Roger Casement's Putomayo Report and The Explanation of Torture," *Comparative Studies in Society and History* 26 (1984): 494, my emphasis added.

24. Leslie W. Rabine, *Reading the Romantic Heroine* (Ann Arbor: University of Michigan Press, 1985), 13.

25. Derek Walcott, *Omeros* (New York: Farrar, Straus, Giroux, 1990).

Index